Machine Learning Engineering with Python

Manage the production life cycle of machine learning models using MLOps with practical examples

Andrew P. McMahon

BIRMINGHAM—MUMBAI

Machine Learning Engineering with Python

Publishing Product Manager: Ali Abidi

Senior Editor: David Sugarman

Content Development Editor: Nathanya Dias

Technical Editor: Sonam Pandey

Copy Editor: Safis Editing

Project Coordinator: Aparna Ravikumar Nair

Proofreader: Safis Editing

Indexer: Sejal Dsilva

Production Designer: Jyoti Chauhan

First published: November 2021

Production reference: 1280921

Published by Packt Publishing Ltd.

Livery Place

35 Livery Street

Birmingham

B3 2PB, UK.

ISBN 978-1-80107-925-9

www.packt.com

5

Deployment Patterns and Tools

6

Scaling Up

Section 3: End-to-End Examples

7

Building an Example ML Microservice

8

Building an Extract Transform Machine Learning Use Case

Other Books You May Enjoy

Index

Preface

Machine Learning (ML) is rightfully recognized as one of the most powerful tools available for organizations to extract value from their data. As the capabilities of ML algorithms have grown over the years, it has become increasingly obvious that implementing them in a scalable, fault-tolerant, and automated way is a discipline in its own right. This discipline, ML engineering, is the focus of this book.

The book covers a wide variety of topics in order to help you understand the tools, techniques, and processes you can apply to engineer your ML solutions, with an emphasis on introducing the key concepts so that you can build on them in your own work. Much of what we will cover will also help you maintain and monitor your solutions, the purview of the closely related discipline of **Machine Learning Operations (MLOps)**.

All the code examples are given in Python, the most popular programming language for data applications. Python is a high-level and object-oriented language with a rich ecosystem of tools focused on data science and ML. Packages such as scikit-learn and pandas often form the backbone of ML modeling code in data science teams across the world. In this book, we will also use these tools but discuss how to wrap them up in production-grade pipelines and deploy them using appropriate cloud and open source tools. We will not spend a lot of time on how to build the best ML model, though some of the tools covered will certainly help with that. Instead, the aim is to understand what to do after you have an ML model.

Many of the examples in the book will leverage services and solutions from **Amazon Web Services (AWS)**. I believe that the accompanying explanations and discussions will, however, mean that you can still apply everything you learn here to any cloud provider or even in an on-premises setting.

Machine Learning Engineering with Python will help you to navigate the challenges of taking ML to production and give you the confidence to start applying MLOps in your organizations.

Who this book is for

This book is for ML engineers, data scientists, and software developers who want to build robust software solutions with ML components. It is also relevant to anyone who manages or wants to understand the production life cycle of these systems. The book assumes intermediate-level knowledge of Python. Basic knowledge of AWS and Bash will also be beneficial.

What this book covers

Chapter 1, *Introduction to ML Engineering*, explains what we mean by ML engineering and how this relates to the disciplines of data science and data engineering. It covers what you need to do to build an effective ML engineering team, as well as what real software solutions containing ML can look like.

Chapter 2, *The Machine Learning Development Process*, explores a development process that will be applicable to almost any ML engineering project. It discusses how you can set your development tooling up for success for later chapters as well.

Chapter 3, *From Model to Model Factory*, teaches you how to build solutions that train multiple ML models during the product life cycle. It also covers drift detection and pipelining to help you start to build out your MLOps practices.

Chapter 4, *Packaging Up*, discusses best practices for coding in Python and how this relates to building your own packages and libraries for reuse in multiple projects.

Chapter 5, *Deployment Patterns and Tools*, teaches you some of the standard ways you can get your ML system into production. In particular, the chapter will focus on hosting solutions in the cloud.

Chapter 6, *Scaling Up*, teaches you how to take your solutions and scale them to massive datasets or large numbers of prediction requests using Apache Spark and serverless infrastructure.

Chapter 7, *Building an Example ML Microservice*, walks through how to use what you have learned elsewhere in the book to build a forecasting service that can be triggered via an API.

Chapter 8, *Building an Extract Transform Machine Learning Use Case*, walks through how to use what you have learned to build a pipeline that performs batch processing. We do this by adding a lot of our newly acquired ML engineering best practices to the simple package created in *Chapter 4*, *Packaging Up*.

To get the most out of this book

To get the most out of the examples in the book, you will need access to a computer or server where you have privileges to install and run Python and Apache Spark applications. For many of the examples, you will also require access to a terminal, such as Bash. The examples in the book were built on a Linux machine running Bash so you may need to translate some pieces for your operating system and terminal. For some examples using AWS, you will require an account where you can enable billing. Examples in the book used Apache Spark v3.0.2.

Software/hardware covered in the book	Operating system requirements
Python 3, Anaconda, Docker	Windows, macOS, or Linux

In *Chapter 5, Deployment Patterns and Tools*, we use the **Managed Workflows with Apache Spark (MWAA)** service from AWS. There is no free tier option for MWAA so as soon as you spin up the example, you will be charged for the environment and any instances. Ensure you are happy to do this before proceeding and I recommend closing down your MWAA instances when finished.

In *Chapter 7, Building an Example ML Microservice*, we build out a use case leveraging the AWS Forecast service, which is only available in a subset of AWS Regions. To check the availability in your Region, and what Regions you can switch to for that example, you can use https://aws.amazon.com/about-aws/global-infrastructure/regional-product-services/.

Technical requirements are given in most of the chapters, but to support this, there are Conda environment .yml files provided in the book repository: https://github.com/PacktPublishing/Machine-Learning-Engineering-with-Python.

If you are using the digital version of this book, we advise you to type the code yourself or access the code from the book's GitHub repository (a link is available in the next section). Doing so will help you avoid any potential errors related to the copying and pasting of code.

Download the example code files

You can download the example code files for this book from GitHub at https://github.com/PacktPublishing/Machine-Learning-Engineering-with-Python. If there's an update to the code, it will be updated in the GitHub repository.

We also have other code bundles from our rich catalog of books and videos available at https://github.com/PacktPublishing/. Check them out!

Download the color images

We also provide a PDF file that has color images of the screenshots and diagrams used in this book. You can download it here: https://static.packt-cdn.com/downloads/9781801079259_ColorImages.pdf.

Conventions used

There are a number of text conventions used throughout this book.

Code in text: Indicates code words in text, database table names, folder names, filenames, file extensions, pathnames, dummy URLs, user input, and Twitter handles. Here is an example: "Mount the downloaded WebStorm-10*.dmg disk image file as another disk in your system."

A block of code is set as follows:

```
html, body, #map {
  height: 100%;
  margin: 0;
  padding: 0
}
```

When we wish to draw your attention to a particular part of a code block, the relevant lines or items are set in bold:

```
[default]
exten => s,1,Dial(Zap/1|30)
exten => s,2,Voicemail(u100)
exten => s,102,Voicemail(b100)
exten => i,1,Voicemail(s0)
```

Any command-line input or output is written as follows:

```
$ mkdir css
$ cd css
```

Bold: Indicates a new term, an important word, or words that you see onscreen. For instance, words in menus or dialog boxes appear in **bold**. Here is an example: "Select **System info** from the **Administration** panel."

> **Tips or important notes**
> Appear like this.

Get in touch

Feedback from our readers is always welcome.

General feedback: If you have questions about any aspect of this book, email us at customercare@packtpub.com and mention the book title in the subject of your message.

Errata: Although we have taken every care to ensure the accuracy of our content, mistakes do happen. If you have found a mistake in this book, we would be grateful if you would report this to us. Please visit www.packtpub.com/support/errata and fill in the form.

Piracy: If you come across any illegal copies of our works in any form on the internet, we would be grateful if you would provide us with the location address or website name. Please contact us at copyright@packt.com with a link to the material.

If you are interested in becoming an author: If there is a topic that you have expertise in and you are interested in either writing or contributing to a book, please visit authors.packtpub.com.

Share Your Thoughts

Once you've read *Machine Learning Engineering with Python*, we'd love to hear your thoughts! Scan the QR code below to go straight to the Amazon review page for this book and share your feedback.

https://packt.link/r/1-801-07925-0

Your review is important to us and the tech community and will help us make sure we're delivering excellent quality content.

Section 1: What Is ML Engineering?

The objective of this section is to provide a discussion of what activities could be classed as *ML engineering* and how this constitutes an important element of using data to generate value in organizations. You will also be introduced to an example software development process that captures the key aspects required in any successful ML engineering project.

This section comprises the following chapters:

- *Chapter 1, Introduction to ML Engineering*
- *Chapter 2, The Machine Learning Development Process*

1
Introduction to ML Engineering

Welcome to *Machine Learning Engineering with Python*, a book that aims to introduce you to the exciting world of making **Machine Learning** (**ML**) systems production-ready.

This book will take you through a series of chapters covering training systems, scaling up solutions, system design, model tracking, and a host of other topics, to prepare you for your own work in ML engineering or to work with others in this space. No book can be exhaustive on this topic, so this one will focus on concepts and examples that I think cover the foundational principles of this increasingly important discipline.

You will get a lot from this book even if you do not run the technical examples, or even if you try to apply the main points in other programming languages or with different tools. In covering the key principles, the aim is that you come away from this book feeling more confident in tackling your own ML engineering challenges, whatever your chosen toolset.

In this first chapter, you will learn about the different types of data role relevant to ML engineering and how to distinguish them; how to use this knowledge to build and work within appropriate teams; some of the key points to remember when building working ML products in the real world; how to start to isolate appropriate problems for engineered ML solutions; and how to create your own high-level ML system designs for a variety of typical business problems.

We will cover all of these aspects in the following sections:

- Defining a taxonomy of data disciplines
- Assembling your team
- ML engineering in the real world
- What does an ML solution look like?
- High-level ML system design

Now that we have explained what we are going after in this first chapter, let's get started!

Technical requirements

Throughout the book, we will assume that Python 3 is installed and working. The following Python packages are used in this chapter:

- Scikit-learn 0.23.2
- NumPy
- pandas
- imblearn
- Prophet 0.7.1

Defining a taxonomy of data disciplines

The explosion of data and the potential applications of that data over the past few years have led to a proliferation of job roles and responsibilities. The debate that once raged over how a *data scientist* was different from a *statistician* has now become extremely complex. I would argue, however, that it does not have to be so complicated. The activities that have to be undertaken to get value from data are pretty consistent, no matter what business vertical you are in, so it should be reasonable to expect that the skills and roles you need to perform these steps will also be relatively consistent. In this chapter, we will explore some of the main data disciplines that I think you will always need in any data project. As you can guess, given the name of this book, I will be particularly keen to explore the notion of *ML engineering* and how this fits into the mix.

Let's now look at some of the roles involved in using data in the modern landscape.

Data scientist

Since the Harvard Business Review declared that being a data scientist was *The Sexiest Job of the 21st Century* (`https://hbr.org/2012/10/data-scientist-the-sexiest-job-of-the-21st-century`), this title has become one of the most sought after, but also hyped, in the mix. A data scientist can cover an entire spectrum of duties, skills, and responsibilities depending on the business vertical, the organization, or even just personal preference. No matter how this role is defined, however, there are some key areas of focus that should always be part of the data scientist's job profile:

- **Analysis**: A data scientist should be able to wrangle, mung, manipulate, and consolidate datasets before performing calculations on that data that help us to understand it. Analysis is a broad term, but it's clear that the end result is knowledge of your dataset that you didn't have before you started, no matter how basic or complex.

- **Modeling**: The thing that gets everyone excited (potentially including you, dear reader) is the idea of modeling data. A data scientist usually has to be able to apply statistical, mathematical, and machine learning models to data in order to explain it or perform some sort of prediction.

- **Working with the customer or user**: The data science role usually has some more business-directed elements so that the results of steps 1 and 2 can support decision making in the organization. This could be done by presenting the results of analysis in PowerPoints or Jupyter notebooks or even sending an email with a summary of the key results. It involves communication and business acumen in a way that goes beyond classic tech roles.

ML engineer

A newer kid on the block, and indeed the subject of this book, is the ML engineer. This role has risen to fill the perceived gap between the analysis and modeling of data science and the world of software products and robust systems engineering.

You can articulate the need for this type of role quite nicely by considering a classic voice assistant. In this case, a data scientist would usually focus on translating the business requirements into a working **speech-to-text** model, potentially a very complex neural network, and showing that it can perform the desired voice transcription task *in principle*. ML engineering is then all about how you take that speech-to-text model and build it into a product, service, or tool that can be used *in production*. Here, it may mean building some software to train, retrain, deploy, and track the performance of the model as more transcription data is accumulated, or user preferences are understood. It may also involve understanding how to interface with other systems and how to provide results from the model in the appropriate formats, for example, interacting with an online store.

Data scientists and ML engineers have a lot of overlapping skill sets and competencies, but have different areas of focus and strengths (more on this later), so they will usually be part of the same project team and may have either title, but it will be clear what hat they are wearing from what they do in that project.

Similar to the data scientist, we can define the key areas of focus for the ML engineer:

- **Translation**: Taking models and research code in a variety of formats and translating this into slicker, more robust pieces of code. This could be done using OO programming, functional programming, a mix, or something else, but basically helps to take the **Proof-Of-Concept** work of the data scientist and turn it into something that is far closer to being trusted in a production environment.

- **Architecture**: Deployments of any piece of software do not occur in a vacuum and will always involve lots of integrated parts. This is true of machine learning solutions as well. The ML engineer has to understand how the appropriate tools and processes link together so that the models built with the data scientist can do their job and do it at scale.

- **Productionization**: The ML engineer is focused on delivering a solution and so should understand the customer's requirements inside out, as well as be able to understand what that means for the project development. The end goal of the ML engineer is not to provide a good model (though that is part of it), nor is it to provide something that *basically works*. Their job is to make sure that the hard work on the data science side of things generates the maximum potential value in a real-world setting.

Data engineer

The most important people in any data team (in my opinion) are the people who are responsible for getting the commodity that everything else in the preceding sections is based on from A to B with high fidelity, appropriate latency, and with as little effort on the part of the other team members as possible. You cannot create any type of software product, never mind a machine learning product, without data.

The key areas of focus for a data engineer are as follows:

- **Quality**: Getting data from A to B is a pointless exercise if the data is garbled, fields are missing, or IDs are screwed up. The data engineer cares about avoiding this and uses a variety of techniques and tools, generally to ensure that the data that left the source system is what lands in your data storage layer.

- **Stability**: Similar to the previous point on quality, if the data comes from A to B but it only does it every second Wednesday if it's not a rainy day, then what's the point? Data engineers spend a lot of time and effort and use their considerable skills to ensure that data pipelines are robust, reliable, and can be trusted to deliver when promised.

- **Access**: Finally, the aim of getting the data from A to B is for it to be used by applications, analyses, and machine learning models, so the nature of the *B* is important. The data engineer will have a variety of technologies to hand for surfacing data and should work with the data consumers (our data scientists and machine learning engineers, among others) to define and create appropriate data models within these solutions:

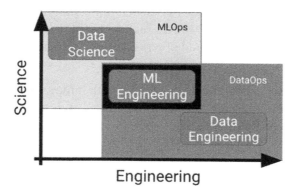

Figure 1.1 – A diagram showing the relationships between data science,
ML engineering, and data engineering

As mentioned previously, this book focuses on the work of the ML engineer and how you can learn some of the skills useful for that role, but it is always important to remember that you will not be working in a vacuum. Always keep in mind the profiles of the other roles (and many more not covered here that will exist in your project team) so that you work most effectively together. Data is a team sport after all!

Assembling your team

There are no set rules about how you should pull together a team for your machine learning project, but there are some good general principles to follow, and gotchas to avoid.

First, always bear in mind that *unicorns do not exist*. You can find some very talented people out there, but do not ever think one person can do everything you will need to the level you require. This is not just a bit unrealistic; it is bad practice and will negatively impact the quality of your products. Even when you are severely resource-constrained, the key is for your team members to have a laser-like focus to succeed.

Secondly, *blended is best*. We all know the benefits of diversity for organizations and teams in general and this should, of course, apply to your machine learning team as well. Within a project, you will need the mathematics, the code, the engineering, the project management, the communication, and a variety of other skills to succeed. So, given the previous point, make sure you cover this in at least some sense across your team.

Third, *tie your team structure to your projects in a dynamic way*. If you are working on a project that is mostly about getting the data in the right place and the actual machine learning models are really simple, focus your team profile on the engineering and data modeling aspects. If the project requires a detailed understanding of the model, and it is quite complex, then reposition your team to make sure this is covered. This is just sensible and frees up team members who would otherwise have been underutilized to work on other projects.

As an example, suppose that you have been tasked with building a system that classifies customer data as it comes into your shiny new data lake, and the decision has been taken that this should be done at the point of ingestion via a streaming application. The classification has already been built for another project. It is already clear that this solution will heavily involve the skills of the data engineer and the ML engineer, but not so much the data scientist since that portion of work has been completed in another project.

In the next section, we will look at some important points to consider when deploying your team on a real-world business problem.

ML engineering in the real world

The majority of us who work in machine learning, analytics, and related disciplines do so for for-profit companies. It is important therefore that we consider some of the important aspects of doing this type of work in the *real world*.

First of all, the ultimate goal of your work is to generate **value**. This can be calculated and defined in a variety of ways, but fundamentally your work has to improve something for the company or their customers in a way that justifies the investment put in. This is why most companies will not be happy for you to take a year to play with new tools and then generate nothing concrete to show for it (not that you would do this anyway, it is probably quite boring) or to spend your days reading the latest papers and only reading the latest papers. Yes, these things are part of any job in technology, and especially any job in the world of machine learning, but you have to be strategic about how you spend your time and always be aware of your value proposition.

Secondly, to be a successful ML engineer in the real world, you cannot just understand the technology; you *must understand the business*. You will have to understand how the company works day to day, you will have to understand how the different pieces of the company fit together, and you will have to understand the people of the company and their roles. Most importantly, you have to understand *the customer*, both of the business and of your work. If you do not know the motivations, pains, and needs of the people you are building for, then how can you be expected to build the right thing?

Finally, and this may be controversial, the most important skill for you being a successful ML engineer in the real world is one that this book will not teach you, and that is the ability to communicate effectively. You will have to work in a team, with a manager, with the wider community and business, and, of course, with your customers, as mentioned above. If you can do this and you know the technology and techniques (many of which are discussed in this book), then what can stop you?

But what kind of problems can you solve with machine learning when you work in the real world? Well, let's start with another potentially controversial statement: *a lot of the time, machine learning is not the answer*. This may seem strange given the title of this book, but it is just as important to know when *not* to apply machine learning as when to apply it. This will save you tons of expensive development time and resources.

Machine learning is ideal for cases when you want to do a semi-routine task faster, with more accuracy, or at a far larger scale than is possible with other solutions. Some typical examples are given in the following table, along with some discussion as to whether or not ML would be an appropriate tool for solving the problem:

Requirement	Is ML Appropriate?	Details
Anomaly detection of energy pricing signals	Yes	You will want to do this on large numbers of points on potentially varying time signals.
Improving data quality in an ERP system	No	This sounds more like a process problem. You can try and apply ML to this but often it is better to make the data entry process more automated or the process more robust.
Forecasting item consumption for a warehouse	Yes	ML will be able to do this more accurately than a human can, so this is a good area of application.
Summarizing data for business reviews	Maybe	This can be required at scale but is not an ML problem - simple queries against your data will do.

Figure 1.2 – Potential use cases for ML

As this table of simple examples hopefully starts to make clear, the cases where machine learning *is* the answer are ones that can usually be very well framed as a mathematical or statistical problem. After all, this is what machine learning really is; a series of algorithms rooted in mathematics that can iterate some internal parameters based on data. Where the lines start to blur in the modern world are through advances in areas such as deep learning or reinforcement learning, where problems that we previously thought would be very hard to phrase appropriately for standard ML algorithms can now be tackled.

The other tendency to watch out for in the real world (to go along with *let's use ML for everything*) is the worry that people have that ML is coming for their job and should not be trusted. This is understandable: a report by PwC in 2018 suggested that 30% of UK jobs will be impacted by automation by the 2030s (*Will Robots Really Steal Our Jobs?*: `https://www.pwc.co.uk/economic-services/assets/international-impact-of-automation-feb-2018.pdf`). What you have to try and make clear when working with your colleagues and customers is that what you are building is there to supplement and augment their capabilities, not to replace them.

Let's conclude this section by revisiting an important point: the fact that you are working for a company means, of course, that the aim of the game is to create value appropriate to the investment. In other words, you need to show a good **Return On Investment (ROI)**. This means a couple of things for you practically:

- You have to understand how different designs require different levels of investment. If you can solve your problem by training a deep neural net on a million images with a GPU running 24/7 for a month, or you know you can solve the same problem with some basic clustering and a bit of statistics on some standard hardware in a few hours, which should you choose?

- You have to be clear about the *value* you will generate. This means you need to work with experts and try to translate the results of your algorithm into actual dollar values. This is so much more difficult than it sounds, so you should take the time you need to get it right. And never, ever over-promise. *You should always under-promise and over-deliver.*

Adoption is not guaranteed. Even when building products for your colleagues within a company, it is important to understand that your solution will be tested every time someone uses it post-deployment. If you build shoddy solutions, then people will not use them, and the value proposition of what you have done will start to disappear.

Now that you understand some of the important points when using ML to solve business problems, let's explore what these solutions can look like.

What does an ML solution look like?

When you think of ML engineering, you would be forgiven for defaulting to imagining working on voice assistance and visual recognition apps (I fell into this trap in previous pages, did you notice?). The power of ML, however, lies in the fact that wherever there is data and an appropriate problem, it can help and be integral to the solution.

Some examples might help make this clearer. When you type a text message and your phone suggests the next words, it can very often be using a natural language model under the hood. When you scroll any social media feed or watch a streaming service, recommendation algorithms are working double time. If you take a car journey and an app forecasts when you are likely to arrive at your destination, there is going to be some kind of regression at work. Your loan application often results in your characteristics and application details being passed through a classifier. These applications are not the ones shouted about on the news (perhaps with the exception of when they go horribly wrong), but they are all examples of brilliantly put-together ML engineering.

In this book, the examples we work through will be more like these; typical scenarios for machine learning encountered in products and businesses every day. These are solutions that, if you can build them confidently, will make you an asset to any organization.

We should start by considering the broad elements that should constitute any ML solution, as indicated in the following diagram:

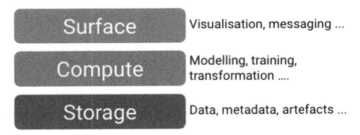

Figure 1.3 – Schematic of the general components or layers of any
ML solution and what they are responsible for

Your **storage layer** constitutes the endpoint of the data engineering process and the beginning of the ML one. It includes your data for training, your results from running your models, your artifacts, and important metadata. We can also consider this as including your stored code.

The **compute layer** is where the *magic* happens and where most of the focus of this book will be. It is where training, testing, prediction, and transformation all (mostly) happen. This book is all about making this layer as well-engineered as possible and interfacing with the other layers. You can blow this layer up to incorporate these pieces as in the following workflow:

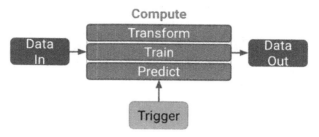

Figure 1.4 – The key elements of the compute layer

> **Important note**
> The details are discussed later in the book, but this highlights the fact that at a fundamental level, your compute processes for any ML solution are really just about taking some data in and pushing some data out.

The **surfacing layer** is where you share your ML solution's results with other systems. This could be through anything from application database insertion to API endpoints, to message queues, to visualization tools. This is the layer through which your customer eventually gets to use the results, so you must engineer your system to provide clean and understandable outputs, something we will discuss later.

And that is it in a nutshell. We will go into detail about all of these layers and points later, but for now, just remember these broad concepts and you will start to understand how all the detailed technical pieces fit together.

Why Python?

Before moving on to more detailed topics, it is important to discuss why Python has been selected as the programming language for this book. Everything that follows that pertains to higher-level topics such as architecture and system design can be applied to solutions using any or multiple languages, but Python has been singled out here for a few reasons.

Python is colloquially known as the *lingua franca* of data. It is a non-compiled, not strongly typed, and multi-paradigm programming language that has clear and simple syntax. Its tooling ecosystem is also extensive, especially in the analytics and machine learning space. Packages such as `scikit-learn`, `numpy`, `scipy`, and a host of others form the backbone of a huge amount of technical and scientific development across the world. Almost every major new software library for use in the data world has a Python API. It is the third most popular programming language in the world, according to the **TIOBE index** (`https://www.tiobe.com/tiobe-index/`) at the time of writing (January 2021).

Given this, being able to build your systems using Python means you will be able to leverage all of the excellent machine learning and data science tools available in this ecosystem, while also ensuring that you build applications that can play nicely with other software.

High-level ML system design

When you get down to the nuts and bolts of building your solution, there are so many options for tools, tech, and approaches that it can be very easy to be overwhelmed. However, as alluded to in the previous sections, a lot of this complexity can be abstracted to understand the bigger picture via some *back-of-the-envelope* architecture and designs. This is always a useful exercise once you know what problem you are going to try and solve, and something I recommend doing before you make any detailed choices about implementation.

To give you an idea of how this works in practice, what follows are a few worked-through examples where a team has to create a high-level ML systems design for some typical business problems. These problems are similar to ones I have encountered before and will likely be similar to ones you will encounter in your own work.

Example 1: Batch anomaly detection service

You work for a tech-savvy taxi ride company with a fleet of thousands of cars. The organization wants to start making ride times more consistent and to understand longer journeys in order to improve customer experience and thereby increase retention and return business. Your ML team is employed to create an anomaly detection service to find rides that have unusual ride time or ride length behaviors. You all get to work, and your data scientists find that if you perform clustering on sets of rides using the features of ride distance and time, you can clearly identify outliers worth investigating by the operations team. The data scientists present the findings to the CTO and other stakeholders before getting the go-ahead to develop this into a service that will provide an outlier flag as a new field in one of the main tables of the company's internal analysis tool.

In this example, we will simulate some data to show how the taxi company's data scientists could proceed. All the code is contained in the Chapter1/batch-anomaly folder in the repository for this book: https://github.com/PacktPublishing/Machine-Learning-Engineering-with-Python/tree/main/Chapter01. This will be true of all code snippets shown in this book:

1. First, let's define a function that will simulate some ride distances based on the random distribution given in numpy and return a numpy array containing the results. The reason for the repeated lines are so that we can create some base behavior and anomalies in the data, and you can clearly compare against the speeds we will generate for each set of taxis in the next step:

```python
def simulate_ride_distances():
    ride_dists = np.concatenate(
        (
            10 * np.random.random(size=370),
            30 * np.random.random(size=10),
            10 * np.random.random(size=10),
            10 * np.random.random(size=10)
        )
    )
    return ride_dists
```

2. We can now do the exact same thing for speeds, and again we have split the taxis into sets of 370, 10, 10, and 10 so that we can create some data with 'typical' behavior and some sets of anomalies, while allowing for clear matching of the values with the distances function:

```python
def simulate_ride_speeds():
    ride_speeds = np.concatenate(
        (
            np.random.normal(loc=30, scale=5, size=370),
            np.random.normal(loc=30, scale=5, size=10),
            np.random.normal(loc=50, scale=10, size=10),
            np.random.normal(loc=15, scale=4, size=10)
        )
    )
    return ride_speeds
```

3. We can now use both of these helper functions inside a function that will call these and bring them together to create a simulated dataset containing ride IDs, speeds, distances, and times. The result is returned as a `pandas` DataFrame for use in modeling:

```
def simulate_ride_data():
    ride_dists = simulate_ride_distances()
    ride_speeds = simulate_ride_speeds()
    ride_times = ride_dists/ride_speeds

    # Assemble into Data Frame
    df = pd.DataFrame(
        {
            'ride_dist': ride_dists,
            'ride_time': ride_times,
            'ride_speed': ride_speeds
        }
    )
    ride_ids = datetime.datetime.now().
strftime("%Y%m%d")+df.index.astype(str)
    df['ride_id'] = ride_ids
    return df
```

We can then run the simulation in lieu of getting the data from the taxi firm's system:

```
df = simulate_ride_data()
```

4. Now, we get to the core of what data scientists produce in their projects, which is a simple function that wraps some `sklearn` code for returning a dictionary with the clustering run metadata and results. We include the relevant imports here for ease:

```
from sklearn.preprocessing import StandardScaler
from sklearn.cluster import DBSCAN
from sklearn import metrics

def cluster_and_label(data, create_and_show_plot=True):
    data = StandardScaler().fit_transform(data)
```

```
    db = DBSCAN(eps=0.3, min_samples=10).fit(data)


    core_samples_mask = np.zeros_like(db.labels_,
dtype=bool)
    core_samples_mask[db.core_sample_indices_] = True
    labels = db.labels_


    n_clusters_ = len(set(labels)) - (1 if -1 in labels
else 0)
    n_noise_ = list(labels).count(-1)


    run_metadata = {
        'nClusters': n_clusters_,
        'nNoise': n_noise_,
        'silhouetteCoefficient': metrics.silhouette_
score(data, labels),
        'labels': labels,
    }
    return run_metadata
```

Finally, if we use the results of the simulation from *Step 4* and apply the machine learning code, we can get the original taxi dataset with a set of labels telling us whether the taxi ride was anomalous ('-1') or not ('0'):

```
    X = df[['ride_dist', 'ride_time']]
    results = cluster_and_label(X, create_and_show_
plot=False)
    df['label'] = results['labels']
```

Then, if you plot the results, with outliers labeled as black triangles, then you get something like *Figure 1.5*:

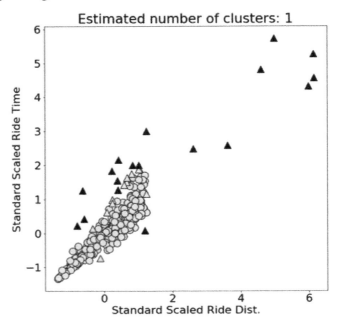

Figure 1.5 – An example set of results from performing clustering on some taxi ride data

Now that you have a basic model that works, you have to start thinking about how to pull this into an engineered solution – how could you do it?

Well, since the solution here is going to support longer-running investigations by another team, there is no need for a very low-latency solution. The stakeholders agree that the insights from clustering can be delivered at the end of each day. Working with the data-science part of the team, the ML engineers (led by you) understand that if clustering is run daily, this provides enough data to give appropriate clusters, but doing the runs any more frequently could lead to poorer results due to smaller amounts of data. So, a daily batch process is agreed upon.

What do you do next? Well, you know the frequency of runs is daily, but the volume of data is still very high, so it makes sense to leverage a distributed computing paradigm. Therefore, you decide to use Apache Spark. You know that the end consumer of the data is a table in a SQL database, so you need to work with the database team to design an appropriate handover of the results. Due to security and reliability concerns, it is not a good idea to write to the production database directly. You therefore agree that another database in the cloud will be used as an intermediate staging area for the data, which the main database can query against on its daily builds.

It might not seem like we have done anything technical here, but actually, you have already performed the high-level system design for your project. The rest of this book tells you how to fill in the gaps in the following diagram!

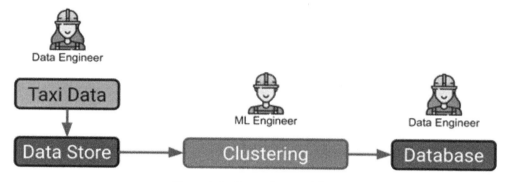

Figure 1.6 – Example 1 workflow

Let's now move on to the next example!

Example 2: Forecasting API

In this example, you are working for the logistics arm of a large retail chain. To maximize the flow of goods, the company would like to help regional logistics planners get ahead of particularly busy periods and to avoid product sell-outs. After discussions with stakeholders and subject matter experts across the business, it is agreed that the ability for planners to dynamically request and explore forecasts for particular warehouse items through a web-hosted dashboard is optimal. This allows the planners to understand likely future demand profiles before they make orders.

The data scientists come good again and find that the data has very predictable behavior at the level of any individual store. They decide to use the Facebook Prophet library for their modeling to help speed up the process of training many different models.

This example will use the open Rossman stores dataset from Kaggle, which can be found here: `https://www.kaggle.com/pratyushakar/rossmann-store-sales`:

1. First, we read in the data from the folder where we have extracted the data. We will perform all the following steps on the `train` dataset provided in the download but treat this as an entire dataset that we wish to split into training and test sets anyway:

    ```
    df = pd.read_csv('./data/rossman/train.csv')
    ```

2. Secondly, the data scientists prepped an initial subset of the data to work with first, so we will do the same. We do some basic tidy up, but the key points are that we select data for store number four in the dataset and only for when it is open:

```python
df['Date'] = pd.to_datetime(df['Date'])
df.rename(columns= {'Date': 'ds', 'Sales': 'y'},
inplace=True)
df_store = df[
    (df['Store']==4) &\
    (df['Open']==1)
].reset_index(drop=True)
df_store = df_store.sort_values('ds', ascending=True)
```

3. The data scientists then developed a little function that will take some supplied data, an index to delineate the size of the training set, and some seasonality parameters before returning a Prophet model trained on the training set:

```python
from fbprophet import Prophet
def train_predict(df, train_index,
seasonality=seasonality):
    # grab split data
    df_train = df.copy().iloc[0:train_index]
    df_test = df.copy().iloc[train_index:]

    model=Prophet(
        yearly_seasonality=seasonality['yearly'],
        weekly_seasonality=seasonality['weekly'],
        daily_seasonality=seasonality['daily'],
        interval_width = 0.95
    )

    # train and predict
    model.fit(df_train)
    predicted = model.predict(df_test)
    return predicted, df_train, df_test
```

4. Before applying this function, we can define the relevant seasonality settings in a dictionary:

```
seasonality = {
    'yearly': True,
    'weekly': True,
    'daily': False
}
```

5. Finally, we can apply the function as the data scientists envisaged:

```
train_index = int(0.8*df_store1.shape[0])
predicted, df_train, df_test = train_predict(
    df = df_store,
    train_index = train_index,
    Seasonality = seasonality
)
```

Running this model and plotting the predicted values against the ground truth gives a plot like that in *Figure 1.7*:

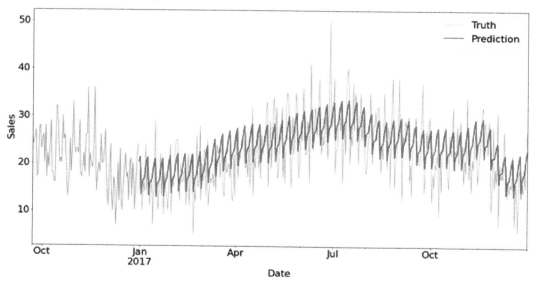

Figure 1.7 – Forecasting store sales

One issue here is that implementing a forecasting model like the one above for every store can quickly lead to hundreds or even thousands of models if the chain gathers enough data. Another issue is that not all stores are on the resource planning system used at the company yet, so some planners would like to retrieve forecasts for other stores they know are similar to their own. It is agreed that if users like this can explore regional profiles they believe are similar with their own data, then they can still make the optimal decisions.

Given this and the customer requirements for dynamic, ad hoc requests, you quickly rule out a full batch process. This wouldn't cover the use case for regions not on the core system and wouldn't allow for dynamic retrieval of up-to-date forecasts via the website, which would allow you to deploy models that forecast at a variety of time horizons in the future. It also means you could save on compute as you don't need to manage the storage and updating of thousands of forecasts every day and your resources can be focused on model training.

Therefore, you decide that actually, a web-hosted API with an endpoint that can return forecasts as needed by the user makes the most sense. To give efficient responses, you have to consider what happens in a typical user session. By workshopping with the potential users of the dashboard, you quickly realize that although the requests are dynamic, most planners will focus on particular items of interest in any one session. They will also not look at many regions. This helps you to design a data, forecast, and model caching strategy that means that after the user makes their first selections, results can be returned more quickly for a better user experience. This leads to the rough system sketch in *Figure 1.8*:

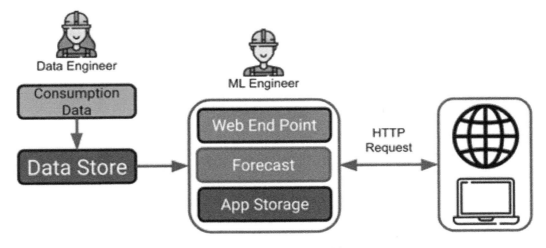

Figure 1.8 – Example 2 workflow

Next, let's look at the final example.

Example 3: Streamed classification

In this final example, you are working for a web-based company that wants to classify users based on their usage patterns as targets for different types of advertising, in order to more effectively target marketing spend. For example, if the user uses the site less frequently, we may want to entice them with more aggressive discounts. One of the key requirements from the business is that the end results become part of the data landed in a data store used by other applications.

Based on these requirements, your team determines that a streaming application is the simplest solution that ticks all the boxes. The data engineers focus their efforts on building the streaming and data store infrastructure, while the ML engineer works to wrap up the classification model the data science team has trained on historical data. The base algorithm that the data scientists settle on is implemented in `sklearn`, which we will work through below by applying it to a marketing dataset that would be similar to that produced in this use case.

This hypothetical example aligns with a lot of classic datasets, including the Bank Marketing dataset from the UCI Machine Learning Repository, `https://archive.ics.uci.edu/ml/datasets/Bank+Marketing#`. The following example code uses this dataset. Remember that all of the following code is available in the book's GitHub repository as in the other examples:

1. First, we will read in the data, which is stored in a folder labeled `data` in the same directory as the script we are building:

```
import pandas as pd
df = pd.read_csv('./data/bank/bank.csv', delimiter=';',
decimal=',')
```

2. Next, we define the features we would like to use in our model and define our feature matrix, X, and target variable vector, y. The target variable will be translated to a numerical value, 1, if the customer went with the proposed product, and 0 if they did not. Note that we assume the features have been selected in this case via robust exploratory data analysis, which is not covered here:

```
cat_feature_cols = ["marital", "education", "contact",
"default", "housing", "loan", "poutcome"]
num_feature_cols = ["age", "pdays", "previous", "emp.var.
rate", "euribor3m", "nr.employed"]
feature_cols = cat_feature_cols + num_feature_cols
X = df[feature_cols].copy()
```

```
y = df['y'].apply(lambda x: 1 if x == 'yes' else
0).copy()
```

3. Before moving on to modeling, we split the data into an 80/20 training and test split:

```
X_train, X_test, y_train, y_test = train_test_split(X, y,
test_size=0.2, random_state=42)
```

4. We then perform some very basic feature engineering and preparation by one-hot encoding all of the categorical variables, being careful to only train the transformer on the training set:

```
from sklearn.preprocessing import OneHotEncoder
enc = OneHotEncoder(handle_unknown='ignore')
X_train_cat_encoded = enc.fit_transform(X_train[cat_
feature_cols])
X_test_cat_encoded = enc.transform(X_test[cat_feature_
cols])
```

5. We then standardize the numerical variables in a similar way:

```
from sklearn.preprocessing import StandardScaler
scaler = StandardScaler()
X_train_num_scaled = scaler.fit_transform(X_train[num_
feature_cols])
X_test_num_scaled = scaler.transform(X_test[num_feature_
cols])
```

6. We then have to bring the numerical and categorical data together into one set:

```
X_train = np.concatenate((X_train_cat_encoded.toarray(),
X_train_num_scaled), axis=1)
X_test = np.concatenate((X_test_cat_encoded.toarray(), X_
test_num_scaled), axis=1)
```

7. Now we are ready to get ready for modeling. The dataset has imbalanced classes, so the data scientists have suggested that we use the SMOTE algorithm, which is contained within the `imblearn` package to perform oversampling of the minority class. This creates a balanced classification dataset:

```
from imblearn.over_sampling import SMOTE
sm = SMOTE()
X_balanced, y_balanced = sm.fit_sample(X_train, y_train)
```

8. The core code that the data scientists created can now be applied. They come up with a series of different variants of code based around a simple random forest classification model:

```
from sklearn.model_selection import KFold
from sklearn.model_selection import cross_val_score
from sklearn.ensemble import RandomForestClassifier
from sklearn.metrics import f1_score


# Define classifier
rfc = RandomForestClassifier(n_estimators=1000)
rfc.fit(X_balanced, y_balanced)
```

When you run this code, you will find that the model performance could be improved. This, along with the need to streamline the preceding code, improve model scalability, and build a solution that can interact with the streaming pipeline, will be the focus of the ML engineer's work for this project. There will also be some subtleties around how often you want to retrain your algorithm to make sure that the classifier does not go stale. We will discuss all of these topics later in this book. Taken together, the outline of the processing steps needed in the solution gives a high-level system design like that in *Figure 1.9*:

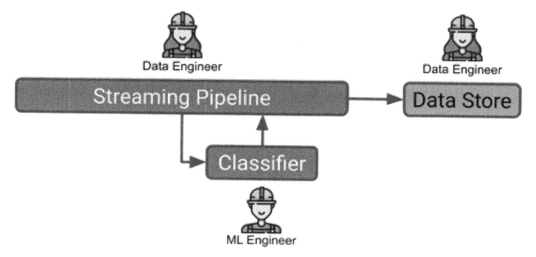

Figure 1.9 – Example 3 workflow

We have now explored three high-level ML system designs and discussed the rationale behind our workflow choices. We have also explored in detail the sort of code that would often be produced by data scientists working on modeling, but which would act as input to future ML engineering work. This section should therefore have given us an appreciation of where our engineering work begins in a typical project and what types of problems we will be aiming to solve. And there you go. You are already on your way to becoming an ML engineer!

Summary

In this chapter, we have introduced the idea of ML engineering and how that fits within a modern team building valuable solutions based on data. There was a discussion of how the focus of ML engineering is complementary to the strengths of data science and data engineering and where these disciplines overlap. Some comments were made about how to use this information to assemble an appropriately resourced team for your projects.

The challenges of building machine learning products in modern real-world organizations were then discussed, along with pointers to help you overcome some of these challenges. In particular, the notion of reasonably estimating value and effectively communicating with your stakeholders were emphasized.

This chapter then rounded off with a taster of the technical content to come in later chapters, in particular, through a discussion of what typical ML solutions look like and how they should be designed (at a high level) for some common use cases.

The next chapter will focus on how to set up and implement your development processes to build the ML solutions you want and provide some insight as to how this is different from standard software development processes. Then there will be a discussion of some of the tools you can use to start managing the tasks and artifacts from your projects without creating major headaches. This will set you up for the technical details of how to build the key elements of your ML solutions in later chapters.

2
The Machine Learning Development Process

In this chapter, we will define how the work for any successful **Machine Learning** (ML) software engineering project can be divided up. Basically, we will answer the question of how do you *actually organize the doing* of a successful ML project? We will not only discuss the process and workflow, but we will also set up the tools you will need for each stage of the process and highlight some important best practices with real ML code examples.

Specifically, this chapter will cover the concept of a *discover, play, develop, deploy* workflow for your ML projects, appropriate development tooling and their configuration and integration for a successful project. We will also cover version control strategies and their basic implementation, setting up **Continuous Integration/Continuous Deployment (CI/CD)** for your ML project. We will also introduce some potential execution environments. At the end of this chapter, you will be set up for success in your Python ML engineering project. This is the foundation on which we will build everything in subsequent chapters.

As usual, we will conclude the chapter by summarizing the main points and highlight what this means as we work through the rest of the book.

Finally, it is also important to note that although we will frame the discussion here in terms of ML challenges, most of what you will learn in this chapter can also be applied to other Python software engineering projects. My hope is that the investment of building out these foundational concepts in detail will be something you can leverage again and again in all of your work.

We will explore all of this in the following sections:

- Setting up our tools
- Concept to solution in four steps

There is plenty of exciting stuff to get through and lots to learn – so let's get started!

Technical requirements

The following software and packages are used in this chapter (versions equal to or greater than these should work):

- Anaconda
- PyCharm Community Edition
- Git
- Jupyter Notebook
- PySpark
- `fbprophet`
- scikit-learn

- MLflow

- pytest

- Flake8

You will also need the following:

- An Atlassian Jira account. We will discuss this more later in the chapter, but you can sign up for one for free at `https://www.atlassian.com/software/jira/free`.

- An AWS account. This will also be covered in the chapter, but you can sign up for an account at `https://aws.amazon.com/`. You will need to add payment details to sign up to AWS, but everything we do in this book will only require the free tier solutions.

The technical steps in this chapter were all executed on a Linux machine running Ubuntu 20.04.1 with a user profile that had admin rights. If you are running the steps on a different system, then you may have to consult the documentation for that specific tool if the steps do not work as planned. Even if this is the case, most of the steps will be almost exactly the same or very similar for most systems. You can also check out all of the code for this chapter under the book repository at `https://github.com/PacktPublishing/Machine-Learning-Engineering-with-Python/tree/main/Chapter02`. The repo will also contain further resources for getting the code examples up and running.

Setting up our tools

To prepare for the work in the rest of this chapter, and indeed the rest of the book, it will be helpful to set up some tools. At a high level, we need the following:

- Somewhere to code

- Something to track our code changes

- Something to help manage our tasks

- Somewhere to provision infrastructure and deploy our solution

Let's look at how to approach each of these in turn:

- **Somewhere to code**: First, although the weapon of choice for coding by data scientists is of course Jupyter Notebook (other solutions are available), once you begin to make the move toward ML engineering, it will be important to have an **Integrated Development Environment (IDE)** to hand. An IDE is basically an application that comes with a series of built-in tools and capabilities to help you to develop the best software that you can. **PyCharm** is an excellent example for Python developers and comes with a wide variety of plugins, add-ons, and integrations useful to the ML engineer. You can download the Community Edition from JetBrains at `https://www.jetbrains.com/pycharm/`. Once you have successfully installed PyCharm, you can create a new project or open an existing one from the **Welcome to PyCharm** window, as shown in *Figure 2.1*:

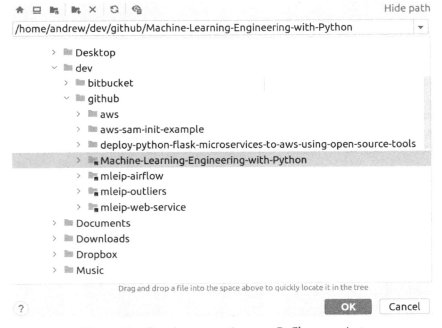

Figure 2.1 – Opening or creating your PyCharm project

- **Something to track code changes**: Next on the list is a code version control system. In this book, we will use **GitHub** but there are a variety of solutions, all freely available, that are based on the same underlying open source **Git** technology. Later sections will discuss how to use these as part of your development workflow but first, if you do not have a version control system set up, you can navigate to github.com and create a free account. Follow the instructions on the site to create your first repository, and you will be shown a screen that looks something as in *Figure 2.2*. To make your life easier later, you should select **Add a README file** and **Add .gitignore** (then select **Python**). The README provides an initial Markdown file for you to get started with and somewhere to describe your project. The .gitignore file tells your Git distribution to ignore certain types of files that in general are not important for version control. It is up to you whether you want the repository to be public or private and what license you wish to use. The repository for this book uses the **MIT license**:

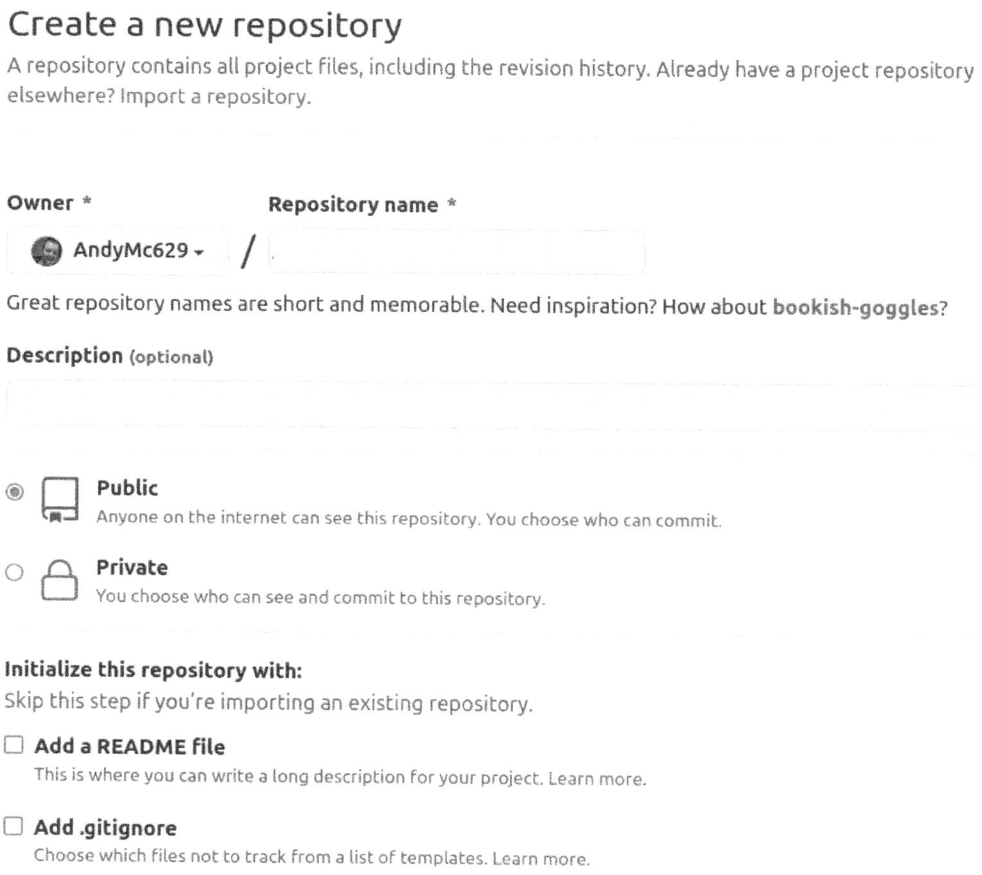

Create a new repository

A repository contains all project files, including the revision history. Already have a project repository elsewhere? Import a repository.

Owner *   **Repository name ***

🔘 AndyMc629 ▾   /

Great repository names are short and memorable. Need inspiration? How about **bookish-goggles**?

Description (optional)

◉ 🗔 **Public**
Anyone on the internet can see this repository. You choose who can commit.

○ 🔒 **Private**
You choose who can see and commit to this repository.

Initialize this repository with:
Skip this step if you're importing an existing repository.

☐ **Add a README file**
This is where you can write a long description for your project. Learn more.

☐ **Add .gitignore**
Choose which files not to track from a list of templates. Learn more.

Figure 2.2 – Setting up your GitHub repository

Once you have set up your IDE and version control system, you need to make them talk to each other by using the Git plugins provided with PyCharm. This is as simple as navigating to **VCS | Enable Version Control Integration** and selecting **Git**. You can edit the version control settings by navigating to **File | Settings | Version Control**; see *Figure 2.3*:

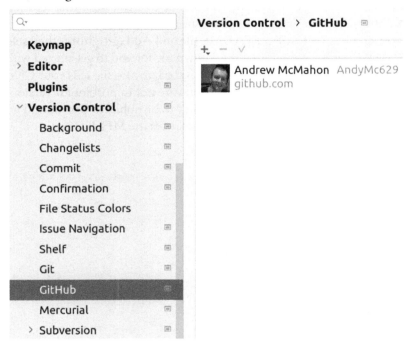

Figure 2.3 – Configuring version control with PyCharm

- **Something to help manage our tasks**: You are now ready to write Python and track your code changes, but are you ready to manage or participate in a complex project with other team members? For this, it is often useful to have a solution where you can track tasks, issues, bugs, user stories, and other documentation and items of work. It also helps if this has good integration points with the other tools you will use. In this book, we will use **Jira** as an example of this. If you navigate to https://www.atlassian.com/software/jira, you can create a free cloud Jira account and then follow the interactive tutorial within the solution to set up your first board and create some tasks. *Figure 2.4* shows the task board for this book project, called **Machine Learning Engineering in Python** (MEIP):

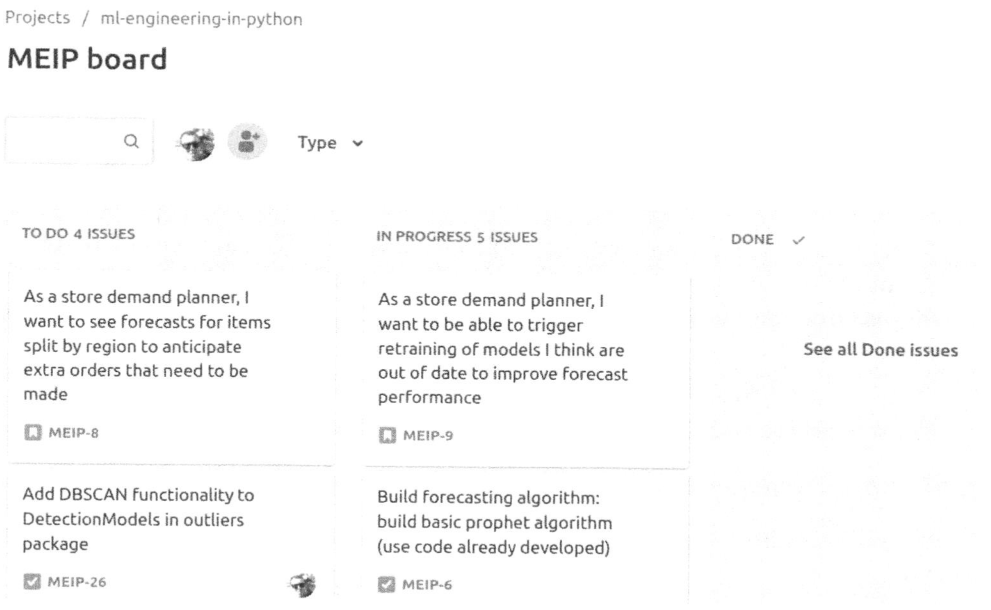

Projects / ml-engineering-in-python

MEIP board

[Q]   Type ∨

TO DO 4 ISSUES

As a store demand planner, I
want to see forecasts for items
split by region to anticipate
extra orders that need to be
made

▢ MEIP-8

Add DBSCAN functionality to
DetectionModels in outliers
package

☑ MEIP-26

IN PROGRESS 5 ISSUES

As a store demand planner, I
want to be able to trigger
retraining of models I think are
out of date to improve forecast
performance

▢ MEIP-9

Build forecasting algorithm:
build basic prophet algorithm
(use code already developed)

☑ MEIP-6

DONE ✓

See all Done issues

Figure 2.4 – The task board for this book in Jira

- **Somewhere to provision infrastructure and deploy our solution**: Everything that you have just installed and set up are tools that will really help take your workflow and software development practices to the next level. The last piece of the puzzle is having the tools, technologies, and infrastructure available for deploying the end solution. Management of computing infrastructure for applications was (and often still is) the provision of dedicated infrastructure teams, but with the advent of public clouds, there has been real democratization of this capability to people working across the spectrum of software roles. In particular, modern ML engineering is very dependent on the successful implementation of cloud technologies, usually through the main public cloud providers such as **Amazon Web Services** (**AWS**), **Microsoft Azure**, or **Google Cloud Platform** (**GCP**). This book will utilize tools found in the AWS ecosystem, but all of the tools and techniques you will find here have equivalents in the other clouds.

The flipside of the democratization of capabilities that the cloud brings is that teams who own the deployment of their solutions have to gain new skills and understanding. I am strong believer in the principle that *you build it, you own it, you run it* as far as possible, but this means that as an ML engineer, you will have to be comfortable with a host of potential new tools and principles, as well as *owning* the performance of your deployed solution. *With great power comes great responsibility* and all that. In *Chapter 5, Deployment Patterns and Tools*, we will dive into this topic in detail.

Let's talk through setting this up.

Setting up an AWS account

As previously stated, you don't have to use AWS, but that's what we're going to use throughout this book. Once it's set up here, you can use it for everything we'll do:

1. To set up an AWS account, navigate to aws.amazon.com and select **Create Account**. You will have to add some payment details but everything we mention in this book can be explored through the *free tier* of AWS, where you do not incur a cost below some set threshold of consumption.

2. Once you have created your account, you can navigate to the AWS Management Console, where you can see all of the services that are available to you (see *Figure 2.5*):

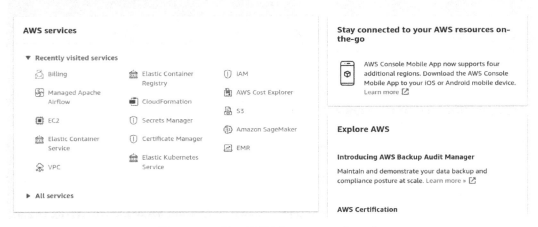

Figure 2.5 – The AWS Management Console

3. Finally, there would be no ML engineering without ML models. So, the final piece of software you should install is one that will help you track and serve your models in a consistent way. For this, we will use **MLflow**, an open source platform from **Databricks** and under the stewardship of the Linux Foundation. Setting up MLflow locally is very simple; all you have to do is find your normal UNIX terminal and run the following code:

```
pip install mlflow
```

Or run the following:

```
conda install -c conda-forge mlflow
```

We will take a look at the difference between `pip` and `conda` later in this chapter, but the key point here is that installing MLflow is really simple. We will discuss the installation of MLflow in the cloud later in the book, but for most of the examples in the book, you can work locally in the first instance.

With our AWS account ready to go, let's look at the four steps that cover the whole process.

Concept to solution in four steps

All ML projects are unique in some way: the organization, the data, the people, and the tools and techniques employed will never be exactly the same for any two projects. This is good, as it signifies progress as well as the natural variety that makes this such a fun space to work in.

That said, no matter the details, broadly speaking, all successful ML projects actually have a good deal in common. They require translation of a business problem into a technical problem, a lot of research and understanding, proofs of concept, analyses, iterations, consolidation of work, construction of the final product, and deployment to an appropriate environment. That is ML engineering in a nutshell!

Developing this a bit further, you can start to bucket these activities into rough categories or stages, the results of each being necessary inputs for later stages. This is shown in *Figure 2.6*:

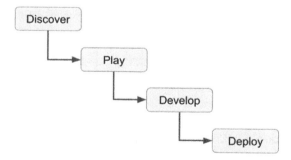

Figure 2.6 – The stages that any ML project goes through as part of the ML development process

Each category of work has a slightly different flavor but taken together, they provide the backbone of any good ML project. The next few sections will develop the details of each of these categories and begin to show you how they can be used to build your ML engineering solutions. As we will discuss later, it is also not necessary that you tackle your entire project in four stages like this; you can actually work through each of these steps for a specific feature or part of your overall project. This will be covered in the *Selecting a software development methodology* section.

Let's make this a bit more real. The main focus and outputs of every stage can be summarized as in the table of *Figure 2.7*:

Stage	Outputs
Discover	Clarity on the business question
	Clear arguments for ML over another approach
	Definition of the KPIs and metrics you want to optimize
	A sketch of the route to value
Play	Detailed understanding of the data
	Working proof of concept
	Agreement on the model/algorithm/logic that will solve the problem
	Evidence that a solution is doable within realistic resource scenarios
	Evidence that good ROI can be achieved
Develop	A working solution that can be hosted on appropriate and available infrastructure
	Thorough test results and performance metrics (for algorithms and software)
	An agreed retraining and model deployment strategy
	Unit tests, integration tests, and regression tests
	Solution packaging and pipelines
Deploy	A working and tested deployment process
	Provisioned infrastructure with appropriate security and performance characteristics
	Mode retraining and management processes
	An end-to-end working solution!

Figure 2.7 – The outputs of the different stages of the ML development process

Important note

You may think that an ML engineer only really needs to consider the latter two stages, *develop*, and *deploy*, and that earlier stages are owned by the data scientist or even a business analyst. We will indeed focus mainly on these stages through this book and this division of labor can work very well. It is, however, crucially important that if you are going to build an ML solution you understand all of the motivations and development steps that have gone before – you wouldn't build a new type of rocket without understanding where you want to go first, would you?

Discover

Before you start working to build any solution, it is vitally important that you understand the problem you are trying to solve. This activity is often termed **discovery** in business analysis and is crucial if your ML project is going to be a success.

The key things to do during the discovery phase are the following:

- *Speak to the customer! And then speak to them again*: You must understand the end user requirements in detail if you are to design and build the right system.

- *Document everything*: You will be judged on how well you deliver against the requirements, so make sure that all of the key points from your discussion are documented and signed off by members of your team and the customer or their appropriate representative.

- *Define the metrics that matter*: It is very easy at the beginning of a project to get carried away and to feel like you can solve any and every problem with the amazing new tool you are going to build. Fight this tendency as aggressively as you can, as it can easily cause major headaches later on. Instead, steer your conversations toward defining a single or very small number of metrics that define what success will look like.

- *Start finding out where the data lives!*: If you can start working out what kind of systems you will have to access to get the data you need, this saves you time later and can help you find any major issues before they derail your project.

Using user stories

Once you have spoken to the customer (a few times), you can start to define some **user stories**. User stories are concise and consistently formatted expressions of what the user or customer wants to see and the acceptance criteria for that feature or unit of work. For example, we may want to define a user story based on the taxi ride example from *Chapter 1, Introduction to ML Engineering*: As a user of our internal web service, I want to see anomalous taxi rides and be able to investigate them further.

Let's begin!

1. To add this in Jira, select the **Create** button.
2. Next, select **Story**.
3. Then, fill in the details as you deem appropriate.

You have now added a user story to your work management tool! This allows you to do things such as create new tasks and link them to this user story or update its status as your project progresses:

Projects / 🕹 ml-engineering-in-py... / ✏ **Add epic** / 🗂 MEIP-14

As a taxi ride analyst, I want to see anomalous journeys so that I can tailor our offers to customers

📎 🔀 🔗 G ⋯

Description

<u>Acceptance criteria (scenario):</u>

Given I have access to data and/or visaulizations of ML results,

where there are anomalous taxi rides,

then the system accurately identifies and labels these rides and I can see them

GitHub integration for Jira

Branches   Pull Requests   Commits   Tags

Figure 2.8 – An example user story in Jira

The data sources you use are particularly crucial to understand. As you know, *garbage in, garbage out*, or even worse, *no data, no go*! The particular questions you have to answer about the data are mainly centered around **access**, **technology**, **quality**, and **relevance**.

For access and technology, you are trying to pre-empt how much work the data engineers have to do to start their pipeline of work and how much this will hold up the rest of the project. It is therefore crucial that you get this one right.

A good example would be if you find out quite quickly that the main bulk of data you will need lives in a legacy internal financial system with no real modern APIs and no access request mechanism for non-finance team members. If its main backend is on-premises and you need to migrate locked-down financial data to the cloud, but this makes your business nervous, then you know you have a lot of work to do before you type a line of code. If the data already lives in your enterprise data lake that your team already has access to, then you are obviously in a better position. Any challenge is surmountable if the value proposition is strong enough, but finding all this out early will save you time, energy, and money later on.

Relevance is a bit harder to find out before you kick off, but you can begin to get an idea. For example, if you want to perform the inventory forecast we discussed in *Chapter 1, Introduction to ML Engineering*, do you need to pull in customer account information? If you want to create the classifier of *premium* or *non-premium* customers as marketing targets, also mentioned in *Chapter 1, Introduction to ML Engineering*, do you need to have data on social media feeds? The question as to what is relevant will often be less clear-cut than these but an important thing to remember is that you can always come back to it if you really missed something important. You are trying to capture the most important design decisions early, so common sense and lots of stakeholder and subject matter expert engagement will go a long way.

Data quality is something that you can try to anticipate a little before moving forward in your project with some questions to current users or consumers of the data or those involved in its entry processes. To get a more quantitative understanding though, you will often just need to get your data scientists working with the data in a hands-on manner.

In the next section, we will look at how we develop proof-of-concept ML solutions in the most research-intensive phase, **play**.

Play

In the play stage of the project, your aim is to work out whether solving the task even at the proof-of-concept level is feasible. To do this, you might employ the usual data science bread-and-butter techniques of exploratory data analysis and explanatory modeling we mentioned in the last chapter before moving on to creating an ML model that does what you need.

In this part of the process, you are not overly concerned with details of implementation, but with exploring the realms of possibility and gaining an in-depth understanding of the data and the problem that goes beyond initial discovery work. Since the goal here is not to create *production-ready* code or to build reusable tools, you should not worry about whether or not the code you are writing is of the highest quality or using sophisticated patterns. For example, it will not be uncommon to see code that looks something as in the following examples (taken, in fact, from the repo for this book):

Prep for Prophet

```
df.rename(columns= {'Datetime': 'ds', 'AEP_MW': 'y'}, inplace=True)
```

```
df['ds']=df['ds'].astype('datetime64[ns]')
```

```
df.dtypes
```

```
#Initialize Split Class, we'll split our data 5 times for cv
ts_splits = TimeSeriesSplit(n_splits=5)
```

Train and Forecast

```
tmp = time_split_train_test(df.sort_values('ds', ascending=True).iloc[-1000:], ts_splits)
```

```
tmp.head()
```

Plot

```
nrow = 5; ncol = 1;
fig, axs = plt.subplots(nrows=nrow, ncols=ncol, figsize=(20,30))
fig.subplots_adjust(hspace=0.4, wspace=0.4)
for i, ax in enumerate(fig.axes):
    split_rmse = tmp[(tmp['split']==i) & (tmp['train']==False)]['rmse'].iloc[0]

    ax.set_title('Split '+str(i)+' - RMSE: '+"{:.2f}".format(split_rmse))

    tmp[(tmp['split']==i) & (tmp['train']==True)].plot(x='ds', y='y', ax=ax, color='blue', marker='o')
    tmp[(tmp['split']==i) & (tmp['train']==False)].plot(x='ds', y='y', ax=ax, color='red', marker='o')
    tmp[(tmp['split']==i) & (tmp['train']==False)].plot(x='ds', y='yhat', ax=ax, color='orange', marker='^')
```

Figure 2.9 – Some example prototype code that will be created during the play stage

Even a quick glance at these screenshots tells you a few things:

- The code is in a Jupyter notebook, which is run by a user interactively in a web browser.

- The code sporadically calls methods to simply check or explore elements of the data (for example, df.head() and df.dtypes).

- There is ad hoc code for plotting (and it's not very intuitive!).

- There is a variable called tmp, which is not very descriptive.

All of this is absolutely fine in this more exploratory phase, but one of the aims of this book is to help you understand what is required to take code like this and make it into something suitable for your production ML pipelines. The next section starts us along this path.

Develop

As we have mentioned a few times already, one of the aims of this book is to get you thinking about the fact that you are building software products that just happen to have ML in them. This means a steep learning curve for some of us who have come from more mathematical and algorithmic backgrounds. This may seem intimidating but do not despair! The good news is that we can reuse a lot of the best practices and techniques honed through the software engineering community over several decades. There is nothing new under the sun.

This section explores several of those methodologies, processes, and considerations that can be employed in the development phase of our ML engineering projects.

Selecting a software development methodology

One of the first things we could and should shamelessly replicate as ML engineers is the software development methodologies that are utilized in projects across the globe. One category of these, often referred to as **Waterfall**, covers project workflows that fit quite naturally with the idea of building something complex (think a building or a car). In Waterfall methodologies, there are distinct and sequential phases of work, each with a clear set of outputs that are needed before moving on to the next phase. For example, a typical Waterfall project may have phases that broadly cover requirements gathering, analysis, design, development, testing, and deployment (sound familiar?). The key thing is that in a Waterfall-flavored project, when you are in the *requirements gathering* phase, you should *only* be working on gathering requirements, when in the testing phase, you should *only* be working on testing, and so on. We will discuss the pros and cons of this for ML in the next few paragraphs after introducing another set of methodologies.

The other set of methodologies, termed **Agile**, began its life after the introduction of the **Agile Manifesto** in 2001 (`https://agilemanifesto.org/`). At the heart of Agile development are the ideas of flexibility, iteration, and incremental updates, failing fast, and adapting to changing requirements. If you are from a research or scientific background, this concept of flexibility and adaptability based on results and new findings may sound familiar.

What may not be so familiar to you if you have this type of scientific or academic background is that you can still embrace these concepts within a relatively strict framework that is centered around delivery outcomes. Agile software development methodologies are all about finding the balance between experimentation and delivery. This is often done by introducing the concepts of **ceremonies** (such as Scrums and Sprint Retrospectives) and **roles** (such as Scrum Master and Product Owner).

Further to this, within Agile development, there are two variants that are extremely popular: **Scrum** and **Kanban**. Scrum projects are centered around short units of work called **Sprints** where the idea is to take additions to the product from ideation through to deployment in that small timeframe. In Kanban, the main idea is to achieve a steady **flow** of tasks from an organized backlog into work in progress through to completed work.

All of these methodologies (and many more besides) have their merits and their detractions. You do not have to be married to any of them; you can chop and change between them. For example, in an ML project, it may make sense to do some *post-deployment* work that has a focus on maintaining an already-existing service (sometimes termed a *business as usual* activity) such as further model improvements or software optimizations in a Kanban framework. It may make sense to do the main delivery of your core body of work in Sprints with very clear outcomes. But you can chop and change and see what fits best for your use cases, your team, and your organization.

But what makes applying these types of workflows to ML projects different? What do we need to think about in this world of ML that we didn't before? Well, some of the key points are the following:

- *You don't know what you don't know*: You cannot know whether you will be able to solve the problem until you have seen the data. Traditional software engineering is not as critically dependent on the data that will flow through the system as ML engineering is. We can know how to solve a problem in principle, but if the appropriate data does not exist in sufficient quantity or is of poor quality, then we can't solve the problem in practice.

- *Your system is alive*: If you build a classic website, with its backend database, shiny frontend, amazing load balancing, and other features, then realistically, if the resource is there, it can just run forever. Nothing fundamental changes about the website and it's running with time. Clicks still get translated to actions and page navigation still happens the same way. Now consider putting some ML-generated advertising content based on typical user profiles in there. What is a *typical user profile* and does that change with time? With more traffic and more users, do behaviors that we never saw before become *the new normal*? Your system is learning all the time and that leads to the problems of *model drift* and *distributional shift* as well as more complex update and rollback scenarios.

- *Nothing is certain*: When building a system that uses rule-based logic, you know what you are going to get each and every time. *If X, then Y* means just that, always. With ML models, it is often very much harder to know what the answer is when you ask the question, which is in fact why these algorithms are so powerful. But it does mean that you can have unpredictable behavior, either for the reasons discussed previously or simply because the algorithm has learned something that is not obvious about the data to a human observer, or because ML algorithms can be based on probabilistic and statistical concepts, results come attached to some uncertainty or *fuzziness*. A classic example is when you apply logistic regression and receive the probability of the data point belonging to one of the classes. It's a probability so you cannot say with certainty that it is the case; just how likely it is! This is particularly important to consider when the outputs of your ML system will be leveraged by users or other systems to make decisions.

Given these issues, in the next section, we'll try and understand what development methodologies can help us when we build our ML solutions. In *Figure 2.10*, we can see some advantages and disadvantages of each of these Agile methodologies for different stages and types of ML engineering projects:

Methodology	Pros	Cons
Agile	Flexibility is expected.	If not well managed, can easily have scope drift.
	Faster dev to deploy cycles.	Kanban or Sprints may not work well for some projects.
Waterfall	Clearer path to deployment.	Lack of flexibility.
	Clear staging and ownership of tasks.	Higher admin overheads.

Figure 2.10 – Agile versus Waterfall for ML development

Let's move on to the next section!

Package management (conda and pip)

If I told you to write a program that did anything in data science or ML without using any libraries or packages and just pure Python, you would probably find this quite difficult to achieve in any reasonable amount of time, and incredibly boring! This is a good thing. One of the really powerful features of developing software in Python is that you can leverage an extensive ecosystem of tools and capabilities relatively easily. The flip side of this is that it would be very easy for managing the dependencies of your code base to become a very complicated and hard-to-replicate task. This is where package and environment managers such as `pip` and `conda` come in.

`pip` is the standard package manager in Python and the one recommended for use by the Python Package Authority. It retrieves and installs Python packages from **PyPI**, the **Python Package Index**. `pip` is super easy to use and is often the suggested way to install packages in tutorials and books.

`conda` is the *package and environment* manager that comes with the Anaconda and Miniconda Python distributions. A key strength of `conda` is that although it comes from the Python ecosystem, and it has excellent capabilities there, it is actually a more general package manager. As such, if your project requires dependencies outside Python (the `numpy` and `scipy` libraries being good examples), then although `pip` can install these, it can't track all the non-Python dependencies, nor manage their versions. With `conda`, this is solved.

You can also use `pip` within `conda` environments, so you can try and get the best of both worlds or use whatever you need for your project. That said, I strongly suggest sticking to installing packages with the `conda` command as much as possible, due to the point about non-Python dependencies, and also for consistency. Throughout this book, we will use `conda` to both manage our Python environments and for package management and installation (you have already seen this in previous sections, for example, when we installed MLflow).

To get started with Conda, if you haven't already, you can download the **Individual** distribution installer from the Anaconda website (`https://www.anaconda.com/products/individual`). Anaconda comes with some Python packages already installed, but if you want to start from a completely empty environment, you can download Miniconda from the same website instead (they have the exact same functionality; you just start from a different base).

The Anaconda documentation is very helpful for getting you up to speed with the appropriate commands, but here is a quick tour of some of the key ones.

First, if we want to create a `conda` environment called `mleng` with Python version 3.8 installed, we simply execute the following in our terminal:

```
conda env --name mleng python=3.8
```

We can then activate the `conda` environment by running the following:

```
source activate mleng
```

This means that any new `conda` or `pip` commands will install packages in this environment and not system-wide.

We often want to share the details of our environment with others working on the same project, so it can be useful to export all the package configurations to a `.yml` file:

```
conda export env > environment.yml
```

The GitHub repository for this book contains a file called `mleng-environment.yml` for you to create your own instance of the `mleng` environment. The following command creates an environment with this configuration using this file:

```
conda env create --file environment.yml
```

These commands, coupled with your classic `install` command, will set you up for your project quite nicely!

```
conda install <package-name>
```

Now that we can successfully configure an environment, we should discuss how we should work in that development environment.

Code version control

If you are going to write code for real systems, you are almost certainly going to do it as part of a team. You are also going to make your life easier if you can have a clean audit trail of changes, edits, and updates so that you can see how the solution has developed. Finally, you are going to want to cleanly and safely separate out the stable versions of the solution that you are building and that can be deployed versus more transient developmental versions. All of this, thankfully, is taken care of by source code version control systems, the most popular of which is **Git**.

We will not go into how Git works under the hood here (there are whole books on the topic!) but we will focus on understanding the key practical elements of using it:

1. You already have a GitHub account from earlier in the chapter, so the first thing to do is to create a repository with Python as the language and initialize README.me and `.gitignore` files. The next thing to do is to get a local copy of this repository by running the following command in your Bash, Git Bash, or other terminal:

    ```
    git clone <repo-name>
    ```

2. Now that you have done this, go into the README.me file and make some edits (anything will do). Then, run the following commands to tell Git to *monitor* this file and to save your changes locally with a message briefly explaining what these are:

```
git add README.m
git commit -m "I've made a nice change …"
```

This now means that your local Git instance has stored what you've changed and is ready to share that with the remote repo.

3. You can then incorporate these changes into the main branch by doing the following:

```
git push origin main
```

If you now go back to the GitHub site, you will see that the changes have taken place in your remote repository, and that the comments you added have accompanied the change.

4. Other people in your team can then get the updated changes by running the following:

```
git pull origin main
```

These steps are the absolute basics of Git and there is a ton more you can learn online. What we will do now, though, is start setting up our repo and workflow in a way that is relevant to ML engineering.

Git strategies

The presence of a strategy for using version control systems can often be a key differentiator between data science and ML engineering aspects of a project. It can sometimes be overkill to define a strict Git strategy for exploratory and basic modeling stages (discover and play) but if you want to engineer something for deployment (and you are reading this book, so this is likely where your head is at), then it is fundamentally important.

Great, but what do we mean by a Git strategy?

Well, let's imagine that we just try to develop our solution without a shared direction in how to organize the versioning and code.

ML engineer *A* wants to start building some of the data science code into a Spark MLlib pipeline (more on this later) so creates a branch from main called pipeline1spark:

```
git checkout -b pipeline1spark
```

She then gets to work in the branch and writes some nice code in a new file called
`pipeline.py`:

```
# Configure an ML pipeline, which consists of three stages:
tokenizer, hashingTF, and lr.
tokenizer = Tokenizer(inputCol="text", outputCol="words")
hashingTF = HashingTF(inputCol=tokenizer.getOutputCol(),
outputCol="features")
lr = LogisticRegression(maxIter=10, regParam=0.001)
pipeline = Pipeline(stages=[tokenizer, hashingTF, lr])
```

Great, she's made some excellent progress in translating some previous `sklearn` code
into Spark, which was deemed more appropriate for the use case. She then keeps working
in this branch because it has all of her additions, and she thinks it's better to do everything
in one place. When she wants to push the branch to the remote repository, she runs the
following commands:

```
git push origin pipelinespark
```

ML engineer *B* comes along, and he wants to use ML engineer *A*'s pipeline code and
build some extra steps around it. He knows she has a branch with this work, so he knows
enough Git to create another branch with her code in it, which he calls `pipeline`:

```
git pull origin pipelinspark
git checkout pipelinespark
git checkout -b pipeline
```

He then adds some code to read the parameters for the model from a variable:

```
lr = LogisticRegression(maxIter=model_config["maxIter"],
regParam=model_config["regParam"])
```

Cool, engineer *B* has made an update that is starting to abstract away some of the
parameters. He then pushes his new branch to the remote repository:

```
git push origin pipeline
```

Finally, ML engineer *C* joins the team and wants to get started on the code. Opening up
Git and looking at the branches, she sees there are three:

```
main
```

```
pipeline1spark
```

```
pipeline
```

So, which one should be taken as the most up to date? If she wants to make new edits, where should she branch from? It isn't clear, but more dangerous than that is if she is tasked with pushing deployment code to the execution environment, she may think that `main` has all the relevant changes. On a far busier project that's been going on for a while, she may even branch off from main and duplicate some of *B* and *C*'s work! In a small project, you would waste time going on this wild goose chase; in a large project with many different lines of work, you would have very little chance of maintaining a good workflow:

```
# Branch pipeline1spark - Commit 1 (Engineer A)
lr = LogisticRegression(maxIter=10, regParam=0.001)
pipeline = Pipeline(stages=[tokenizer, hashingTF, lr])
```

```
# Branch pipeline - Commit 2 (Engineer B)
lr = LogisticRegression(maxIter=model_config["maxIter"],
regParam=model_config["regParam"])
pipeline = Pipeline(stages=[tokenizer, hashingTF, lr])
```

If these commits both get pushed to the main branch at the same time, then we will get what is called a **merge conflict**, and in each case the engineer will have to choose which piece of code to keep, the current or new example. This would look something like this if engineer *A* pushed their changes to main first:

```
<<<<<<< HEAD
lr = LogisticRegression(maxIter=10, regParam=0.001)
pipeline = Pipeline(stages=[tokenizer, hashingTF, lr])
=======
lr = LogisticRegression(maxIter=model_config["maxIter"],
regParam=model_config["regParam"])
pipeline = Pipeline(stages=[tokenizer, hashingTF, lr])
>>>>>>> pipeline
```

The delimiters in the code show that there has been a merge conflict and that it is up to the developer to select which of the two versions of the code they want to keep.

Important note

Although in this simple case we could potentially trust the engineers to select the *better* code, allowing situations like this to occur very frequently is a huge risk to your project. This not only wastes a huge amount of precious development time, but it could also mean that you actually end up with worse code!

The way to avoid confusion and extra work like this is to have a very clear strategy for use of your version control system in place, such as the one we will now explore.

Gitflow Workflow

The biggest problem with the previous example was that all of our hypothetical engineers were actually working on the same piece of code in different places. To stop situations like this, you have to create a process that your team can all follow – in other words, a version control strategy or workflow.

One of the most popular of these strategies is the **Gitflow Workflow**. This builds on the basic idea of having branches that are dedicated to features and extends it to incorporate the concept of releases and hotfixes, which are particularly relevant to projects with a continuous deployment element.

The main idea is we have the following types of branches:

- Main
- Dev
- Release
- Feature
- Hotfix

The creation of each is for a clear and extremely specific reason. Some general pointers to get started with this methodology are as follows:

- **Main** contains your official releases and should only contain the stable version of your code.

- **Dev** acts as the main point for branching from and merging to for most work in the repository; it contains the ongoing development of the code base and acts as a staging area before main.

- **Feature** branches should not be merged straight into the main branch; everything should branch off from dev and then be merged back into dev.

- **Release** branches are created from dev to kick off a build or release process, before being merged into main and dev and then deleted.

- **Hotfix** branches are for removing bugs in deployed or production software. You can branch this from main before merging into main and dev when done.

This can all be summarized diagrammatically as in *Figure 2.11*, which shows how the different branches contribute to the evolution of your code base in the Gitflow Workflow:

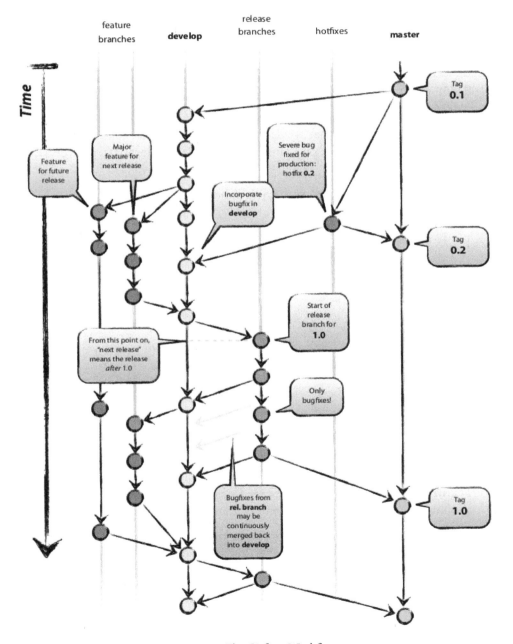

Figure 2.11 – The Gitflow Workflow

This diagram is taken from `https://lucamezzalira.com/2014/03/10/git-flow-vs-github-flow/`. More details can be found at `https://www.atlassian.com/git/tutorials/comparing-workflows/gitflow-workflow`.

If your ML project can follow this sort of strategy (and you don't need to be completely strict about this if you want to adapt it), you will likely see a drastic improvement in productivity, code quality, and even documentation:

```
∨  ⊹ 9 ▪▪▪▫ chapter1/bad-git/pipeline.py ▢

...    ...    @@ -1,9 +1,14 @@
1             - # EXAMPLE BELOW TAKEN FROM THE SPARK API DOCS, BEFORE BEING UPDATE FOR THE BOOK
       1      + # EXAMPLE BELOW ADAPTED FROM THE SPARK DOCS
2      2      # https://spark.apache.org/docs/latest/ml-pipeline.html#pipeline
3      3      from pyspark.ml import Pipeline
4      4      from pyspark.ml.classification import LogisticRegression
5      5      from pyspark.ml.feature import HashingTF, Tokenizer
6      6
       7      + import json
       8      +
       9      + with open("model_config.json") as f:
       10     +     model_config = json.load(f)
       11     +
7      12     # Prepare training documents from a list of (id, text, label) tuples.
8      13     training = spark.createDataFrame([
9      14         (0, "a b c d e spark", 1.0),

⊹             @@ -15,7 +20,7 @@
15     20     # Configure an ML pipeline, which consists of three stages: tokenizer, hashingTF, and lr.
16     21     tokenizer = Tokenizer(inputCol="text", outputCol="words")
17     22     hashingTF = HashingTF(inputCol=tokenizer.getOutputCol(), outputCol="features")
18            - lr = LogisticRegression(maxIter=10, regParam=0.001)
       23     + lr = LogisticRegression(maxIter=model_config['maxIter'], regParam=model_config['regParam'])
19     24     pipeline = Pipeline(stages=[tokenizer, hashingTF, lr])
```

Figure 2.12 – Example code changes upon a pull request in GitHub

One important aspect we haven't discussed yet is the concept of code reviews. These are triggered in this process by what is known as a **pull request**, where you make known your intention to merge into another branch and allow another team member to review your code before this executes. This is the natural way to introduce code review to your workflow. You do this whenever you want to merge your changes and update them into dev or main branches. The proposed changes can then be made visible to the rest of the team, where they can be debated and iterated on with further commits before completing the merge. This enforces code review to improve quality, as well as creating an audit trail and safeguards for updates. *Figure 2.12* shows an example of how changes to code are made visible for debate during a pull request in GitHub.

Now that we have discussed some of the best practices for applying version control to your code, let's explore how to version control the models you produce during your ML project.

Model version control

In any ML engineering project, it is not only code changes that you have to track clearly, but also changes in your models. You want to track changes not only in the modeling approach but also in performance when new or different data is fed into your chosen algorithms. One of the best tools for tracking these kinds of changes and providing version control of ML models is **MLflow**, which we installed earlier in this chapter.

The main aim of MLflow is to provide a platform via which you can log model experiments, artifacts, and performance metrics. It does this through some very simple APIs provided by the Python `mlflow` library, interfaced to selected storage solutions through a series of centrally developed and community plugins. It also comes with functionality for querying, analyzing, and importing/exporting data via a **Graphical User Interface (GUI)**, which will look something like *Figure 2.13*:

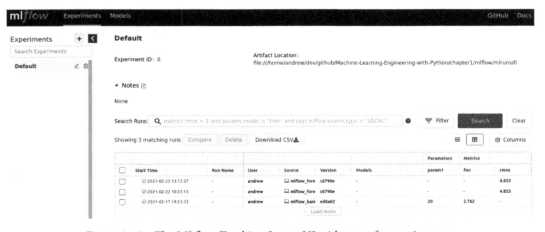

Figure 2.13 – The MLflow Tracking Server UI with some forecasting runs

The library is extremely easy to use. In the following example, we will take the sales forecasting example from *Chapter 1*, *Introduction to ML Engineering*, and add some basic MLflow functionality for tracking performance metrics and saving the trained Prophet model:

1. First, we make the relevant imports, including MLflow's `pyfunc` module, which acts as a general interface for saving and loading models that can be written as Python functions. This facilitates working with libraries and tools not natively supported in MLflow (such as the `fbprophet` library):

```
import pandas as pd
from fbprophet import Prophet
from fbprophet.diagnostics import cross_validation
from fbprophet.diagnostics import performance_metrics
import mlflow
import mlflow.pyfunc
```

2. To create a more seamless integration with the forecasting models from `fbprophet`, we define a small wrapper class that inherits from the `mlflow.pyfunc.PythonModel` object:

```
class FbProphetWrapper(mlflow.pyfunc.PythonModel):
    def __init__(self, model):
        self.model = model
        super().__init__()

    def load_context(self, context):
        from fbprophet import Prophet
        return

    def predict(self, context, model_input):
        future = self.model.make_future_
dataframe(periods=model_input["periods"][0])
        return self.model.predict(future)
```

We now wrap the functionality for training and prediction into a single helper function called `train_predict()` to make running multiple times simpler. We will not define all of the details inside this function here but let's run through the main pieces of MLflow functionality contained within it.

3. First, we need to let MLflow know that we are now starting a training run we wish to track:

```
with mlflow.start_run():
    # Do stuff ...
```

4. Inside this loop, we then define and train the model, using parameters defined elsewhere in the code:

```
# create Prophet model
model = Prophet(
    yearly_seasonality=seasonality_params['yearly'],
    weekly_seasonality=seasonality_params['weekly'],
    daily_seasonality=seasonality_params['daily']
)
# train and predict
model.fit(df_train)
```

5. We then perform some cross-validation to calculate some metrics we would like to log:

```
# Evaluate Metrics
df_cv = cross_validation(model, initial="730 days",
period="180 days", horizon="365 days")
df_p = performance_metrics(df_cv)
```

6. We can log these metrics, for example, here the **Root Mean Squared Error (RMSE)**, to our MLflow server:

```
# Log parameter, metrics, and model to MLflow
mlflow.log_metric("rmse", df_p.loc[0, "rmse"])
```

7. Then, finally, we can use our model wrapper class to log the model and print some information about the run:

```
mlflow.pyfunc.log_model("model", python_
model=FbProphetWrapper(model))
print(
    "Logged model with URI: runs:/{run_id}/model".format(
        run_id=mlflow.active_run().info.run_id
    )
)
```

With only a few extra lines, we have started to perform version control on our models and track the statistics of different runs!

There are many different ways to save the ML model you have built to MLflow (and in general), which is particularly important when tracking model versions. Some of the main options are as follows:

- **pickle**: `pickle` is a Python library for object serialization that is often used for the export of ML models that are written in scikit-learn or pipelines in the wider `scipy` ecosystem (`https://docs.python.org/3/library/pickle.html#module-pickle`). Although it is extremely easy to use, you must be careful when exporting your models to `pickle` files because of the following:

  a) **Versioning**: When you pickle an object, you have to unpickle it in other programs using the *same version of pickle* for stability reasons. This adds more complexity to managing your project.

  b) **Security**: The documentation for `pickle` states clearly that it is *not secure* and that it is very easy to construct malicious pickles that will execute dangerous code upon unpickling. This is a very important consideration, especially as you move toward production.

- **joblib**: `joblib` is a general-purpose pipelining library in Python that is very powerful but lightweight. It has a lot of really useful capabilities centered around caching, parallelizing, and compression that make it a very versatile tool for saving and reading in your ML pipelines. We will use `joblib` more in later chapters.

- **JSON**: If `pickle` and `joblib` aren't appropriate, you can serialize your model and its parameters in JSON format. This is good because JSON is a standardized text serialization format that is commonly used across a variety of solutions and platforms. The caveat to using JSON serialization of your models is that you often have to manually define the JSON structure with the relevant parameters you want to store. So, it can create a lot of extra work. Several ML libraries in Python have their own export to JSON functionality, for example, the deep learning package Keras, but they can all result in quite different formats.

- **MLeap**: MLeap is a serialization format and execution engine based on the **Java Virtual Machine** (**JVM**). It has integrations with Scala, PySpark, and scikit-learn but you will often see it used in examples and tutorials for saving Spark pipelines, especially for models built with Spark MLlib. This focus means it is not the most flexible of formats but is very useful if you are working in the Spark ecosystem.

- **ONNX**: The **Open Neural Network Exchange** (**ONNX**) format is aimed at being completely cross-platform and allowing the exchange of models between the main ML frameworks and ecosystems. The main downside of ONNX is that (as you can guess from the name) it is mainly aimed at neural network-based models, with the exception of its scikit-learn API. It is an excellent option if you are building a neural network though.

In *Chapter 3, From Model to Model Factory*, we will export our models to MLflow using some of these formats, but they are all compatible with MLfl and so you should feel comfortable using them as part of your ML engineering workflow.

The final section of this chapter will introduce some important concepts for planning how you wish to deploy your solution, prefacing more detailed discussions later in the book.

Deploy

The final stage of the ML development process is the one that really matters: how do you get the amazing solution you have built out into the real world and solve your original problem? The answer has multiple parts, some of which will occupy us more thoroughly later in this book but will be outlined in this section. If we are to successfully deploy our solution, first of all, we need to know our deployment options: what infrastructure is available and is appropriate for the task? We then need to get the solution from our development environment onto this production infrastructure so that, subject to appropriate orchestration and controls, it can execute the tasks we need it to and surface the results where it has to. This is where the concepts of DevOps and MLOps come into play.

Let's elaborate on these two core concepts, laying the groundwork for later chapters and exploring how to begin deploying our work.

Knowing your deployment options

In *Chapter 5, Deployment Patterns and Tools*, we will cover in detail what you need to get your ML engineering project from the **develop** to **deploy** stage, but to pre-empt that and provide a taster of what is to come, let's explore the different types of deployment options we have at our disposal:

- **On-premises deployment**: The first option we have is to ignore the public cloud altogether and deploy our solutions in-house on owned infrastructure. This option is particularly popular and necessary for a lot of large institutions with a lot of legacy software and strong regulatory constraints on data location and processing. The basic steps for deploying on-premises are the same as deploying on the cloud but often require a lot more involvement from other teams with particular specialties. For example, if you are in the cloud, you often do not need to spend a lot of time configuring networking or implementing load balancers, whereas on-premises solutions will require these.

  The big advantage of on-premises deployment is security and peace of mind that none of your data is going to traverse your company firewall. The big downsides are that it requires a larger investment upfront for hardware and that you have to expend a lot of effort to successfully configure and manage that hardware effectively. We will not be discussing on-premises deployment in detail in this book, but all of the concepts we will employ around software development, packaging, environment management, and training and prediction systems still apply.

- **Infrastructure-as-a-Service (IaaS)**: If you are going to use the cloud, one of the lowest levels of abstraction you have access to for deployment is IaaS solutions. These are typically based around the concept of virtualization, such that servers with a variety of specifications can be spun up at the user's will. These solutions often abstract away the need for maintenance and operations as part of the service. Most importantly, they allow extreme scalability of your infrastructure as you need it. Have to run 100 more servers next week? No problem, just scale up your IaaS request and there it is. Although IaaS solutions are a big step up from fully managed on-premises infrastructure, there are still several things you need to think about and configure. The balance in cloud computing is always over how easy you want things to be versus what level of control you want to have. IaaS maximizes control but minimizes (relative) ease compared to some other solutions. In AWS, **Simple Storage Service (S3)** and **Elastic Compute Cloud (EC2)** are good examples of IaaS offerings.

- **Platform-as-a-Service (PaaS)**: PaaS solutions are the next level up in terms of abstraction and usually provide you with a lot of capabilities without needing to know exactly what is going on under the hood. This means you can focus solely on the development tasks that the platform is geared up to support, without worrying about underlying infrastructure at all. One good example is AWS Lambda functions, which are serverless functions that can scale almost without limit. All you are required to do is enter the main piece of code you want to execute inside the function. Another good example is Databricks, which provides a very intuitive UI on top of the Spark cluster infrastructure, with the ability to provision, configure, and scale up these clusters almost seamlessly.

Being aware of these different options and their capabilities can help you design your ML solution and ensure that you focus your team's engineering effort where it is most needed and will be most valuable. If your ML engineer is working on configuring routers, for example, you have definitely gone wrong somewhere.

But once you have selected the components you'll use and provisioned the infrastructure, how do you integrate these together and manage your deployment and update cycles? This is what we will explore now.

DevOps and MLOps

A very powerful idea in modern software development is that your team should be able to continuously update your code base as needed, while testing, integrating, building, packaging, and deploying your solution should be as automated as possible. This then means these processes can happen on an almost continual basis without big pre-planned buckets of time being assigned to update cycles. This is the main idea behind **CI/CD**. CI/CD is a core part of **DevOps** and its ML-focused cousin **MLOps**, which both aim to bring together software development and post-deployment operations. Several of the concepts and solutions we will develop in this book will be built up so that they naturally fit within an MLOps framework.

The CI part is mainly focused on the stable incorporation of ongoing changes to the code base while ensuring functionality remains stable. The CD part is all about taking the resultant stable version of the solution and pushing it to the appropriate infrastructure. *Figure 2.14* shows a high-level view of this process:

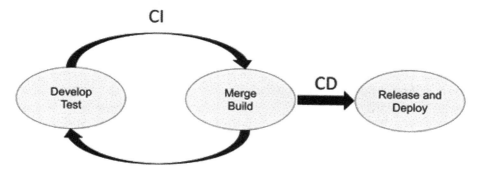

Figure 2.14 – A high-level view of CI/CD processes

In order to make CI/CD a reality, you need to incorporate tools that help automate tasks that you would traditionally perform manually in your development and deployment process. For example, if you can automate the running of tests upon merging of code, or the pushing of your code artifacts/models to the appropriate environment, then you are well on your way to CI/CD.

We will use GitHub Actions as our CI/CD tool in this book, but there are several other tools available that do the same job.

When using GitHub Actions, you have to create a `.yml` file that tells GitHub when to perform the required actions and, of course, what actions to perform. In the following code, we will build up an example `.yml` file for a Python project where we automatically install dependencies, run a **linter** (a solution to check for bugs, syntax errors, and other issues), and then run some unit tests. This example comes from the GitHub Starter Workflows repository (`https://github.com/actions/starter-workflows/blob/main/ci/python-package-conda.yml`):

1. First, you define the name of the GitHub Actions workflow and what Git event will trigger it:

    ```
    name: Python package

    on: [push]
    ```

2. You then list the jobs you want to execute as part of the workflow, as well as their configuration. For example, here we have one job called `build`, which we want to run on the latest Ubuntu distribution, and we want to attempt the build using several different versions of Python:

```
jobs:
  build:


    runs-on: ubuntu-latest
    strategy:
      matrix:
        python-version: [2.7, 3.5, 3.6, 3.7, 3.8]
```

3. You then define the steps that execute as part of the job. Each step is separated by a hyphen and is executed as a separate command. It is important to note that the `uses` keyword grabs standard GitHub Actions; for example, in the first step, the workflow uses the `v2` version of the checkout action and the second step sets up the Python versions we want to run in the workflow:

```
steps:
- uses: actions/checkout@v2
- name: Set up Python ${{ matrix.python-version }}
  uses: actions/setup-python@v2
  with:
    python-version: ${{ matrix.python-version }}
```

4. The next step installs the relevant dependencies for the solution using `pip` and a `requirements.txt` file (but you can use `conda` of course!):

```
- name: Install dependencies
  run: |
    python -m pip install --upgrade pip
    pip install flake8 pytest
    if [ -f requirements.txt ]; then pip install -r requirements.txt; fi
```

5. We then run some linting:

```
- name: Lint with flake8
  run: |
```

```
        # stop the build if there are Python syntax
errors or undefined names
        flake8 . --count --select=E9,F63,F7,F82 --show-
source --statistics
        # exit-zero treats all errors as warnings. The
GitHub editor is 127 chars wide
        flake8 . --count --exit-zero --max-complexity=10
--max-line-length=127 --statistics
```

6. Finally, we run our tests using our favorite Python testing library:

```
- name: Test with pytest
  run: |
      pytest
```

And that, in a nutshell, is how you start building your CI/CD pipelines. Later in the book, we will build workflows specific to our ML solutions.

Summary

This chapter was all about building a solid foundation for future work. We discussed the development steps common to all ML engineering projects, which we called discover, play, develop, deploy. In particular, we outlined the aim of each of these steps and their desired outputs.

This was followed by a high-level discussion of tooling, and a walkthrough of the main setup steps. We set up the tools for developing our code, keeping track of the changes of that code, managing our ML engineering project, and finally, deploying our solutions.

In the rest of the chapter, we went through the details for each of the four stages we outlined previously, with a particular focus on the *develop* and *deploy* stages. Our discussion covered everything from the pros and cons of Waterfall and Agile development methodologies to environment management and then software development best practices. We also discussed how to apply testing to our ML code. We finished off with an exploration of how to package your ML solution and what deployment infrastructure is available for you to use and outlined the basics of setting up your DevOps and MLOps workflows.

In the next chapter, we will turn our attention to how to build out the software for performing the automated training and retraining of your models using a lot of the techniques we have been discussing here.

Section 2: ML Development and Deployment

This section focuses on the technical details of developing your ML solutions, including examples of building your own training systems, coding your own ML wrapper libraries, designing your cloud-based architecture, and finally, scaling up your solutions to large organizational datasets. This section will also give you the knowledge you need to feel confident in building robust solutions that use machine learning to solve real-world problems.

This section comprises the following chapters:

- *Chapter 3, From Model to Model Factory*
- *Chapter 4, Packaging Up*
- *Chapter 5, Deployment Patterns and Tools*
- *Chapter 6, Scaling Up*

3
From Model to Model Factory

This chapter is all about one of the most important concepts in ML engineering: how do you take the difficult task of training and fine-tuning your models and make it something you can automate, reproduce, and scale for production systems?

We will recap the main ideas behind training different ML models at a theoretical and practical level, before providing motivation for retraining, namely the idea that ML models will not perform well forever. This concept is also known as **drift**. Following this, we will cover some of the main concepts behind feature engineering, which is a key part of any ML task. Next, we will deep dive into how ML works and how it is, at heart, a series of optimization problems. We will explore how, when setting out to tackle these optimization problems, you can do so with a variety of tools at various levels of abstraction. In particular, we will discuss how you can provide the direct definition of the model you want to train, which I term *hand cranking*, or how you can perform hyperparameter tuning or **Automated ML (AutoML)**. We will look at examples of using different libraries and tools that do all of these, before exploring how to implement them for later use in your training workflow. We will then build on the introductory work we did in *Chapter 2, The Machine Learning Development Process*, on MLflow by showing you how to interface with the different MLflow APIs to manage your models and update their statuses in MLflow's Model Registry.

We will end this chapter by discussing the utilities that allow you to chain all of your ML model training steps into single units known as **pipelines**, which can help act as more compact representations of all the steps we have discussed previously. The summary at the end will recap the key messages and also outline how what we have done here will be built upon further in *Chapter 4*, *Packaging Up*, and *Chapter 5*, *Deployment Patterns and Tools*.

In essence, this chapter will tell you *what* you need to stick together in your solution, while later chapters will tell you *how* to stick them together robustly. We will cover this in the following sections:

- Defining the model factory
- Designing your training system
- Retraining required
- Learning about learning
- Persisting your models
- Building the model factory with pipelines

Technical requirements

To complete this chapter, you will need to have installed the following Python packages and tools:

- MLflow version >= 1.15.0 (the Model Registry examples require later versions of MLflow)
- TensorFlow
- `auto-keras`
- Hyperopt
- Optuna
- `auto-sklearn`
- `alibi-detect`

Defining the model factory

If we want to develop solutions that move away from ad hoc, manual, and inconsistent execution and toward ML systems that can be automated, robust, and scalable, then we have to tackle the question of how we will create and curate the star of the show: the models themselves.

In this chapter, we will discuss the key components that have to be brought together to move toward this vision and provide some examples of what these may look like in code. These examples are not the only way to implement these concepts, but they will enable us to start building up our ML solutions toward the level of sophistication we will need if we want to deploy in the *real world*.

The main components we are talking about here are as follows:

- *Training system*: A system for robustly training our models on the data we have in an automated way. This consists of all the code we have developed to train our ML models on data.

- *Model store*: A place to persist successfully trained models and a place to share production-ready models with components that will run the predictions.

- *Drift detector*: A system for detecting changes in model performance to trigger training runs.

These components, combined with their interaction with the deployed prediction system, encompass the idea of a model factory. This is shown schematically in the following diagram:

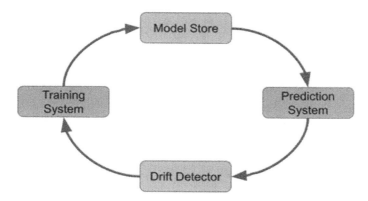

Figure 3.1 – The components of the model factory

For the rest of this chapter, we will explore the three components we mentioned previously in detail. Prediction systems will be the focus of later chapters, especially *Chapter 5, Deployment Patterns and Tools*.

First, let's explore what it means to train a ML model and how we can build systems to do so.

Designing your training system

Viewed at the highest level, ML models go through a life cycle with two stages: a **training** phase and an **output** phase. During the training phase, the model is fed data to learn from the dataset. In the prediction phase, the model, complete with its optimized parameters, is fed new data in order and returns the desired output.

These two phases have very different computational and processing requirements. In the training phase, we have to expose the model to as much data as we can to gain the best performance, all while ensuring subsets of data are kept aside for testing and validation. Model training is fundamentally an optimization problem, which requires several incremental steps to get to a solution. Therefore, this is computationally demanding, and in cases where the data is relatively large (or compute resources are relatively low), it can take a long time. Even if you had a small dataset and a lot of computational resources, training is still not a low-latency process. Also, it is a process that is often run in batches and where small additions to the dataset will not make that much difference to model performance (there are exceptions to this). Prediction, on the other hand, is a more straightforward process and can be thought of in the same way as running any calculation or function in your code: inputs go in, a calculation occurs, and the result comes out. This (in general) is not computationally demanding and is low latency.

Taken together, this means that, firstly, it makes sense to separate these two steps (training and prediction) both logically and in code. Secondly, it means we have to consider the different execution requirements for these two stages and build this into our solution designs. Finally, we need to make choices about our training regime, including whether we schedule training in batches, use incremental learning, or whether we should trigger training based on model performance criteria. These are the key parts of your training system.

Training system design options

Before we create any detailed designs of our training system, some general questions will always apply:

- Is there infrastructure available that is appropriate to the problem?

- Where is the data and how will we feed it to the algorithm?

- How am I testing the performance of the model?

In terms of infrastructure, this can be very dependent on the model and data you are using for training. If you are going to train a linear regression on data with three features and your dataset contains only 10,000 tabular records, you can likely run this on laptop-scale hardware without much thought. This is not a lot of data, and your model does not have a lot of free parameters. If you are training on a far larger dataset, such as one that contains 100 million tabular records, then you could benefit from parallelization across something such as a Spark cluster. If, however, you are training a 100-layer deep convolutional neural network on 1,000 images, then you are likely going to want to use a GPU. There are plenty of options, but the key is choosing the right thing for the job.

Regarding the question of how we feed data to the algorithm, this can be non-trivial. Are we going to run a SQL query against a remotely hosted database? If so, how are we connecting to it? Does the machine we're running the query on have enough RAM to store the data? If not, do we need to consider using an algorithm that can learn incrementally? For classic algorithmic performance testing, we need to employ the well-known tricks of the ML trade and perform train/test/validation splits on our data. We also need to decide what cross-validation strategies we may want to employ. We then need to select our model performance metric of choice and calculate it appropriately. As ML engineers, however, we will also be interested in *other* measures of performance, such as training time, efficient use of memory, latency, and (dare I say it) cost. We will need to understand how we can measure and then optimize these as well.

So long as we bear these things in mind as we proceed, we will be in a good position. Now, onto the design.

As we mentioned in the introduction to this section, we have two fundamental pieces to consider: the training and output processes. There are two ways in which we can put these together for our solution. We will discuss this in the next section.

Train-run

Option 1 is to perform training and prediction in the same process, with training occurring in either batch or incremental mode. This is shown schematically in the following diagram. This pattern is called *train-run*:

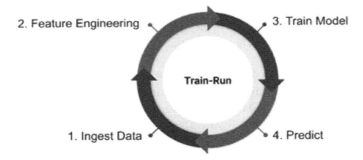

Figure 3.2 – The train-run process

This pattern is the simpler of the two but also the least desirable for real-world problems since it does not embody the *separation of concerns* principle we mentioned previously. This does not mean it is an invalid pattern, and it does have the advantage of often being simpler to implement. Here, we run our entire training process before making our predictions, with no real *break* in between. Given our previous discussions, we can automatically rule out this approach if we have to serve prediction in a very low-latency fashion; for example, through an event-driven or streaming solution (more on these later).

Where this approach *could* be completely valid, though (and I've seen this a few times in practice), is either in cases where the algorithms you are applying are actually very lightweight to train and you need to keep using very recent data, or where you are running a large batch process relatively infrequently.

Although this is a simple approach and does not apply to all cases, it does have distinct advantages:

- Since you are training as often as you predict, you are doing everything you can to protect against modern performance degradation, meaning that you are combatting *drift* (see later sections in this chapter).

- You are significantly reducing the complexity of your solution. Although you are tightly coupling two components, which should generally be avoided, the training and prediction stages may be so simple to code that if you just stick them together, you will save a lot of development time. This is a non-trivial point because *development time costs money*.

Now, let's look at the other case.

Train-persist

Option 2 is that training runs in batch, while prediction runs in whatever mode is deemed appropriate, with the prediction solution reading in the trained model from a store. We will call this design pattern *train-persist*. This is shown in the following diagram:

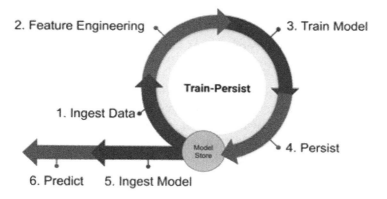

Figure 3.3 – The train-persist process

If we are going to train our model and then persist the model so that it can be picked up later by a prediction process, then we need to ensure a few things are in place:

- What are our model storage options?

- Is there a clear mechanism for accessing our model store (writing to and reading from)?

- How often should we train versus how often will we predict?

In our case, we will solve the first two questions by using MLflow, which we introduced in *Chapter 2, The Machine Learning Development Process*, but will revisit in later sections. There are also lots of other solutions available. The key point is that no matter what you use as a model store and *handover* point between your train and predict processes, it should be used in a way that is robust and accessible.

The third point is trickier. You could potentially just decide at the outset that you want to train on a schedule, and you stick to that. Or you could be more sophisticated and develop trigger criteria that must be met before training occurs. Again, this is a choice that you, as an ML engineer, need to make with your team. Later in this chapter, we will discuss mechanisms for scheduling your training runs.

In the next section, we will explore what you have to do if you want to trigger your training runs based on how your model's performance could be degrading over time.

Retraining required

You wouldn't expect that after finishing your education, you never read a paper or book or speak to anyone again, which means you wouldn't be able to make informed decisions about what is happening in the world. So, you shouldn't expect a ML model to be trained once and then be performant forever afterward.

This idea is intuitive, but it represents a formal problem for ML models known as **drift**. Drift is a term that covers a variety of reasons for your model's performance dropping over time. It can be split into two main types:

- **Concept drift**: This happens when there is a change in the fundamental relationship between the features of your data and the outcome you are trying to predict. Sometimes, this is also known as *covariate drift*. An example could be that at the time of training, you only have a subsample of data that seems to show a linear relationship between the features and your outcome. If it turns out that, after gathering a lot more data post-deployment, the relationship is non-linear, then concept drift has occurred. The mitigation against this is retraining with data that is more representative of the correct relationship.

- **Data drift**: This happens where there is a change in the statistical properties of the variables you are using as your features. For example, you could be using *age* as a feature in one of your models but at training time, you only have data for 16–24-year-olds. If the model gets deployed and your system starts ingesting data for a wider age demographic, then you have data drift.

Detecting drift in your deployed models is a key part of MLOps and should be at the forefront of your mind as a ML engineer. If you can build your training systems so that retraining is triggered based on an informed understanding of the drift in your models, you will save a lot of computational resources by only training when required.

The next section will discuss some of the ways we can detect drift in our models. This will help us start building up a smart retraining strategy in our solution.

Detecting drift

So far, we have defined drift, and we know that detecting it is going to be important if we want to build sophisticated training systems. The next logical question is, *how do we do this?*

The definitions of drift we gave in the previous section were very qualitative; we can start to make these statements a bit more quantitative as we explore the calculations and concepts that can help us detect drift.

In this section, we will rely heavily on the `alibi-detect` Python package from Seldon, which, at the time of writing, was not available from `Anaconda.org` but is available on PyPI. To acquire this package, use the following commands:

```
pip install alibi
pip install alibi-detect
```

It is very easy to use the `alibi-detect` package. In the following example, we will work with the `wine` dataset from `sklearn`, which will be used elsewhere in this chapter. In this first example, we will split the data 50/50 and call one set the *reference* set and the other the *test* set. We will then use the Kolmogorov-Smirnov test to show that there hasn't been data drift between these two datasets, as expected, and then artificially add some drift to show that it has been successfully detected:

1. First, we must import the `TabularDrift` detector from the `alibi-detect` package, as well as the relevant packages for loading and splitting the data:

    ```
    from sklearn.datasets import load_wine
    from sklearn.model_selection import train_test_split

    import alibi
    from alibi_detect.cd import TabularDrift
    ```

2. Next, we must get and split the data:

    ```
    wine_data = load_wine()
    feature_names = wine_data.feature_names
    X, y = wine_data.data, wine_data.target

    X_ref, X_test, y_ref, y_test = train_test_split(X, y,
                                               test_size=0.50,
                                               random_state=42)
    ```

3. Next, we must initialize our drift detector using the reference data and by providing the p-value we want to be used by the statistical significance tests. If you want to make your drift detector trigger when smaller differences occur in the data distribution, you must select a larger `p_val`:

    ```
    cd = TabularDrift(X_ref=X_ref, p_val=.05 )
    ```

4. We can now check for drift in the test dataset against the reference dataset:

```
preds = cd.predict(X_test)
labels = ['No', 'Yes']
print('Drift: {}'.format(labels[preds['data']['is_
drift']]))
```

This returns `'Drift: No'`.

So, we have not detected drift here, as expected (see the following *Important note* for more on this).

5. Although there was no drift in this case, we can easily simulate a scenario where the chemical apparatus being used for measuring the chemical properties experienced a calibration error, and all the values are recorded as 10% higher than their true values. In this case, if we run drift detection again on the same reference dataset, we will get the following output:

```
X_test_cal_error = 1.1*X_test
preds = cd.predict(X_test_cal_error)
labels = ['No', 'Yes']
print('Drift: {}'.format(labels[preds['data']['is_
drift']]))
```

This returns `'Drift: Yes'`, showing that the drift has been successfully detected.

> **Important note**
>
> This example is very artificial but is useful for illustrating the point. In a standard dataset like this, there won't be data drift between 50% of the randomly sampled data and the other 50% of the data. This is why we have to artificially *shift* some of the points to show that the detector does indeed work. In real-world scenarios, data drift can occur naturally due to everything from updates to sensors being used for measurements; to changes in consumer behavior; all the way through to changes in database software or schemas. So, be on guard as many drift cases won't be as easy to spot as in this case!

This example shows how, with a few simple lines of Python, we can detect a change in our dataset, which means our ML model may start to degrade in performance if we do not retrain to take the new properties of the data into account. We can also use similar techniques to track when the performance metrics of our model, for example accuracy or mean squared error, are drifting as well. In this case we have to make sure we periodically calculate performance on new test or validation datasets. Now, we can start to build this into solutions that will automatically trigger our ML model being retrained, as shown in the following diagram:

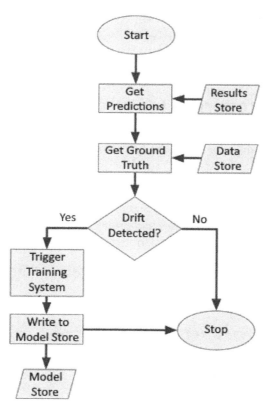

Figure 3.4 – An example of drift detection and the training system process

Next, we'll look at how to engineer specific features for data consumption.

Engineering features for consumption

Before we feed any data into a ML model, it has to be transformed into a state that can be *understood* by our models. We also need to make sure we only do this on the data we deem useful for improving the performance of the model, as it is far too easy to explode the number of features and fall victim to the *curse of dimensionality*. This refers to a series of related observations where, in high-dimensional problems, data becomes increasingly sparse in the feature space, so achieving statistical significance can require exponentially more data. In this section, we will not cover the theoretical basis of feature engineering. Instead, we will focus on how we, as ML engineers, can help automate some of the steps in production. To this end, we will quickly recap the main types of feature preparation and feature engineering steps so that we have the necessary pieces to add to our pipelines later in this chapter.

Engineering categorical features

Categorical features are those that form a non-numerical set of distinct objects, such as the day of the week or hair color. They can be distributed in a variety of ways throughout your data.

For an ML algorithm to be able to *digest* a categorical feature we need to translate the feature into something numerical, while also ensuring that the numerical representation *does not produce bias or weigh our values inappropriately*. An example of this would be if we had a feature that contained different products sold in a supermarket:

```
data = [['Bleach'], ['Cereal'], ['Toilet Roll']]
```

Here, we can map each to a positive integer using sklearn's OrdinalEncoder:

```
from sklearn import preprocessing
ordinal_enc = preprocessing.OrdinalEncoder()
ordinal_enc.fit(data)
# Print returns [[0.]
#     [1.]
#     [2.]]
print(ordinal_enc.transform(data))
```

This is what is called **ordinal encoding**. We have mapped these features to numbers, so there's a big tick there, but is the representation appropriate? Well, if you think about it for a second, not really. These numbers seem to suggest that cereal is to bleach as toilet roll is to cereal, and that the average of toilet roll and bleach is cereal. These statements don't make sense (and I don't want bleach and toilet roll for breakfast), so this suggests we should try a different approach. This representation would be appropriate, however, in cases where we wanted to maintain the notion of ordering in the categorical features. An excellent example would be if we had a survey, and the participants were asked their opinion of the statement *breakfast is the most important meal of the day*. If the participants were then told to select one option from the list *Strongly Disagree, Disagree, Neither Disagree nor Agree, Agree*, and *Strongly Agree* and we ordinally encoded this data to map to the numerical list of *1, 2, 3, 4*, and *5*, then we could more intuitively answer questions such as *was the average response more in agreement or disagreement?* and *how widespread was the opinion on this statement?*. Ordinal encoding would help here, but as we mentioned previously, it's not necessarily correct in this case.

What we could do is consider the list of items in this feature, and then provide a binary number to represent whether the value is or isn't that particular value in the original list. So, here, we will decide to use sklearn's `OneHotEncoder`:

```
onehot_enc = preprocessing.OneHotEncoder()
onehot_enc.fit(data)
# Print returns [[1. 0. 0.]
#     [0. 1. 0.]
#     [0. 0. 1.]]
print(onehot_enc.transform(data).toarray())
```

This representation is known as a **one-hot encoding**. There are a few benefits to this method of encoding, including the following:

- There are no enforced orderings of the values.

- All the feature vectors have unit norms (more on this later).

- Every unique feature is orthogonal to the others, so there are no weird averages or distance statements that are implicit in the representation.

One of the disadvantages of this approach is that if your categorical list contains a lot of instances, then the size of your feature vector will easily blow up, and we have to both store and work with extremely sparse vectors and matrices at the algorithmic level. This can very easily lead to issues in several implementations and is another manifestation of the dreaded curse of dimensionality.

In the next section, numerical features are discussed.

Engineering numerical features

Preparing numerical features is slightly easier since we already have numbers, but there are a few steps we still need to take to prepare for many algorithms. For most ML algorithms, the features must be all on similar scales; for example, they must have a magnitude between -1 and 1 or 0 and 1. This is for the relatively obvious reason that some algorithms taking in a feature for house price values of up to a million dollars and another for the square footage of the house will automatically weigh the larger dollar values more. This also means that we lose the helpful notion of where specific values sit in their distributions. For example, some algorithms will benefit from scaling features so that the median dollar value and the median square footage value are both represented by 0.5 rather than 500,000 and 350. Or we may want all of our distributions to have the same meaning if they were normally distributed, which allows our algorithms to focus on the shape of the distributions rather than their locations.

So, what do we do? Well, as always, we are not starting from scratch and there are some standard techniques we can apply. Some very common ones are listed here, but there are far too many to include all of them:

- **Standardization**: This is a transformation of a numerical feature and assumes that the distribution of values is normal or Gaussian before scaling the variance to be 1 and the average to be 0. If your data is indeed normal or Gaussian, then this is a good technique to use. The mathematical formula for standardization is very simple, so I've provided it here, where z represents the transformed value, x is the original value, and μ and σ are the average and standard deviation, respectively:

$$z_i = \frac{x_i - \mu}{\sigma}$$

- **Min-max normalization**: In this case, we want to scale the numerical features so that they're always between 0 and 1, irrespective of the type of distribution that they follow. This is intuitively easy to do, as you just need to subtract the minimum of the distribution from any given value and then divide by the range of the data (maximum minus minimum). You can think of this first step as making sure that all the values are greater than or equal to 0. The second step involves making sure that their maximum size is 1. This can be written with a simple formula, where the transformed number, x_i, is the original number, and x_i represents the entire distribution of that feature:

$$x_i' = \frac{x_i - \min(x)}{\max(x) - \min(x)}$$

- **Feature vector normalization**: Here, you scale every single sample in your dataset so that they have norms equal to 1. This can be very important if you are using algorithms where the distance or cosine similarity between features is an important component, such as in clustering. It is also commonly used in text classification in combination with other feature engineering methods, such as the TF-IDF statistic. In this case, assuming your entire feature is numerical, you just calculate the appropriate norm for your feature vector and then divide every component by that value. For example, if we use the Euclidean or L2-norm of the feature vector, $||x||$, then we would transform each component, x_j, via the following formula:

$$x_j' = \frac{x_j}{||x||}$$

To highlight the improvements these simple steps can make to your model's performance, we will look at a simple example from the `sklearn wine` dataset. Here, we will be training a Ridge classifier on data that has not been standardized and then on data that has been standardized. Once we've done this, we will compare the results:

1. First, we must import the relevant libraries and set up our training and test data:

```
from sklearn.model_selection import train_test_split
from sklearn.preprocessing import StandardScaler
from sklearn.linear_model import RidgeClassifier
from sklearn import metrics
from sklearn.datasets import load_wine
from sklearn.pipeline import make_pipeline


X, y = load_wine(return_X_y=True)
```

2. Then, we must make a typical 70/30 train/test split:

```
X_train, X_test, y_train, y_test =\
train_test_split(X, y, test_size=0.30, random_state=42)
```

3. Next, we must train a model without any standardization in the features and predict on the test set:

```
no_scale_clf = make_pipeline(RidgeClassifier(tol=1e-2,
solver="sag"))
no_scale_clf.fit(X_train, y_train)
y_pred_no_scale = no_scale_clf.predict(X_test)
```

4. Finally, we must do the same but with a standardization step added in:

```
std_scale_clf = make_pipeline(StandardScaler(),
RidgeClassifier(tol=1e-2, solver="sag"))
std_scale_clf.fit(X_train, y_train)
y_pred_std_scale = std_scale_clf.predict(X_test)
```

5. Now, if we print some performance metrics, we will see that without scaling, the accuracy of the predictions is at 0.76, while the other metrics, such as the weighted averages of precision, recall, and f1-score, are 0.83, 0.76, and 0.68, respectively:

```
print('\nAccuracy [no scaling]')
print('{:.2%}\n'.format(metrics.accuracy_score(y_test, y_
pred_no_scale)))


print('\nClassification Report [no scaling]')
print(metrics.classification_report(y_test, y_pred_no_
scale))
```

This produces the following output:

```
Accuracy [no scaling] 75.93%



Classification Report [no scaling]
              precision    recall  f1-score   support


           0       0.90      1.00      0.95        19
           1       0.66      1.00      0.79        21
           2       1.00      0.07      0.13        14


    accuracy                           0.76        54
```

macro avg	0.85	0.69	0.63	54
weighted avg	0.83	0.76	0.68	54

6. In the case where we standardized the data, the metrics are far better across the board, with the accuracy and weighted averages of the precision, recall, and f1-score all at 0.98:

```
print('\nAccuracy [scaling]')
print('{:.2%}\n'.format(metrics.accuracy_score(y_test, y_
pred_std_scale)))


print('\nClassification Report [scaling]')
print(metrics.classification_report(y_test, y_pred_std_
scale))
```

This produces the following output:

```
Accuracy [scaling]
98.15%
```

Classification Report [scaling]	precision	recall	f1-score	support
0	0.95	1.00	0.97	19
1	1.00	0.95	0.98	21
2	1.00	1.00	1.00	14
accuracy			0.98	54
macro avg	0.98	0.98	0.98	54
weighted avg	0.98	0.98	0.98	54

Here, we can see a significant jump in performance, just by adding one simple step to our ML training process.

Now, let's look at how training works at its core. This will help us make sensible choices for our algorithms and training approaches.

Learning about learning

At their heart, ML algorithms all contain one key feature: an optimization of some kind. The fact that these algorithms *learn* (meaning that they iteratively improve their performance concerning an appropriate metric upon exposure to more observations) is what makes them so powerful and exciting. This process of learning is what we refer to when we say *training*.

In this section, we will cover the key concepts underpinning training, the options we can select in our code, and what these mean for the potential performance and capabilities of our training system.

Defining the target

We have just stated that training is an optimization, but what exactly are we optimizing? Let's consider supervised learning. In training, we provide the labels or values that we would want to predict for the given feature so that the algorithms can learn the relationship between the features and the target. To optimize the internal parameters of the algorithm during training, it needs to know how *wrong* it would be with its current set of parameters. The optimization is then all about updating the parameters so that this measure of *wrongness* gets smaller and smaller. This is exactly what is captured by the concept of a loss function.

Loss functions come in a variety of forms, and you can even define your own if you need to with a lot of packages, but there are some standard ones that it helps to be aware of. The names of some of these are mentioned here.

For regression problems, you can use the following:

- Mean squared error/L2 loss
- Mean absolute error/L1 loss

For binary classification problems, you can use the following:

- Log loss/logistic loss/cross-entropy loss
- Hinge loss

For multi-class classification problems, you can use the following:

- Multi-class across entropy loss
- Kullback Leibler Divergence loss

After defining your loss function, you then need to optimize it. This is what we will look at in the next section.

Cutting your losses

At this point, we know that training is all about optimizing, and we know what to optimize, but we have not covered *how* to optimize yet.

As usual, there are plenty of options to choose from. In this section, we will look at some of the main approaches.

The following are the **constant learning rate** approaches:

- **Gradient descent**: This algorithm works by calculating the derivative of our loss function regarding our parameters, and then uses this to construct an update that moves us in the direction of decreasing loss.

- **Batch gradient descent**: The gradient that we use to make our move in the parameter space is found by taking the average of all the gradients found. It does this by looking at each data point in our training set and checking whether the dataset is not too large, and the loss function is relatively smooth and convex. This can pretty much reach the global minimum.

- **Stochastic gradient descent**: The gradient is calculated using one randomly selected data point at each iteration. This is faster at getting to the global minimum of the loss function, but it is more susceptible to sudden fluctuations in the loss after each optimization step.

- **Mini-batch gradient descent**: This is a mixture of both the batch and stochastic cases. In this case, updates to the gradient for each update to the parameters use several points greater than one but smaller than the entire dataset. This means that the size of the batch is now a parameter that needs to be tuned. The larger the batch, the more we approach batch gradient descent, which provides a better gradient estimate but is slower. The smaller the batch, the more we approach stochastic gradient descent, which is faster but not as robust. Mini-batch allows us to decide where in between the two we want to be. Batch sizes may be selected with a variety of criteria in mind. These can take on a range of memory considerations. Batches processed in parallel and larger batches will consume more memory while providing improved generalization performance for smaller batches. See *Chapter 8* of the book *Deep Learning* by Ian Goodfellow, Yoshua Bengio, and Aaron Courville at https://www.deeplearningbook.org/ for more details.

Then, there are the **adaptive learning rate methods**. Some of the most common are as follows:

- **AdaGrad**: The learning rate parameters are dynamically updated based on the properties of the learning updates during the optimization process.

- **AdaDelta**: This is an extension of AdaGrad that does not use all the previous gradient updates. Instead, it uses a rolling window on the updates.

- **RMSprop**: This works by maintaining a moving average of the square of all the gradient steps. It then divides the latest gradient by the square root of this.

- **Adam**: This is an algorithm that is supposed to combine the benefits of AdaGrad and RMSprop.

The limits and capabilities of all these optimization approaches are important for us, as ML engineers, because we want to ensure that our training systems use the right tool for the job and are optimal for the problem at hand. Just having the awareness that there are multiple options for your internal optimization will also help you focus your efforts and increase performance.

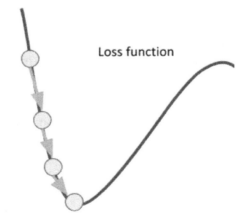

Figure 3.5 – Simple representation of training as the optimization of a loss function

Now, let's think about what level of control we can have over the training process as we build out our solutions.

Hierarchies of automation

One of the main reasons that ML is now a common part of software development, as well as a major business and academic activity, is because of the plethora of tools available now. All of the packages and libraries containing working and optimized implementations of sophisticated algorithms have allowed people to build on top of these, rather than have to reimplement the basics every time there is a problem to solve. This is a powerful expression of the idea of **abstraction** in software development, where lower-level units can be leveraged and engaged with at higher levels of implementation.

This idea can be extended even further to the entire enterprise of training itself. At the lowest level of implementation (but still very high level in the sense of the underlying algorithms), we can provide details about how we want the training process to go. We can manually define the exact set of hyperparameters (see the next section on *Optimizing hyperparameters*) to use in the training run in our code. I call this **hand cranking**. We can then move one level of abstraction up and supply ranges and bounds for our hyperparameters to tools designed to efficiently sample and test our model's performance for each of these; for instance, *automated hyperparameter tuning*. Finally, there is one higher level of abstraction that has created a lot of media excitement over the past few years, where we optimize over which algorithm to run. This is known as **automated ML** or **AutoML**.

There's a lot of hype surrounding AutoML, with some people proclaiming the eventual automation of all ML development job roles. In my opinion, this is just not realistic, as selecting your model and hyperparameters is only one aspect of a hugely complex engineering challenge (hence this being a book and not a leaflet!). AutoML is, however, a very powerful tool that should be added to your arsenal of capabilities when you go into your next ML project.

We can summarize all of this quite handily as a *hierarchy of automation*; basically, how much control do you, as the ML engineer, want in the training process? I once heard this described in terms of gear control in a car (credit: *Databricks at Spark AI 2019*). Hand cranking is the equivalent of driving a manual car with full control over the gears: there's more to think about, but it can be very efficient if you know what you're doing. One level up, you have automatic cars: there's less to worry about so that you can focus more on getting to your destination, traffic, and other challenges. This is a good option for a lot of people but still requires you to have sufficient knowledge, skills, and understanding. Finally, we have self-driving cars: sit back, relax, and don't even worry about how to get where you're going. You can focus on what you are going to do once you get there.

This *hierarchy of automation* is shown in the following diagram:

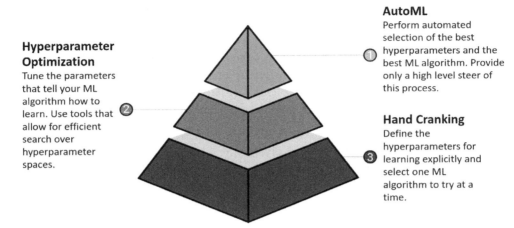

AutoML
Perform automated selection of the best hyperparameters and the best ML algorithm. Provide only a high level steer of this process.

Hyperparameter Optimization
Tune the parameters that tell your ML algorithm how to learn. Use tools that allow for efficient search over hyperparameter spaces.

Hand Cranking
Define the hyperparameters for learning explicitly and select one ML algorithm to try at a time.

Figure 3.6 – The hierarchy of automation of ML model optimization, with AutoML as the most automated possibility

That, in a nutshell, is how the different levels of training abstraction link together.

In the next few sections, we will discuss implementations of these in detail. First, we will focus on the *automatic car* option of automated hyperparameter tuning.

Optimizing hyperparameters

When you fit some sort of mathematical function to data, some values are tuned during the fitting or training procedure: these are called **parameters**. For ML, there is a further level of abstraction where we have to define the values that tell the algorithms we are employing *how they should update the parameters*. These values are called **hyperparameters**, and their selection is one of the important *dark arts* of training ML algorithms.

The following tables list some hyperparameters that are used for common ML algorithms to show you the different forms they may take. These lists are not exhaustive but are there to highlight that hyperparameter optimization is not a trivial exercise:

Algorithm	Hyperparameters	What This Controls
Decision Trees and Random Forests	• Tree depth • Min/max leaves	• How many levels are in your trees • How much **branching** can occur at each level
Support Vector Machines	• **C** • **Gamma**	• Penalty for misclassification • The radius of influence of the training points for **Radial Basis Function** (**RBF**) kernels
Neural Networks (numerous architectures)	• Learning rate • Number of hidden layers • Activation function • Many more	• Update step sizes • How **deep** your network is • The *firing* conditions of your neurons
Logistic Regression	• Solver • Regularization type • Regularization prefactor	• How to minimize the loss • How to prevent overfitting/make the problem well behaved • The *strength* of the regularization type

Figure 3.7 – Some hyperparameters and what they control for some supervised algorithms

Further examples can be seen in the following table:

Algorithm	Hyperparameters	What This Controls
K-Nearest Neighbors	• **K** • Distance metric	• The number of clusters • How to define the distance between points
DBSCAN	• **Epsilon** • Minimum number of samples • Distance metric	• The max distance to be considered **neighbors** • How many neighbors are required to be considered **core** • How to define the distance between points

Figure 3.8 – Some hyperparameters and what they control for some unsupervised algorithms

All of these hyperparameters have their own specific set of values they can take. This range of hyperparameter values for the different potential algorithms you want to apply to your ML solution means that there are a lot of ways to define a *working* model (meaning, one that doesn't break the implementation you are using), but how do you find the *optimal* model?

This is where hyperparameter search comes in. The concept is that for a finite number of hyperparameter value combinations, we want to find the set that gives the best model performance. This is another optimization problem that's similar to that of training in the first place!

In the following sections, we will discuss two very popular hyperparameter optimization libraries and show you how to implement them in a few lines of Python.

> **Important note**
>
> It is important to understand which algorithms are being used for optimization in these hyperparameter libraries, as you may want to use a couple of different implementations from each to compare different approaches and assess performance. If you didn't look at how they were working under the hood, you could easily make unfair comparisons – or worse, you could be comparing almost the same thing without knowing it! If you have some deeper knowledge of how these solutions work, you will also be able to make better judgment calls as to when they will be beneficial and when they will be overkill. Aim to have a working knowledge of a few of these algorithms and approaches, since this will help you design more holistic training systems with algorithm tuning approaches that complement one another.

Hyperopt

Hyperopt is an open source Python package that bills itself as being *for serial and parallel optimization over awkward search spaces, which may include real-valued, discrete, and conditional dimensions*. Check out the following link for more information: `https://github.com/Hyperopt/Hyperopt`. At the time of writing, version 0.2.5 comes packaged with three algorithms for performing optimization over user-provided search spaces:

- **Random search**: This algorithm essentially selects random numbers within your provided ranges of parameter values and tries them. It then evaluates which sets of numbers provide the best performance according to your chosen objective function.

- **Tree of Parzen Estimators** (**TPE**): This is a Bayesian optimization approach that models distributions of hyperparameters below and above a threshold for the objective function (roughly *good* and *bad* scorers), and then aims to draw more values from the *good* hyperparameter distribution.

- **Adaptive TPE**: This is a modified version of TPE that allows for some optimization of the search, as well as the ability to create a ML model to help guide the optimization process.

The Hyperopt repository and documentation contain several nice and detailed worked examples. We will not go through these here. Instead, we will learn how to use this for a simple classification model, such as the one we defined in *Chapter 1, Introduction to ML Engineering*. Let's get started:

1. In Hyperopt, we must define the hyperparameters that we want to optimize across. For example, for a typical logistic regression problem, we could define the space of hyperparameters to cover, whether we want to reuse parameters that were learned from the previous model runs each time (`warm_start`), whether we want the model to include a bias in the decision function (`fit_intercept`), the tolerance set for deciding when to stop the optimization (`tol`), the regularization parameter (`C`), which `solver` we want to try, and the maximum number of iterations, `max_iter`, in any training run:

    ```python
    from Hyperopt import hp
    space = {
        'warm_start' : hp.choice('warm_start', [True,
    False]),
        'fit_intercept' : hp.choice('fit_intercept', [True,
    False]),
        'tol' : hp.uniform('tol', 0.00001, 0.0001),
        'C' : hp.uniform('C', 0.05, 2.5),
        'solver' : hp.choice('solver', ['newton-cg', 'lbfgs',
    'liblinear']),
        'max_iter' : hp.choice('max_iter', range(10,500))
    }
    ```

2. Then, we have to define an objective function to optimize. In the case of our classification algorithm, we can simply define the `loss` function we want to minimize as 1 minus the f1-score. Note that Hyperopt allows your objective function to supply run statistics and metadata via your return statement if you are using the `fmin` functionality. The only requirement if you do this is that you return a value labeled `loss` and a valid status value from the list of `Hyperopt.STATUS_STRING` (ok by default and `fail` if there is an issue in the calculation that you want to call out as a failure):

    ```python
    def objective(params, n_folds, X, y):

        # Perform n_fold cross validation with hyperparameters
        clf = LogisticRegression(**params, random_state=42)
        scores = cross_val_score(clf, X, y, cv=n_folds,
    ```

```
scoring='f1_macro')

    # Extract the best score
    max_score = max(scores)

    # Loss must be minimized
    loss = 1 - max_score

    # Dictionary with information for evaluation
    return {'loss': loss, 'params': params, 'status':
STATUS_OK}
```

3. Now, we must optimize using the `fmin` method with the **TPE** algorithm:

```
# Trials object to track progress
trials = Trials()

# Optimize
best = fmin(
    fn=partial(objective, n_folds=n_folds, X=X_train, y=y_
train),
    space=space,
    algo=tpe.suggest,
    max_evals=16,
    trials=trials
)
```

4. The content of `best` is a dictionary containing all the best hyperparameters in the search space you defined. So, in this case, we have the following:

```
{'C': 0.26895003542493234,
 'fit_intercept': 1,
 'max_iter': 452,
 'solver': 2,
 'tol': 1.863336145787027e-05,
 'warm_start': 1}
```

You can then use these hyperparameters to define your model for training on the data.

Optuna

Optuna is a software package that has an extensive series of capabilities based around some core design principles, such as its **define-by-run** API and modular architecture. *Define-by-run* here refers to the fact that, when using Optuna, the user does not have to define the full set of parameters to test, which is *define-and-run*. Instead, they can provide some initial values and ask Optuna to suggest its own set of experiments to run. This saves the user time and reduces the code footprint (two big pluses for me!).

Optuna contains four basic search algorithms: **grid search**, **random search**, **TPE**, and the **Covariance Matrix Adaptation Evolution Strategy** (**CMA-ES**) algorithm. We covered the first three previously, but CMA-ES is an important addition to the mix. As its name suggests, this is based on an evolutionary algorithm and draws samples of hyperparameters from a multivariate Gaussian distribution. Then, it uses the rankings of the evaluated scores for the given objective function to dynamically update the parameters of the Gaussian distribution (the covariance matrix being one set of these) to help find an optimum over the search space quickly and robustly.

The key thing that makes Optuna's optimization process different from Hyperopt, however, is in its application of **pruning** or **automated early stopping**. During optimization, if Optuna detects evidence that a trial of a set of hyperparameters will not lead to a better overall trained algorithm, it terminates that trial. The developers of the package suggest that this leads to overall efficiency gains in the hyperparameter optimization process by reducing unnecessary computation.

Here, we're looking at the same example we looked at previously, but we are now using Optuna instead of Hyperopt:

1. First, when using Optuna, we can work using an object known as Study, which provides us with a convenient way to fold our search space into our objective function:

```
def objective(trial, n_folds, X, y):
    """Objective function for tuning logistic regression
hyperparameters"""
    params = {
        'warm_start': trial.suggest_categorical('warm_
start', [True, False]),
        'fit_intercept': trial.suggest_categorical('fit_
intercept', [True, False]),
        'tol': trial.suggest_uniform('tol', 0.00001,
0.0001),
        'C': trial.suggest_uniform('C', 0.05, 2.5),
```

```
        'solver': trial.suggest_categorical('solver',
['newton-cg', 'lbfgs', 'liblinear']),
        'max_iter': trial.suggest_categorical('max_iter',
range(10, 500))
    }
    # Perform n_fold cross validation with
hyperparameters
    clf = LogisticRegression(**params, random_state=42)
    scores = cross_val_score(clf, X, y, cv=n_folds,
scoring='f1_macro')


    # Extract the best score
    max_score = max(scores)


    # Loss must be minimized
    loss = 1 - max_score


    # Dictionary with information for evaluation
    return loss
```

2. Now, we must set up the data in the same way as we did in the Hyperopt example:

```
n_folds = 5
X, y = datasets.make_classification(n_samples=100000, n_
features=20,n_informative=2, n_redundant=2)


train_samples = 100  # Samples used for training the
models


X_train = X[:train_samples]
X_test = X[train_samples:]
y_train = y[:train_samples]
y_test = y[train_samples:]
```

3. Now, we can define this `Study` object that we mentioned and tell it how we wish to optimize the value that's returned by our objective function, complete with guidance on how many trials to run in the study. Here, we will use the TPE sampling algorithm again:

```
from optuna.samplers import TPESampler

study = optuna.create_study(direction='minimize',
sampler=TPESampler())
study.optimize(partial(objective, n_folds=n_folds, X=X_
train, y=y_train), n_trials=16)
```

4. Now, we can access the best parameters via the `study.best_trial.params` variable, which gives us the following values for the best case:

```
{'warm_start': False,
 'fit_intercept': False,
 'tol': 9.866562116436095e-05,
 'C': 0.08907657649508408,
 'solver': 'newton-cg',
 'max_iter': 108}
```

As you can see, Optuna is also very simple to use and very powerful. Now, let's look at the final level of the hierarchy of automation: AutoML.

> **Important note**
>
> You will notice that these values are different from the ones returned by Hyperopt. This is because we have only run 16 trials in each case, so we are not effectively subsampling the space. If you run either of the Hyperopt or Optuna samples a few times in a row, you can get quite different results for the same reason. The example given here is just to show the syntax, but if you are keen, you can set the number of iterations to be very high (or create smaller spaces to sample), and the results of the two approaches should roughly converge.

AutoML

The final level of our hierarchy is the one where we, as the engineer, have the least direct control over the training process, but where we also potentially get a good answer for very little effort!

The development time that's required to search through many hyperparameters and algorithms for your problem can be large, even when you code up reasonable-looking search parameters and loops.

Given this, the past few years have seen the deployment of several AutoML libraries and tools in a variety of languages and software ecosystems. The hype surrounding these techniques has meant they have had a lot of airtime, which has led to several data scientists questioning when their jobs will be automated away. As we mentioned previously in this chapter, in my opinion, declaring the death of data science is extremely premature and also dangerous from an organizational and business performance standpoint. These tools have been given such a pseudo-mythical status that many companies could believe that simply using them a few times will solve all their data science and ML problems.

They are wrong, but they are also right.

These tools and techniques *are* very powerful and *can* help make some things better, but they are not a magical *plug-and-play* panacea. Let's explore these tools and start to think about how to incorporate them into our ML engineering workflow and solutions.

Auto-sklearn

One of our favorite libraries, good old scikit-learn, was always going to be one of the first targets for building a popular AutoML library. One of the very powerful features of auto-sklearn is that its API has been designed so that the main objects that optimize and section models and hyperparameters can be swapped seamlessly into your code.

As usual, an example will show this more clearly. In the following example, we will assume that the wine dataset (a favorite for this chapter) has already been retrieved and split into train and test samples in line with other examples, such as the one in the *Detecting drift* section:

1. First, since this is a classification problem, the main thing we need to get from auto-sklearn is the autosklearn.classification object:

```
import numpy as np
import sklearn.datasets
import sklearn.metrics
import autosklearn.classification
```

2. We must then define our `auto-sklearn` object. This provides several parameters that help us define how the model and hyperparameter tuning process will proceed. In this example, we will provide an upper time limit in seconds for running the overall optimization and an upper time limit in seconds for any single call to the ML model:

```
automl = autosklearn.classification.
AutoSklearnClassifier(
    time_left_for_this_task=60,
    per_run_time_limit=30
)
```

3. Then, just like we would fit a normal sklearn classifier, we can fit the `auto-sklearn` object. As we mentioned previously, the `auto-sklearn` API has been designed so that this looks familiar:

```
automl.fit(X_train, y_train, dataset_name='wine')
```

Now that we've fit the object, we can start to dissect what has been achieved by the object during its optimization run.

4. First, we can see which models were tried and which were kept in the object as part of the final ensemble:

```
print(automl.show_models())
```

5. We can then get a readout of the main statistics from the run:

```
print(automl.sprint_statistics())
```

6. Then, we can predict some text features, as expected:

```
predictions = automl.predict(X_test)
```

7. Finally, we can check how well we did by using our favorite metrics calculators – in this case, the `sklearn metrics` module:

```
sklearn.metrics.accuracy_score(y_test, predictions)
```

As you can see, it is very straightforward to start using this powerful library, especially if you are already comfortable working with `sklearn`.

Next, let's discuss how we extend this concept to neural networks, which have an extra layer of complexity due to their different potential model architectures.

Auto-Keras

A particular area where AutoML has been a big hit is in neural networks. This is because for a neural network, the question of *what is the best model?* is a very complicated one. For our typical classifiers, we can usually think of a relatively short, finite list of algorithms to try. For a neural network, we don't have this finite list. Instead, we have an essentially infinite set of possible neural network *architectures*; for instance, for organizing the neurons into layers and the connections between them. Searching for the optimal neural network architecture is a problem in which powerful optimization can make your life, as an ML engineer or data scientist, a whole lot easier.

In this instance, we are going to explore an AutoML solution built on top of the very popular neural network API library known as Keras. Unbelievably, the name of this package is – you guessed it – `auto-keras`!

For this example, we will, once again, assume that the `wine` dataset has been loaded so that we can focus on the details of the implementation. Let's get started:

1. First, we must import the `autokeras` library:

    ```
    import autokeras as ak
    ```

2. Now, it's time for the fun and, for `auto-keras`, the extremely simple bit! Since our data is structured (tabular with a defined schema), we can use the `StructuredDataClassifier` object, which wraps the underlying mechanisms for automated neural network architecture and hyperparameter search:

    ```
    clf = ak.StructuredDataClassifier(max_trials=5)
    ```

3. Then, all we then have to do is fit this classifier object, noticing its similarity to the `sklearn` API. Remember that we assume that the training and test data exist in pandas DataFrames, as in the other examples in this chapter:

    ```
    clf.fit(x=X_train, y=y_train)
    ```

4. The training objects in `auto-keras` have a convenient evaluation method wrapped within them. Let's use this to see how accurate our solution was:

    ```
    accuracy=clf.evaluate(x=X_train, y=y_train)
    ```

    With that, we have successfully performed a neural network architecture and hyperparameter search in a few lines of Python. As always, read the solution documentation for more information on the parameters you can provide to the different methods.

Now that we've covered how to create performant models, in the next section, we will learn how to persist these models so that they can be used in other programs.

Persisting your models

In the previous chapter, we introduced some of the basics of model version control using MLflow. In particular, we discussed how to log metrics for your ML experiments using the MLflow Tracking API. We are now going to build on this knowledge and consider the touchpoints our training systems should have with model control systems in general.

First, let's recap what we're trying to do with the training system. We want to automate (as far as possible) a lot of the work that was done by the data scientists in finding the first working model, so that we can continually update and create new model versions that still solve the problem in the future. We would also like to have a simple mechanism that allows the results of the training process to be shared with the part of the solution that will carry out the prediction when in production. We can think of our model version control system as a bridge between the different stages of the ML development process we discussed in *Chapter 2, The Machine Learning Development Process*. In particular, we can see that the ability to track experiment results allows us to keep the results of the **Play** phase and build on these during the **Develop** phase. We can also track more experiments, test runs, and hyperparameter optimization results in the same place during the **Develop** phase. Then, we can start to tag the performant models as ones that are good candidates for deployment, thus bridging the gap between the **Develop** and **Deploy** development phases. If we focus on MLflow for now (though plenty of other solutions are available that fulfill the need for a model version control system), then MLflow's Tracking and Model Registry functionalities nicely slot into these bridging roles. This is represented schematically in the following diagram:

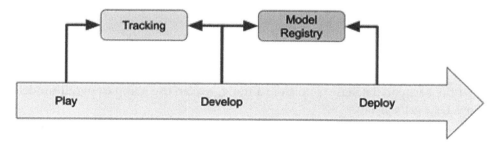

Figure 3.9 – How the MLflow Tracking and Model Registry functionalities can help us progress through the different stages of the ML development process

In *Chapter 2, The Machine Learning Development Process*, we only explored the basics of the MLflow Tracking API for storing experimental model run metadata. Now, we will briefly dive into how to store production-ready models in a very organized way so that you can start to perform model staging. This is the process whereby models can be progressed through stages of readiness, and you can swap models in and out of production if you wish to. This is an extremely important part of any training system that supplies models and will run as part of a deployed solution, which is what this book is all about!

As alluded to previously, the functionality that we need in MLflow is called Model Registry, one of MLflow's four main functionalities. Here, we will walk through examples of how to take a logged model and push it to the registry, how to update information such as the model version number in the registry, and then how to progress your model through different life cycle stages. We will finish this section by learning how to retrieve a given model from the registry in other programs – a key point if we are to share our models between separate training and prediction services.

Before we dive into the Python code for interacting with Model Registry, we have one important piece of setup to perform. The registry only works if a database is being used to store the model metadata and parameters. This is different from the basic Tracking API, which works with just a file backend store. This means that before pushing models to Model Registry, we have to fire up an MLflow server with a database backend. You can do this with a SQLite database running locally by executing the following command in your terminal. You will have to run this before the code snippets in the rest of this section (this command is stored in a short Bash script in this book's GitHub repository, under `https://github.com/PacktPublishing/Machine-Learning-Engineering-with-Python/blob/main/Chapter03/mlflow-advanced/start-mlflow-server.sh`):

```
mlflow server \
    --backend-store-uri sqlite:///mlflow.db \
    --default-artifact-root ./artifacts \
    --host 0.0.0.0
```

Now that the backend database is up and running, we can use it as part of our model workflow. Let's get started:

1. Let's begin by logging some metrics and parameters for one of the models we trained earlier in this chapter:

    ```
    with mlflow.start_run(run_name="YOUR_RUN_NAME") as run:
        params = {
    ```

```
            'tol': 1e-2,
            'solver': 'sag'
        }

        std_scale_clf = make_pipeline(StandardScaler(),
RidgeClassifier(**params))
        std_scale_clf.fit(X_train, y_train)
        y_pred_std_scale = std_scale_clf.predict(X_test)

        mlflow.log_metrics(
            {
                'accuracy': metrics.accuracy_score(y_
test, y_pred_std_scale),
                'precision': metrics.precision_score(y_
test, y_pred_std_scale, average='macro'),
                'f1': metrics.f1_score(y_test, y_pred_
std_scale, average='macro'),
                'recall': metrics.recall_score(y_test, y_
pred_std_scale, average='macro')
            }
        )
        mlflow.log_params(params)
```

2. Inside the same code block, we can now log the model to Model Registry, providing a name for the model to reference later:

```
        mlflow.sklearn.log_model(
            sk_model=std_scale_clf,
            artifact_path="sklearn-model",
            registered_model_name="sk-learn-std-scale-
clf"
        )
```

3. Now, let's assume we are running a prediction service and we want to retrieve the model and predict using it. Here, we have to write the following:

```
    model_name = "sk-learn-std-scale-clf"
    model_version = 1
    model = mlflow.pyfunc.load_model(
        model_uri=f"models:/{model_name}/{model_version}"
```

```
    )
    model.predict(X_test)
```

4. By default, newly registered models in Model Registry are assigned the `'Staging'` stage value. Therefore, if we want to retrieve the model based on knowing the stage but not the model version, we could execute the following code:

```
stage = 'Staging'
model = mlflow.pyfunc.load_model(
    model_uri=f"models:/{model_name}/{stage}"
)
```

5. Based on all of our discussions in this chapter, the result of our training system must be able to produce a model we are happy to deploy to production. The following piece of code promotes the model to a different stage, called `"Production"`:

```
client = MlflowClient()
client.transition_model_version_stage(
    name="sk-learn-std-scale-clf",
    version=1,
    stage="Production"
)
```

These are the most important ways to interact with Model Registry and we have covered the basics of how to register, update, promote, and retrieve your models in your training (and prediction) systems.

Now, we will learn how to chain our main training steps together into single units called **pipelines**. We will cover some of the standard ways of doing this inside single scripts, which will allow us to build our first training pipelines. In *Chapter 5*, *Deployment Patterns and Tools*, we will cover tools for building more generic software pipelines for your ML solution (of which your training pipeline may be a single component).

Building the model factory with pipelines

The concept of a software pipeline is intuitive enough. If you have a series of steps chained together in your code, so that the next step consumes or uses the output of the previous step or steps, then you have a pipeline.

In this section, when we refer to a pipeline, we will be specifically dealing with steps that contain processing or calculations that are appropriate to ML. For example, the following diagram shows how this concept may apply to some of the steps the marketing classifier mentioned in *Chapter 1, Introduction to ML Engineering*:

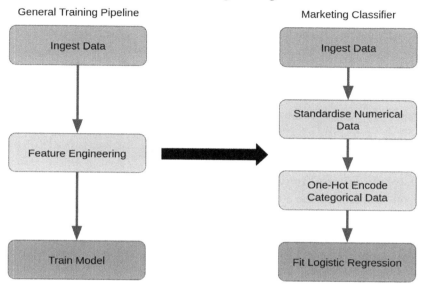

Figure 3.10 – The main stages of any training pipeline and how this maps to a specific case from Chapter 1, Introduction to ML Engineering

Let's discuss some of the standard tools for building up your ML pipelines in code.

Scikit-learn pipelines

Our old friend scikit-learn comes packaged with some nice pipelining functionality. At the time of writing, scikit-learn versions greater than 0.20 also contain the `ColumnTransformer` object, which allows you to build pipelines that perform different actions on specific columns. This is exactly what we want to do with the logistic regression marketing model example we were discussing previously, where we want to standardize our numerical values and one-hot encode our categorical variables. Let's get started:

1. To create this pipeline, you need to import the `ColumnTransformer` and `Pipeline` objects:

```
from sklearn.compose import ColumnTransformer
from sklearn.pipeline import Pipeline
```

2. To show you how to chain steps inside the transformers that make up the pipeline, we will add some imputation later. For this, we need to import the `SimpleImputer` object:

```
from sklearn.impute import SimpleImputer
```

3. Now, we must define the numerical transformer sub-pipeline, which contains the two steps for imputation and scaling. We must also define the names of the numerical columns this will apply to so that we can use them later:

```
numeric_features = ['age', 'balance']
numeric_transformer = Pipeline(steps=[
    ('imputer', SimpleImputer(strategy='median')),
    ('scaler', StandardScaler())])
```

4. Next, we must perform similar steps for the categorical variables, but here, we only have one transformation step to define for the one-hot encoder:

```
categorical_features = ['job', 'marital', 'education',
'contact', 'housing', 'loan', 'default','day']
categorical_transformer = OneHotEncoder(handle_
unknown='ignore')
```

5. We must bring all of these preprocessing steps together into a single object, called `preprocessor`, using the `ColumnTransformer` object. This will apply our transformers to the appropriate columns of our DataFrame:

```
preprocessor = ColumnTransformer(
    transformers=[
        ('num', numeric_transformer, numeric_features),
        ('cat', categorical_transformer, categorical_
features)])
```

6. Finally, we want to add the ML model step at the end of the previous steps and finalize the pipeline. We will call this `clf_pipeline`:

```
clf_pipeline = Pipeline(steps=[('preprocessor',
preprocessor),
                    ('classifier', LogisticRegression())])
```

This is our first ML training pipeline. The beauty of the scikit-learn API is that the `clf_pipeline` object can now be called as if it was a standard algorithm from the rest of the library. So, this means we can write the following:

```
clf_pipeline.fit(X_train, y_train)
```

This will run the `fit` methods of all of the pipeline steps in turn. The ability to abstract the steps that are performing feature engineering and training your model into a single object is very powerful, as it means you can export and import this pipeline in various places, without knowing the details of the implementation. Abstraction is a good thing!

Spark ML pipelines

There is another toolset we have been using throughout this book that will be particularly important when we discuss scaling up our solutions: Apache Spark and its ML ecosystem. We will see that building a similar pipeline with Spark ML requires a slightly different set of syntax, but the key concepts look very similar to the sklearn case.

There are a few important points to mention about PySpark pipelines. Firstly, in line with good programming practices in Scala, which Spark is written in, objects are treated as **immutable**, so transformations do not occur *in place*. Instead, new objects are created. This means that the output of any transformation will require new columns to be created in your original DataFrame (or indeed new columns in a new DataFrame).

Secondly, the Spark MLlib estimators (that is, the ML algorithms) all require the features to be assembled into one tuple-like object in a single column. This contrasts with scikit-learn, where you can keep all the features in their columns in your data object. This means that you need to become comfortable with the use of **assemblers**, utilities for pulling disparate feature columns together, especially when you are working with mixed categorical and numerical features that must be transformed in different ways before being invested by the algorithm.

Thirdly, Spark has many functions that use **lazy evaluation**, meaning that they are only executed when they're triggered by specific actions. This means that you can build up your entire ML pipeline and not have to transform any data. The reason for lazy evaluation is that the computational steps in Spark are stored in a **Directed Acyclic Graph (DAG)** so that the execution plan can be optimized before you perform the computational steps, making Spark very efficient.

Finally – and this is a small point – it is commonplace to write PySpark variables using *camel case* rather than the common *snake case*, which is often used for Python variables (for instance, `variableName` versus `variable_name`). This is done to keep the code in line with the PySpark functions that inherit this convention from the underlying Scala code behind Spark. Let's take a look:

1. First, we must one-hot encode the categorical features for the previous example using the following syntax:

```
from pyspark.ml import Pipeline, PipelineModel
categoricalColumns = ["job", "marital", "education",
"contact", "housing", "loan", "default", "day"]
for categoricalCol in categoricalColumns:
    stringIndexer = StringIndexer(inputCol=categoricalCol,
                                outputCol=categoricalCol
+ "Index").setHandleInvalid(
        "keep")
    encoder = OneHotEncoder(inputCols=[stringIndexer.
getOutputCol()], outputCols=[categoricalCol +
"classVec"])

    stages += [stringIndexer, encoder]
```

2. For the numerical columns, we must perform imputation:

```
numericalColumns = ["age", "balance"]
numericalColumnsImputed = [x + "_imputed" for x in
numericalColumns]
imputer = Imputer(inputCols=numericalColumns,
outputCols=numericalColumnsImputed)
stages += [imputer]
```

3. Then, we must perform standardization. Here, we need to be a bit clever about how we apply `StandardScaler` as it only applies to one column at a time. Therefore, we need to create a scaler for each numerical feature after pulling our numerically imputed features into a single feature vector:

```
from pyspark.ml.feature import StandardScaler
numericalAssembler =
VectorAssembler(inputCols=numericalColumnsImputed,
outputCol='numerical_cols_imputed')
stages += [numericalAssembler]
```

```
scaler = StandardScaler(inputCol='numerical_cols_
imputed', outputCol="numerical_cols_imputed_scaled")
stages += [scaler]
```

4. Then, we have to assemble the numerical and categorical transformed features into one feature column:

```
assemblerInputs = [c + "classVec" for c in
categoricalColumns] + ["numerical_cols_imputed_scaled"]

assembler = VectorAssembler(inputCols=assemblerInputs,
outputCol="features")
stages += [assembler]
```

5. Finally, we can define our model step, add this to the pipeline, and then train on and transform the appropriate data:

```
lr = LogisticRegression(labelCol="label",
featuresCol="features", maxIter=10)
stages += [lr]

(trainingData, testData) = data.randomSplit([0.7, 0.3],
seed=100)

clfPipeline = Pipeline().setStages(stages).
fit(trainingData)
clfPipeline.transform(testData)
```

And that is how we can build a training pipeline in PySpark.

Summary

In this chapter, we learned about the important topic of how to build up our solutions for training and surfacing the ML models that we want to run in production. We split the components of such a solution into pieces that tackled training the models, the persistence of the models, serving the models, and triggering retraining for the models.

We conducted a detailed investigation into the reasons why you may want to separate your training and running components for performance reasons. We then discussed how you can perform drift detection on your model performance and data statistics to understand whether retraining should be triggered. We then summarized some of the key concepts of feature engineering, or how you transform your data into something that a ML model can understand. We then went into a deep dive on how ML models learn and what you can control about that process, and then finished up that section by looking at some tools that allow you to exercise that control. We then covered how to persist and retrieve models using simple Python commands that can be executed from your training and prediction systems. Finally, we covered the concept of training pipelines and how these objects simplify your training solution.

In the next chapter, we will find out how to package up some of these concepts in a Pythonic way so that they can be deployed and reused seamlessly in other projects.

4
Packaging Up

In previous chapters, we introduced a lot of the tools and techniques you will need to use to successfully build working **Machine Learning** (**ML**) products. We also introduced a lot of example pieces of code that helped us to understand how to implement these tools and techniques. So far, this has all been about *what* we need to program, but this chapter will focus on *how* to program. In particular, we will introduce and work with a lot of the techniques, methodologies, and standards that are prevalent in the wider Python software development community and apply them to ML use cases. The conversation will be centered around the concept of developing *user-defined libraries and packages*, reusable pieces of code that you can use for deploying your ML solutions or for developing new ones. It is important to note that everything we discuss here can be applied to all of your Python development activities across your ML project development life cycle. If you are working on some exploratory data analysis in a notebook or some modeling scripts for the research portion of your project, your work will still benefit immensely from the concepts we are about to introduce.

In this chapter, we will recap some of the basic points of programming in Python, before discussing the concept of coding standards and some pointers for writing high-quality Python code. We will also touch upon the difference between object-oriented and functional programming in Python, and where this has strengths and points of synergy with other tools that you may want to use in your solution. We will discuss some good use cases for writing your own ML packages and go through the options for packaging up. Next will be a discussion of testing, logging, and error handling in your code, which are important concepts for building code that can be trusted not just to work, but to be diagnosable when it doesn't. This will be followed by a deep dive into the logical flow of our package. Finally, we will perform an exploration of how we ensure we do not reinvent the wheel and use functionality that already exists elsewhere.

In this chapter, we will cover the following topics:

- Writing good Python

- Choosing a style

- Packaging your code

- Building your package

- Testing, logging, and error handling

- Not reinventing the wheel

> **Important note**
> There isn't a clearly defined difference between a package and a library in Python. The general consensus seems to be that *library* often refers to any collection of code you want to reuse in other projects, whereas *package* refers to a collection of Python modules (covered in this chapter). We will often use the two interchangeably here with the understanding that when we say library, we are usually referring to a bunch of code that is cleanly put together and contains at least one package. This means that we won't count single scripts with some code you reuse later as a library for our purposes here.

Who doesn't want to write more robust, clean, readable, testable, and performant code that can be used by our colleagues, the ML community, or even our customers? Let's get started!

Technical requirements

In order to run the examples in this chapter you will need to make sure you have installed:

- Scikit-learn
- the Unix make(P-code) utility

Writing good Python

As discussed throughout this book, Python is an extremely popular and very versatile programming language. Some of the most widely used software products in the world, and some of the most widely used ML engineering solutions in the world, use Python as a core language. Given this scope and scale, it is clear that if we are to write similarly amazing pieces of ML-driven software, we should once again follow the best practices and standards already adopted by these solutions. In the following sections, we will explore what packaging up means in practice, and start to really level up our ML code in terms of quality and consistency.

Recapping the basics

Before we get stuck into some more advanced concepts, let's make sure we are all on the same page and go over some of the basic terminology of the Python world. This will ensure that we apply the right thought processes to the right things and that we can feel confident when writing our code.

In Python, we have the following objects:

- **Variable**: An object that stores data of one of a variety of types. In Python, variables can be created through assignment without specifying the type, for example:

```
numerical_variable = 10
string_variable = 'string goes here'
```

- **Function**: Unit of code that is self-contained and performs logical steps on variables (or another object). Defined by the def keyword in Python and can return any Python object. Functions are *first-class citizens* in Python, which means you can reference them using their object name (and re-reference them) and that functions can pass and return functions. So, for example, if we create a function that calculates some simple statistics from a pandas DataFrame, we can do the following. First, define it:

```
def calculate_statistics(df):
    return df.describe()
```

Then run it using the original name and a dataframe called X_train:

```
calculate_statistics(X_train)
```

Then you can re-assign the function using a new name and similarly call it:

```
new_statistics_calculator = calculate_statistics
new_statistics_calculator(X_train)
```

You can then pass the function around even more. For example, if you pass the function into a new function that takes the result and returns a JSON object, then you can call that!

```
def make_func_result_json(func ,df):
    return func(df).to_json
make_func_result_json(calculate_statistics, X_train)
```

This can help build up some simple pieces of code into something relatively complex quite quickly.

- **Module**: This is a file containing definitions and statements of functions, variables, and other objects where the contents can be imported into other Python code. For example, if we put the functions defined in the previous example into a file called module.py, we can then type the following in another Python program (or the Python interpreter) in order to use the functionality contained within it:

```
import module
module.calculate_statistics(df)
module.make_func_result_json(module.calcualate_
statistics, df)
```

- **Class**: We will discuss classes in detail in the *Object-oriented programming* section, but for now just know that these are the basic units of object-oriented programming, and act as a nice way of containing logically related functionality.

- **Package**: This is a collection of modules that are coupled together via their directory structure and is built such that modules in the package are accessed through the dot syntax. For example, if we have a package called feature that contains modules for helping us to do feature engineering, it could be organized as follows:

```
feature/
|-- numerical/
    |-- analyze.py
    |-- aggregate.py
    |-- transform.py
```

```
|-- categorical/
    |-- analyze.py
    |-- aggregate.py
    |-- transform.py
```

Then, if we wanted to use the functionality contained within the numerical or categorical sub-modules, we would use the `dot` syntax like so:

```
import feature.categorical.analyze
import feature.numerical.transform
```

Now let's move onto discuss some general Python tips and tricks.

Tips and tricks

Let's now discuss some tips and tricks of using Python that can often be overlooked, even by those quite familiar with the language. The following concepts can help you write more compact and performant code, so it's good to have them to hand. Note that this list is definitely not exhaustive:

- **Generators**: These are convenience functions for helping us create syntax that iterates in some sense. They save us writing a lot of boilerplate code, are memory efficient, and have very useful properties, such as the ability to pause execution and save the internal state automatically. Then you can resume iterating with it later in your program. Generators are created in Python whenever we define a function that use the `yield` statement. For example, here we can define a generator that will filter a given list of values based on a predicate called `condition`:

```
def filter_data(data, condition):
    for x in data:
        if condition(x):
            yield x
```

In action, we could apply this to a simple list of the integers from zero to ninety-nine called `data_vals` and filter out values below a certain threshold:

```
for x in filter_data(data_vals, lambda x: x > 50):
    print(x)
```

This will return the integers from fifty to ninety-nine.

The other way to define a generator expression is by using an iterative statement in round brackets. For example, here we can define a generator that iterates over the squares from zero to nine:

```
gen1 = (x**2 for x in range(10))
for i in gen1:
    print(i)
```

Note that you can only execute your generators once; after that, they are *empty*. This is because they only store what they need in memory for each step of the iteration, so once it is complete, nothing is stored!

Generators are really powerful ways for creating data manipulation steps that are memory efficient and can be used to define custom pipelines in frameworks such as **Apache Beam**. We will not cover this here, but it is definitely worth checking out. As an example, take a look at the article at https://medium.com/analytics-vidhya/building-a-data-pipeline-with-python-generators-a80a4d19019e.

- **List comprehension**: This is syntax that allows us to take any iterable we have to hand (a dict, a list, a tuple, and a str are all examples) and build a list from it in an extremely compact way. This can save you from writing long, clunky loops and can help create some more elegant code. List comprehensions create the entire list in memory, so they are not as efficient as generators. So use them wisely, and only to create small lists if you can. You perform list comprehension by writing your iteration logic in square brackets, as opposed to the round brackets of generators. As an example, we can create the data used in the first generator example:

```
data_vals = [x for x in range(100)]
```

- **Containers and collections**: Python has a useful set of built-in types that are known as **containers**, these being dict, set, list, and tuple. Beginners in Python learn how to use these from their first time playing with the language, but what we can often forget is their augmented counterparts: **collections**. These allow for additional behavior on top of the standard containers that can be useful. The table shown in *Figure 4.1* summarizes some useful containers mentioned in the Python 3 documentation on python.org at https://docs.python.org/3/library/collections. html. These are useful to have to hand when you are working through some data manipulations and can often save you a couple of lines of code:

Container	Description
deque	This is a double-ended queue and allows you to add and remove elements to either end of the object in a scalable way. It's useful if you want to add to the beginning or end of large data lists or if you want to search for the last occurrences of X in your data.
Counter	Counters take in iterables such as dicts or lists and return the count of each of the elements. They're really useful to get quick summaries of the content of these objects.
OrderedDict	The standard dict object does not maintain order, so OrderedDict introduces this functionality. This can be really useful if you need to loop back over a dictionary you have created in the same order as it was created for new processing.

Figure 4.1 – Some useful types in the collections module in Python 3

- *args and **kwargs: When we want to call a function in Python, we often supply it with arguments. We have seen plenty of examples of this in this book already. But what happens if you define a function for which you would like to apply to a varying number of arguments? This is where the *args and **kwargs patterns come in. For example, imagine we want to initialize a class called Address that uses information gathered from an online web form to create a single string giving an address. We may not know how many elements are going to be in each text box used by the user for the address ahead of time. We could then use the *args pattern (you don't have to call it args, so here we've called it address). Here's the class:

```python
class Address(object):
    def __init__(self, *address):
        if not address:
            self.address = None
            print('No address given')
        else:
            self.address = ' '.join(str(x) for x in address)
```

Then your code will work absolutely fine in both of these cases, even though there are a variable number of arguments to the constructor:

```python
address1 = Address('62', 'Lochview', 'Crescent')
address2 = Address('The Palm', '1283', 'Royston', 'Road')
```

Then address1.address will be given by '62 Lochview Crescent' and address2.address will be given by 'The Palm 1283 Royston Road'.

**kwargs extends this idea to allow a variable number of keyword arguments. This is particularly useful if you have functions where you may want to define a variable number of parameters, but you need names attached to those parameters. For example, we may want to define a class for containing ML model hyperparameter values, the number, and names of which will vary by algorithm. We can therefore do something like the following:

```python
class ModelHyperparameters(object):
    def __init__(self, **hyperparams):
        if not hyperparams:
            self.hyperparams = None
        else:
            self.hyperparams = hyperparams
```

Then the code will allow us to define instances such as the following:

```python
hyp1 = ModelHyperparameters(eps=3, distance='euclidean')
hyp2 = ModelHyperparameters(n_clusters=4, max_iter=100)
```

And then hyp1.hyperparams will be given by {'eps': 3, 'distance': 'euclidean'} and hyp2.hyperparams by {'n_clusters': 4, 'max_iter': 100}.

There are many more concepts that are important to understand for a detailed understanding of how Python works. For now, these pointers will be enough for us to build upon throughout the chapter.

Now we will consider how to define and organize these elements in a way that makes your code readable and consistent.

Adhering to standards

When you say something like *adhering to standards,* in most contexts you would be forgiven for half-expecting a sigh and a gigantic eye roll from whoever you were talking to. Standards sound boring and tedious, but they are in fact an extremely important part of making sure that your work is consistent and high quality.

In Python, the *de facto* standard for coding style is **Python Enhancement Proposal 8 (PEP-8)**, written by Guido Van Rossum (the creator of Python), Barry Warsaw, and Nick Coghlan (`https://www.python.org/dev/peps/pep-0008/`). It is essentially a collection of guidelines, tips, tricks, and suggestions for making code that is consistent and readable. Some of the benefits of adhering to the PEP-8 style guide in your Python projects are as follows:

- **Greater consistency**: This will help you write code that is less likely to break once you have deployed it, as it is much easier to follow the flow of your programs and identify errors and bugs. Consistency also helps simplify the design of extensions and interfaces to your code.

- **Improved readability**: This begets efficiency, as colleagues and even users of your solutions can understand what is being done and how to use it more effectively.

So, what is in the PEP-8 style guide? And how should you think about applying it to your ML project? For the full details, I recommend you read the PEP-8 documentation given earlier. But in the next few paragraphs, we will go into some of the details that will give you the greatest improvement to your code for the least effort.

First, let's cover **naming conventions**. When you write a piece of code you will have to create several variables, files, and other objects, such as classes, and these all have to have a name. Making sure that these names are readable and consistent is the first part of making your code of a very high standard.

Some of the key pointers from PEP-8 are as follows:

- **Variables and function names**: It is recommended that these consist of all lowercase words, separated by underscores. They should also help us understand what they are for. As an example, if you are building a regression model and you want to put some of your feature engineering steps inside a function to simplify reuse and readability elsewhere in the code, you may call it something like `Makemydata()`:

```python
def Makemydata():
    # steps go here …
    return result
```

Calling your function `Makemydata()` is not a great idea, whereas naming it something like `transform_features` is better:

```python
def transform_features()
    # steps go here …
    return result
```

This function name is compliant with PEP-8.

- **Modules and packages**: The recommendation is that these have all short lowercase names. Some great examples are ones you are familiar with, such as `pandas`, `numpy`, and `scipy`. Scikit-learn may seem like it breaks this rule, but it actually doesn't as the package name is `sklearn`. The style guide mentions that modules can have underscores to improve readability, but packages should not. If we had a module in a package called `transform_helpers`, then this is acceptable, but an entire package called `marketing_outlier_detection` would be terrible!

- **Classes**: Classes should have names such as `OutlierDetector`, `Transformer`, or `PipelineGenerator`, which clearly specify what they do and also follow the upper CamelCase or PascalCase (both mean the same thing) style.

These are some of the most commonly used naming conventions you should be aware of. The PEP-8 document also covers a lot of good points on whitespace and the formatting of lines that we will not go into here. We will finish this section with a discussion of some of the author's favorite suggestions from the *programming recommendations* of PEP-8. These are often overlooked and, if forgotten, can make for some code that is both horrible to read and likely to break, so take heed!

A good point to remember in all of this talk about style is that at the top of the PEP-8 document, it states that *Foolish Consistency is the Hobgoblin of Little Minds* and that there are good reasons to ignore these style suggestions in certain circumstances. Again, read the PEP-8 document for the full works, but if you follow these points then, in general, you will write clean and readable code.

Next, we will cover how some of these rules do not really apply when we are using the Python API for Apache Spark.

Writing good PySpark

In this section, we draw attention to one particular flavor of Python that is very important in the world of data science and ML. PySpark code has already been used in examples throughout this book since it is the go-to tool for distributing your data workloads, including your ML models. In *Chapter 6, Scaling Up*, we will learn more about PySpark, but here we will just briefly mention some points on coding style.

As mentioned in the section on *Spark ML pipelines* in *Chapter 3, From Model to Model Factory*, since Spark is written in Scala, the syntax of PySpark (which is just the Python API for Spark) has inherited a lot of the syntactical style from that underlying language. This means in practice that many of the methods you use will be written in CamelCase, meaning that it also makes sense to define your variables using CamelCase rather than the standard Python PEP-8 naming convention of words separated by underscores. This is behavior that we should encourage as it helps people reading our code to clearly see which sections are PySpark code and which are (more) vanilla Python. To emphasize this, when we used the `StringIndexer` object from the `pyspark.ml` package before, we used `StringIndexer` instead of the more idiomatic Python, `string_indexer`:

```
from pyspark.ml.feature import StringIndexer
stringIndexer = StringIndexer(inputCol=categoricalCol,
                              outputCol=categoricalCol)
```

Another important point about PySpark code is that because Spark is written in a functional paradigm, it also makes sense that your code also follows this style. We will understand a bit more of what this means in the next section.

Choosing a style

This section will provide a summary of two coding styles or paradigms, which make use of different organizational principles and capabilities of Python. Whether you write your code in an object-orientated or functional style could just be an aesthetic choice. This choice, however, can also provide other benefits, such as code that is more aligned with the logical elements of your problem, code that is easier to understand, or even more performant code.

In the following sections, we will outline the main principles of each paradigm and allow you to choose for yourself based on your use case.

Object-oriented programming

Object-Oriented Programming (OOP) is a style where the code is organized around, you guessed it, abstract objects with relevant attributes and data instead of around the logical flow of your solution. The subject of OOP is worth a book (or several books!) in itself, so we will focus on the key points that are relevant for our ML engineering journey.

First, in OOP, you have to define your `objects`. This is done in Python through the core OOP principle of classes, which are definitions of structures in your program that keep together related data and logical elements. A class is a template for defining the objects in OOP. As an example, consider a very simple class that groups together some methods for calculating numerical outliers on a dataset. For example, if we consider the pipelines that we looked into in *Chapter 3, From Model to Model Factory*, we may want to have something that makes this even easier to apply in a production setting. We may therefore want to wrap up some of the functionality provided by tools such as scikit-learn into a class of its own that could have bespoke steps specific to our problem. In the simplest case, if we wanted a class to wrap the standardization of our data and then apply a generic outlier detection model, it could look something like this:

```python
class OutlierDetector(object):
    def __init__(self, model=None):
        if model is not None:
            self.model = model
        self.pipeline = make_pipeline(StandardScaler(), self.
model)
    def detect(self, data):
        return self.pipeline.fit(data).predict(data)
```

All this example does is allow a user to skip writing out some of the steps that they may have to otherwise write to get the job done. The code doesn't disappear, it just gets placed inside a handy object with a clear logical definition. In this case, the pipeline shown is extremely simple, but we can imagine extending this to something very complex and containing logic that's specific to our use case. Therefore, if we have already defined an outlier detection model (or retrieved from a model store, such as MLFlow, as discussed in *Chapter 3, From Model to Model Factory*) we can then feed this into this class and run quite complex pipelines just with a single line of code, no matter the complexity contained within the class:

```python
model = IsolationForest(behaviour='new',
                        contamination=outliers_fraction,
                        random_state=42)

detector = OutlierDetector(model=model)

result = detector.detect(data)
```

As you can see from the example, this pattern of implementation seems familiar, and that's because it should be! Scikit-learn has a lot of OOP in it, and you use this paradigm every time you create a model. The act of creating a model is a case of you instantiating a class object, and the process of you calling `fit` or `predict` on your data are examples of calling class methods. So, the reason the preceding code may not seem alien is because it shouldn't! We've already been using OOP if we have done any ML with scikit-learn.

Despite what we have just said, using objects and understanding how to build them are obviously two different challenges. So, let's go through the core concepts of building your own classes. This will set us up later for building more classes of relevance for our own ML solutions.

First, you see from the preceding code snippet that a class is defined with the `class` keyword and that the PEP-8 convention is to use upper CamelCase for the class name. It is also good practice to make your class names clear definitions of *things that do stuff*. For example, `OutlierDetector`, `ModelWrapper`, and `DataTransformer` are good class names, but `Outliers` or `Calculation` are not. You will also notice that we have something in brackets after the name of the class. This tells the class which object to inherit functionality from. In the preceding example, we can see that this class inherits from something called `object`. This is actually the built-in base class in Python from which *all other objects inherit*. Therefore, since the class we defined does not inherit from anything more complex than `object`, you can think of this as essentially saying *the class we are about to build will have all of the functionality it needs defined within it; we do not need to use more complex functionality already defined in other objects for this class*. The syntax showing the inheritance from `object` is actually superfluous as you can just omit the brackets and write `OutlierDetector`, but it can be good practice to make the inheritance explicit.

Next, you can see that the functionality we want to group together is defined inside the class. Functions that live inside a class are called **methods**. You can see that `OutlierDetector` has only one method called `detect`, but you are not limited in how many methods your class can have. Methods contain your class's abilities to interact with data and other objects, so their definition is where most of the work of building up your class goes.

You might think we have missed a method, the one called `__init__()`. This is in fact not a method (or you can think of it as a very special method) and is called the *constructor*. The constructor does what it says—it constructs! Its job is to perform all of the relevant setup tasks (some of which occur in the background, such as memory allocation) for your class when it gets initialized as an object. When the example defines `detector`, the constructor is called. As you can see, you can pass variables and then these variables can be used within the class. Classes in Python can be created without defining an explicit constructor, but one will be created in the background. The final point we will make on constructors is that they are not allowed to return anything other than `None`, so it's common to leave the `return` statement unwritten.

You will also have seen in the example that there are variables inside the class and there is a somewhat mysterious `self` keyword. This allows methods and operations inside the class to refer to the particular instance of the class. So, if you define two or a hundred instances of the `OutlierDetector` object, it is possible for them all to have different values for their internal attributes but still have the same functionality.

We will create some more involved OOP styles for your ML solution later, but for now, let's discuss the other programming paradigm that we may want to use – functional programming.

Functional programming

Functional programming is based on the concept of, you guessed it, functions. At its core, this programming paradigm is about trying to write pieces of code that only take in data and output data, doing so without creating any internal state that can be changed. One of the goals of functional programming is to write code that has no unintended side effects due to mismanagement of state. It also has the benefit of making sure that the data flow in your programs can be understood completely by looking at the `return` statements of the functions you have written.

It uses the idea of the data in your program not being allowed to change in place. This concept is known as **immutability**. If your data (or any object) is immutable, it means that there is no internal state to modify and if you want to do something with the data you actually have to create new data. For example, in the section on *Object-oriented programming*, we again revisited the concept of standardizing data. In a functional program, standardized data cannot overwrite unstandardized data; you would need to store this new data somewhere, for example, in a new column in the same data structure.

Some programming languages are designed with functional principles at their core, such as F# and Haskell, but Python is a general-purpose language that can accommodate both paradigms quite nicely.

You will likely have seen some other functional programming concepts in other Python code. For example, if you have ever used a lambda function then this can be a powerful aspect of a functionally programmed piece of code as it is how you define *anonymous functions* (those without a specified name). So, you may have seen code that looks like something like this:

```
df['data_squared'] = df['data'].apply(lambda x: x**2)
```

In the preceding code block, `df` is a pandas dataframe and `data` is just a column of numbers. This is one of the tools that helps make functional programming in Python easier. Other such tools are the built-in functions `map()`, `reduce()`, and `filter()`.

As an example, imagine that we have some address data similar to that in the *Recapping the basics* section, where we discussed the concepts of `args` and `**kwargs`:

```
data = [
    ['The', 'Business', 'Centre', '15', 'Stevenson', 'Lane'],
    ['6', 'Mossvale', 'Road'],
    ['Studio', '7', 'Tottenham', 'Court', 'Road']
]
```

Now, we might want to write some code that returns a list of lists with the same shape as this data, but every entry now contains the number of characters in each string. This could be a stage in a data preparation step in one of our ML pipelines. If we wanted to write some code to do this functionally, we could define a function that takes a list and returns a new list with the string lengths for the entries like this:

```
def len_strings_in_list(data_list):
    return list(map(lambda x: len(x), data_list))
```

This embodies functional programming because the data is immutable (there is no change of internal state) and the function is pure (it only uses data within the scope of the function). We can then use another concept from functional programming called higher-order functions, where you supply functions as the arguments of other functions. For example, we may want to define a function that can apply any list-based function but to a list of lists:

```
def list_of_list_func_results(list_func, list_of_lists):
    return list(map(lambda x: list_func(x), list_of_lists))
```

Note that this is completely generic; as long as the `list_func()` can be applied to a list, this will work on a list of lists. We can therefore get the original result we wanted by calling the following:

```
list_of_list_func_results(len_strings_in_list, data)
```

This returns the desired result:

```
[[3, 8, 6, 2, 9, 4], [1, 8, 4], [6, 1, 9, 5, 4]]
```

Spark, a tool that's already been used multiple times in this book, is written in the Scala language, which is also general-purpose and can accommodate both object-oriented and functional programming. Spark is predominantly written in a functional style; its aim of distributing computation is more easily accommodated if principles such as immutability are respected. This means that when we have been typing PySpark code through this book we have subtly been picking up some functional programming practices (did you notice?).

In fact, in *Chapter 3*, *From Model to Model Factory*, the example PySpark pipeline we built had code like this:

```
data = data.withColumn('label', f.when((f.col("y") == "yes"),
1).otherwise(0))
```

This is functional since the `data` object we create is actually a new dataframe with the new column added—we can't just add a column in place. There was also code that formed part of our pipelines from the Spark MLlib library:

```
scaler = StandardScaler(inputCol='numerical_cols_imputed',
outputCol="numerical_cols_imputed_scaled")
```

This is defining how to take a series of columns in a dataframe and perform a scaling transformation on them. Note how you define input columns and output columns, and *these cannot be the same*. That's immutability in action—you have to create new data rather than transform it in place.

Hopefully, this gives you a taste of functional programming in Python. This is not the main paradigm we will use in this book, but it will be used for some pieces of code and, in particular, remember that when we use PySpark we are often implicitly using functional programming.

We will now discuss ways of packaging the code that you have written.

Packaging your code

In some ways, it is interesting that Python has taken the world by storm. It is dynamically typed and non-compiled, so it can be quite different to work with compared to Java or C++. This particularly comes to the fore when we think about packaging our Python solutions. For a compiled language, the main target is to produce a compiled artifact that can run on the chosen environment, a Java `jar` for example. Python requires that the environment you run in has an appropriate Python interpreter and the ability to install the libraries and packages you need. There is also no single compiled artifact created, so you often need to deploy your whole code base as is.

Despite this, Python has indeed taken the world by storm, especially for ML. As we are ML engineers thinking about taking models to production, we would be remiss to not understand how to package and share Python code in a way that helps others to avoid repetition, to trust in the solution, and to be able to easily integrate it with other projects.

In the following sections, we are first going to discuss what we mean by a user-defined library and some of the advantages of packaging your code this way. We are then going to define the main ways you can do this so that you can run your ML code in production.

Why package?

Before we discuss in detail exactly what a package or library is in Python, we can articulate the advantages by using a working definition of *a collection of Python code that can be run without detailed knowledge of its implementation.*

You will have already picked up from this definition the nature of the first reason to do this: **abstraction**.

Bringing together your code into a library or package that can be reused by other developers and data scientists in your team, organization, or the wider community allows these user groups to solve problems more quickly. Since the details of the work are abstracted away, anyone using your code can focus on implementing the capabilities of your solution, rather than trying to understand and dissect every line. This will lead to reduced development and deployment time in projects, as well as encourage the usage of your code in the first place!

The second advantage is that by consolidating the functionality you need into a library or package; you bring all of the implementation details to one place and therefore *improvements scale*. What we mean by this is if 40 projects are using your library and someone discovers a minor bug, you only need to patch it *once* and then redeploy or update the package in those 40 implementations. This is way more scalable than explaining the issue to the relevant teams and getting 40 different fixes at the implementation end. This consolidation also means that once you have thoroughly tested all the components, you can more confidently assume that this solution will be running smoothly in those 40 different projects, without knowing anything about the details under the hood.

Figure 4.2 helps to show how packages helpfully allow a *write once, use many* philosophy for your code, which is incredibly important if you want to engineer ML solutions that can solve multiple problems in a scalable fashion:

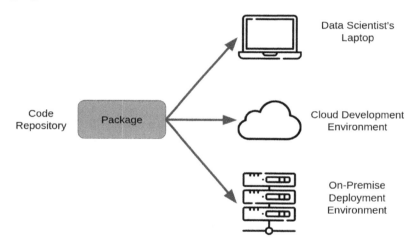

Figure 4.2 – Developing packages for your ML solutions allows you to write the code once but use it many times in different environments

The next section will build on these main ideas about packaging to discuss specified use cases in which packaging our code can be beneficial.

Selecting use cases for packaging

First things first, not all of your solutions should be libraries. If you have an extremely simple use case, you may only need one simple script to run on a schedule for the core of your ML solution. You can still write a well-engineered system and performant code in this case, but it's not a library. Similarly, if your problem is best solved by a web app, then although there will be lots of components, it will not naturally be a library.

Some good reasons you may want to write up your solution as a library or package are as follows:

- The problem your code solves is a common one that many come up in multiple projects or environments.

- You want to abstract away implementation details so that execution and development are decoupled, making it easier for others to use your code.

- To minimize the number of places and number of times you need to change code to implement bug fixes.

- To make testing simpler.

- To simplify your **Continuous Integration/Continuous Development (CI/CD)** pipeline.

We will now dive into how we might go about designing our packages.

Designing your package

The layout of your code base is far more than just a stylistic consideration. It is something that will determine how your code is used in every instance of the project – no pressure!

This means that it is important to put some thought into how you want to lay out your code and how this influences usage patterns. You need to ensure that all of the main components you need have a presence in the code base and are easy to find.

Let's work this through with an example based on the outlier detection case we worked through in the previous sections.

First, we need to decide what kind of solution we want to create. Are we building something that will run a web application or a standalone executable with lots of functionality, or are we building a library for others to use in their ML projects? In fact, we can choose to do more than one thing! For this case, let's build a package that can be imported for use in other projects but can also run in a standalone execution mode.

To set the context for the development of our package, imagine we have been asked to start building a solution that can run a set of selected unsupervised outlier detection models. The data scientists have found that, for the problem at hand, `Isolation Forest` models are most performant, but they must be retrained on every run and the users of the package should be able to edit the configuration of the models through a config file. Only `sklearn` models have been studied so far, but the business and users of the package would like this functionality to be extensible to other modeling tools if needed. Technical requirements for the project mean we cannot use MLflow for this project. Don't worry; in later chapters when we build more examples, we will relax this constraint to show how it all fits together:

1. The package we are going to build is all about outliers, so let's call it `outliers` (I know, inventive, right?). Just to make it clear how everything hangs together, we will start to build the `outliers` package in a folder called `outlier_package`:

   ```
   outlier_package/
        outliers
   ```

2. Our package design will be based on the functionality we want the solution to have, so in this case we want something that detects outliers, so let's create a sub-package called `detectors`:

   ```
   outlier_package/
        outliers/
             detectors
   ```

3. Within this, we will put some code that wraps (more on this later) around some basic models from external libraries. We will also want some code that gets data for us to analyze, so we will add a sub-package for that too:

   ```
   outlier_package/
        outliers/
             detectors
             data
   ```

4. We can already see our package taking shape. Finally, we will want to have somewhere to store configuration information and somewhere to store helper functions that may be used across the package, so let's add a directory and sub-package for those too:

   ```
   outlier_package/
   outliers/
   detectors
   ```

```
data
configs
utils
```

Now, this layout is not sacrosanct or dictated in any way. We can create the layout however we want and do whatever we think makes sense. It is important when doing this, though, to always remember the principles of **Don't Repeat Yourself** (**DRY**), **Keep It Simple Stupid** (**KISS**), and the Python mantra of *there should preferably be only one way to do something*. If you stick to these principles, you will be fine. For more information on these principles, see https://code.tutsplus.com/tutorials/3-key-software-principles-you-must-understand--net-25161 and https://www.python.org/dev/peps/pep-0020/.

So, what actually goes in each of these sub-packages? Well, the underlying code of course!

5. In this case, we will want something to provide an interface between our detector implementations and the syntax for creating a pipeline and calling them, so we will build a simple class and keep it in pipelines.py. pipelines.py contains the following code:

```python
from sklearn.preprocessing import StandardScaler
from sklearn.pipeline import make_pipeline


class OutlierDetector(object):
    def __init__(self, model=None):
        if model is not None:
            self.model = model

        self.pipeline = make_pipeline(StandardScaler(),
    self.model)


    def detect(self, data):
        return self.pipeline.fit(data).predict(data)
```

6. We then also need something to define the models we want to interface with. In this case, we will create code that uses information stored in a configuration file to decide which of a select few models to instantiate. We put all this functionality in a class called `DetectionModels`. For brevity, we omit the details of each of the functions in the class in this first instance:

```python
import json
from sklearn.ensemble import IsolationForest


class DetectionModels(object):
    def __init__(self, model_config_path=None):
    ...

    def create_model(self, model_name=None, params=None):
    .....


    def get_models(self):
    .....
```

7. The initialization method is expanded here. Notice that we wrote this code so that we could define a series of models in the `config` file:

```python
class DetectionModels(object):
    def __init__(self, model_config_path=None):
        if model_config_path is not None:
            with open(model_config_path) as w:
                self.model_def = json.load(w)
```

8. Then the `create_model` method is able to instantiate the model based on parameter and model name information. We have also built this so that we can actually pull in configuration information for models from different libraries if we wanted to; we would just need to add the appropriate implementation logic in this `create_model` function, checking that `sklearn` or another model was defined and running the appropriate syntax in each case. We would also have to make sure the pipeline generated in `OutlierDetector` was appropriate in each case as well:

```python
    def create_model(self, model_name=None, params=None):
        if model_name is None and params is None:
            return None
```

```
        if model_name == 'IsolationForest' and params is
not None:
            return IsolationForest(**params)
```

9. Finally, we bring the preceding methods together through the `get_models` method, which returns a list of all models defined in the appropriate config file, instantiated as a `sklearn` object via the `create_model` method:

```
    def get_models(self):
        models = []
        for model_definition in self.model_def:
            defined_model = self.create_model(
                model_name=model_definition['model'],
                params=model_definition['params']
            )
            models.append(defined_model)
        return models
```

You may be thinking *why not just read in the appropriate model and apply it, no matter what it is?* That could be a viable solution, but what we have done here means that only model types and algorithms that have been approved by the team working on the project can make it through to production, as well as permitting the use of heterogeneous model implementations.

10. To see how this could all work in practice, let's define a script called `__main__.py` at the uppermost level of the package that can act as the main entry point for execution of modeling runs:

```
from utils.data import create_data
from detectors.detection_models import DetectionModels
import detectors.pipelines
from definitions import MODEL_CONFIG_PATH


if __name__ == "__main__":
    data = create_data()
    models = DetectionModels(MODEL_CONFIG_PATH).get_
models()
    for model in models:
        detector = detectors.pipelines.
OutlierDetector(model=model)
```

```
        result = detector.detect(data)
        print(result)
```

11. The model_config.json file referred to here is given by the following code:

```
[
    {
        "model": "IsolationForest",
        "params": {
          "behaviour": "new",
          "contamination": 0.15,
          "random_state": 42
        }
    }
]
```

12. The definitions.py file is a file that holds relevant paths and other variables that we want to make globally accessible in the package without polluting the namespace:

```
import os
ROOT_DIR = os.path.dirname(__file__)
MODEL_CONFIG_PATH = os.path.join(ROOT_DIR, "configs/
model_config.json")
```

We can see that we don't really do anything with the results, we just print them to show that output is produced, but in reality you will either push these results elsewhere or calculate statistics on them.

This script can be run by typing this in your terminal:

```
python __main__.py
```

Alternatively, you could type the following:

```
python -m outliers
```

And that is how you can package functionality into classes, modules, and packages. The example given was relatively constrained, but it does give us an awareness of how the different pieces can be brought together and executed.

> **Important note**
> The example given here has been built up to show you how to hang your
> code together by using some of the techniques discussed in this chapter. It is
> not necessarily the only way to bring all of these bits together, but it does act
> as a good illustration of how to create your own package. So, just remember
> that if you see a way to improve this implementation or adapt it to your own
> purposes, then brilliant!

In the next section, we will explore how to build distributions of this code and how to
allow ourselves and users to install the `outliers` package as a normal Python package
that we can use in other projects.

Building your package

In our example, we can package up our solution using the `setuptools` library. In
order to do this, you must create a file called `setup.py` that contains the important
metadata for your solution, including the location of the relevant packages it requires. An
example of `setup.py` is shown in the following code block. This shows how to do this
for a simple package that wraps some of the outlier detection functionality we have been
mentioning in this chapter:

```
from setuptools import setup

setup(name='outliers',
      version='0.1',
      description='A simple package to wrap some outlier
detection functionality',
      author='Andrew McMahon',
      license='MIT',
      packages=['outliers'],
      zip_safe=False)
```

We can see that `setuptools` allows you to supply metadata such as the name of the
package, the version number, and the software license. Once you have this file in the root
directory of your project, you can then do a few things:

1. First, you can install the package locally as an executable. This will mean you can
   import your library like any other Python library in code you want to run:

   ```
   pip install .
   ```

2. You can create a source distribution of the package so that all of the code is bundled together efficiently. For example, if you run the following command at the root of your project, a `gzipped tarball` is created in a folder called `dist`:

```
python setup.py sdist
```

3. You can create a built distribution of the package, which is an object that can be unpacked and used immediately by the user without them having to run the `setup.py` script as in a source distribution. The most appropriate built distribution is what is known as a Python wheel. Running the following command in the root directory of your project creates the wheel and puts it in the `dist` folder:

```
python setup.py bdist_wheel
```

4. If you are going to distribute your code using `pip`, then it makes sense to package both a source distribution and a wheel and let the user decide what to do. So, you can build both and then use a package called `twine` to upload both distributions to PyPI. If you want to do this, then you need to register for a PyPI account at `https://pypi.org/account/register/`. Just run the previous two commands together in the root directory of your project and use the `twine upload` command:

```
python setup.py sdist bdist_wheel
twine upload dist/*
```

For a lot more information on packaging, you can read through the information and tutorials at `https://www.pypa.io/en/latest/`, provided by the **Python Packaging Authority** (**PyPA**).

The next section touches briefly on how we can automate a few of the steps around building and testing our packages using Makefiles.

Makefiles

If we are on a UNIX system and we have the `make` utility installed, then we can further automate a lot of the steps we want to run for our solution in different scenarios using Makefiles. For example, in the following code block we have a Makefile that allows us to run our module's main entry point, run our test suite, or clean up any artifacts using the `run`, `test`, and `clean` targets:

```
MODULE := outliers
run:
    @python -m $(MODULE)
test:
```

```
    @pytest
.PHONY: clean test
clean:
            rm -rf .pytest_cache .coverage .pytest_cache
coverage.xml
```

This is a very simple Makefile, but we can make it as complex as needed by layering more and more commands. If we want to `run` a specific target set of commands, we simply call `make`, then the target name:

```
make test
make run
```

This is a powerful way to abstract out a lot of terminal commands you would otherwise have to manually enter in each case. It also acts as documentation for other users of the solution!

Next, let's cover some of the steps we can take to ensure that our packages are robust and can be trusted to work or to fail gracefully and be diagnosable if there is an issue.

Testing, logging, and error handling

Building code that performs an ML task may seem like the end goal, but it is only one piece of the puzzle. We also want to be confident that this code will work and if it doesn't, we will be able to fix it. This is where the concepts of testing, logging, and error handling come in, which the next few sections cover at a high level.

Testing

One of the most important features that sets your ML engineered code apart from typical research scripts is the presence of robust testing. It is critical that any system you are designing for deployment can be trusted not to fall down all the time and that you can catch issues during the development process.

Luckily, since Python is a general-purpose programming language, it is replete with tools for performing tests on your software. In this chapter, we will use **PyTest**, which is one of the most popular, powerful, and easy-to-use testing toolsets for Python code available. PyTest is particularly useful if you are new to testing because it focuses on building tests as standalone Python functions that are quite readable, whereas other packages can sometimes lead to the creation of clunky testing classes and complex `assert` statements. Let's dive into an example.

First, let's start by writing tests for some pieces of code defined in the rest of this chapter from our `outliers` package. We can define a simple test to ensure that our data helper function actually creates some numerical data that can be used for modeling. To run this sort of test in PyTest, we first create a file with `test_` or `_test` in the name somewhere in our test's directory—PyTest will automatically find files that have this in their name. So, for example, we may write a test script called `test_create_data.py` that contains the logic we need to test all of the functions that refer to creating data within our solution. Let's make this explicit with an example:

1. Import the relevant modules we will need from the package and anything else we need for testing. Here, we import `pytest` because we will use some functionality from it in later steps but, in general, you don't need to import this:

    ```
    import numpy
    import pytest
    import outliers.utils.data
    ```

2. Then, since we want to test the function for creating data, it would be good to only generate the data once, then test its attributes in a variety of ways. To do this, we employ the `fixture` decorator from PyTest, which allows us to define an object that can be read into several of our tests. Here, we use this so that we can apply our tests using `dummy_data`, which is just the output of the `create_data` function:

    ```
    @pytest.fixture()
    def dummy_data():
        data = outliers.utils.data.create_data()
        return data
    ```

3. Finally, we can actually write the tests. Here are two examples that test if the dataset created by the function is a `numpy` array and if it has more than `100` rows of data:

    ```
    def test_data_is_numpy(dummy_data):
        assert isinstance(dummy_data, numpy.ndarray)


    def test_data_is_large(dummy_data):
        assert len(dummy_data)>100
    ```

    We can write as many of these tests and as many of these types of test modules as we like. This allows us to create a high degree of **test coverage** across our package.

4. You can then enter the following command in the terminal at the top level of your project in order to run all the tests in the package:

```
$ pytest
```

Then you will see a message like this, telling us what tests have run and which have passed and failed:

```
======================================================================== test session starts ======
platform linux -- Python 3.8.5, pytest-6.1.1, py-1.9.0, pluggy-0.13.1 -- /home/andrew/anaconda3/envs/mleng/bin/python
cachedir: .pytest_cache
rootdir: /home/andrew/dev/github/Machine-Learning-Engineering-with-Python/chapter4/outlier_package
collected 2 items

outliers/tests/test_create_data.py::test_data_is_numpy PASSED
outliers/tests/test_create_data.py::test_data_is_large PASSED

====================================================================================== 2 passed in 0.45s =======
```

Figure 4.3 – The output of a successful unit test in PyTest

The previous example showed how to write and execute some basic tests on our data utilities. We can now expand on this by testing some of the more sophisticated functionality in the package, namely the model creation process.

5. Similarly to the previous case, we create a script for holding our tests in `tests/ test_detectors.py`. Since we are testing more complex functionality, we will have to import more pieces of the package into the script:

```
import pytest
from outliers.detectors.detection_models import
DetectionModels
from outliers.detectors.pipelines import OutlierDetector
from outliers.definitions import MODEL_CONFIG_PATH
import outliers.utils.data
import numpy as np
```

6. We will have the same fixture for dummy data created as in *Step 2*, but now we also have a fixture for creating some example models to use in tests:

```
@pytest.fixture()
def example_models():
    models = DetectionModels(MODEL_CONFIG_PATH)
    return models
```

7. Our final fixture creates an example detector instance for us to use, based on the previous models fixture:

```
@pytest.fixture()
def example_detector(example_models):
    model = example_models.get_models()[0]
    detector = OutlierDetector(model=model)
    return detector
```

8. And now we are ready to test some of the model creation functionality. First, we can test that the models we created are not empty objects:

```
def test_model_creation(example_models):
    assert example_models is not None
```

9. We can then test that we can successfully retrieve models using the instance of DetectionModels created in *step 6*:

```
def test_model_get_models(example_models):
    example_models.get_models() is not None
```

10. Finally, we can test that the results found by applying the model pass some simple tests. This shows that the main pieces of our package are working for an end-to-end application:

```
def test_model_evaluation(dummy_data, example_detector):
    result = example_detector.detect(dummy_data)
    assert len(result[result == -1]) == 39 #number of
anomalies to detect
    assert len(result) == len(dummy_data) #same numbers
of results
    assert np.unique(result)[0] == -1
    assert np.unique(result)[1] == 1
```

11. As in *Step 4*, we can run the full test suite from the command line. We add a verbosity flag to show the individual tests that pass. This helps confirm that both our data utility and our model tests are being triggered:

```
pytest --verbose
```

The output is shown in the following screenshot:

```
================================================================================= test session starts ======
platform linux -- Python 3.8.5, pytest-6.1.1, py-1.9.0, pluggy-0.13.1 -- /home/andrew/anaconda3/envs/mleng/bin/python
cachedir: .pytest_cache
rootdir: /home/andrew/dev/github/Machine-Learning-Engineering-with-Python/chapter4/outlier_package
collected 5 items

outliers/tests/test_create_data.py::test_data_is_numpy PASSED
outliers/tests/test_create_data.py::test_data_is_large PASSED
outliers/tests/test_detectors.py::test_model_creation PASSED
outliers/tests/test_detectors.py::test_model_get_models PASSED
outliers/tests/test_detectors.py::test_model_evaluation PASSED
```

Figure 4.4 – Output of successful tests on both data and model functionality

The running of these tests can be automated either via the inclusion of `githooks` in our repository or through the use of other tools, such as the `Makefile` used for the project.

We now move on to consider how we can log information about our code as it runs, which can help with debugging and with general monitoring of your solution.

Logging

Next, it is important to ensure that as your code is running, the status of the different operations is reported, as well as any errors which occur. This helps make your code more maintainable and helps you debug when there is an issue. For this, you can use the Python `logging` library.

Loggers can be instantiated in your code via logic like this:

```
import logging

logging.basicConfig(filename='outliers.log',
                    level=logging.DEBUG,
                    format='%(asctime)s | %(name)s |
%(levelname)s | %(message)s')
```

This code defines our format for the logging messages and specifies that logging messages of level DEBUG or higher will go to the `outliers.log` file. We can then log output and information relevant to our code's running status using the very easy-to-use syntax that comes with the `logging` library:

```
logging.debug('Message to help debug ...')
logging.info('General info about a process that is running
...')
logging.warning('Warn, but no need to error ...')
```

With the settings shown in the first `logging` snippet, this will result in the following logging messages being written to `outliers.log`:

```
2021-08-02 19:58:53,501 | root | DEBUG | Message to help debug
...
2021-08-02 19:58:53,501 | root | INFO | General info about a
process that is running ...
2021-08-02 19:58:53,501 | root | WARNING | Warn, but no need to
error ...
```

This only scratches the surface of what is possible when it comes to logging, but this will allow you to get started.

Now, we move onto what we need to do in our code to handle scenarios where things go wrong!

Error handling

The last piece of *housekeeping* to cover in this section is error handling. It is important to remember that when you are an ML engineer, your aim is to build products and services that work, but an important part of this is recognizing that things do not always work! It is therefore important that you build in patterns that allow for the escalation of (inevitable) errors during run time. In Python, this is typically done via the concept of *exceptions*. Exceptions can be raised by the core Python functions and methods you are using. For example, imagine you ran the following code without defining the variable x:

```
y = 10*x
```

The following exception would be raised:

```
NameError: name 'x' is not defined
```

The important point for us as engineers is that we should build solutions in which we can confidently control the flow of errors. We may not always want our code to break when an error occurs, or we may want to ensure that very specific messages and logging occurs upon certain expected edge cases. The simplest technique for doing this is via `try except` blocks, as seen in the following code block:

```
try:
    do_something()
except:
    do_something_else()
```

In this case, `do_something_else()` is executed if `do_something()` runs into an error.

We will now finish with a comment on how to be efficient when building your solutions.

Not reinventing the wheel

You will already have noticed through this chapter (or I hope you have!) that a lot of the functionality that you need for your ML and Python project has already been built. One of the most important things you can learn as an ML engineer is that you are not supposed to build everything from scratch. You can do this in a variety of ways, the most obvious of which is to use other packages in your own solution and then build functionality that enriches what is already there. As an example, you do not need to build basic regression modeling capabilities since they exist in a variety of packages, but you might have to add a new type of regressor or use some specific domain knowledge or trick you have developed. In this case, you would be justified in writing your own code on top of the existing solution. You can also use a variety of concepts from Python, such as wrapper classes or decorators, as well. The key message is that although there is a lot of work for you to do when building your ML solutions, it is important that you do not feel the need to build everything from scratch. It is far more efficient to focus on where you can create added value and build on what has gone before!

Summary

This chapter has been all about best practices for when you write your own Python packages for your ML solutions. We went over some of the basic concepts of Python programming as a refresher before covering some tips and tricks and good techniques to bear in mind. We covered the importance of coding standards in Python and PySpark. We then performed a comparison between object-oriented and functional programming paradigms for writing your code. We moved onto the details of taking the high-quality code you have written and packaging it up into something you can distribute across multiple platforms and use cases. To do this, we looked into different tools, designs, and setups you could use to make this a reality. This included a brief discussion of how to find good use cases for packaging up. We continued with a summary of some housekeeping tips for your code, including how to test, log, and monitor in your solution. We finished with a brief *philosophical* point on the importance of not reinventing the wheel.

In the next chapter, we will take a deep dive into the world of deployment. This will be all about how you take scripts, packages, libraries, and apps that you have written and run them on appropriate infrastructure and tools.

5
Deployment Patterns and Tools

In this chapter, we will dive into some important concepts around the deployment of your **Machine Learning** (**ML**) solution. We will begin to close the circle of the ML development life cycle and lay the groundwork for getting your solutions out into the world.

The act of deploying software, of taking it from a demo you can show off to a few stakeholders to a service that will ultimately impact customers or colleagues, is a very exhilarating but often challenging exercise. It also remains one of the most difficult aspects of any ML project and getting it right can ultimately make the difference between generating value or just hype.

We are going to explore some of the main concepts that will help your ML engineering team cross the chasm between a fun proof-of-concept to solutions that can run on scalable infrastructure in an automated way.

In this chapter, we will cover the following topics:

- Architecting systems
- Exploring the unreasonable effectiveness of patterns
- Containerizing
- Hosting your own microservice on **Amazon Web Services** (**AWS**)
- Pipelining 2.0

The next section will discuss how we can architect and design our ML systems with deployment in mind. Let's go!

Technical requirements

To work through the examples in this chapter, we require the following tools to be installed:

- AWS CLI v2
- Postman
- Docker

Architecting systems

No matter how you are working to build your software, it is always important to have a design in mind. This section will highlight the key considerations we must bear in mind when architecting ML systems.

Consider a scenario where you are contracted to organize the building of a house. We would not simply go out and hire a team of builders, buy all the supplies, hire all the equipment, and just tell everyone to *start building*. We would also not assume we knew exactly what the client who hired us wants without first speaking to them.

Instead, we would likely try to understand what the client wanted in detail, and then try to design the solution that would fit their requirements. We would potentially iterate this plan a few times with them and with appropriate experts who knew the details of pieces that fed into the overall design. Although we are not interested in building houses (or maybe you are, but there will not be any in this book!), we can still see the analogy with software. Before building anything, we should create an effective and clear design. This design provides the direction of travel for the solution and helps the build team know exactly what components they will work on. This means that we will be confident that what we build will solve the end user's problem.

This, in a nutshell, is what software architecture is all about.

If we did the equivalent of the above example for our ML solution, some of the following things may happen. We could end up with a very confusing code base, with some ML engineers in our team building elements and functionality that are already covered by the work that other engineers have done. We may also build something that fundamentally cannot work later in the project; for example, if we have selected a tool that has specific environmental requirements we cannot meet due to another component. We may also struggle to anticipate what infrastructure we need to be provisioned ahead of time, leading to a disorganized scramble within the project to get the correct resource. We may also underestimate the amount of work required and miss our deadline. All of these are outcomes we wish to avoid and can be avoided if we are following a good design.

In order to be effective, the architecture of a piece of software should provide at least the following things to the team working on building the solution:

- It should define the functional components required to solve the problem in totality.

- It should define how these functional components will interact, usually through the exchange of some form of data.

- It should show how the solution can be extended in future to include further functionality the client may require.

- It should provide guidance on which tools should be selected to implement each of the components outlined in the architecture.

- It should stipulate the process flow for the solution, as well as the data flow.

This is what a piece of good architecture should do, but what does this actually mean in practice?

There is no strict definition of how an architecture has to be compiled. The key point is that it acts as a design against which building can progress. So, for example, this might take the form of a nice diagram with boxes, lines, and some text, or it could be a several-page document. It might be compiled using a formal modeling language such as **Unified Modeling Language** (**UML**), or not. This often depends on the business context in which you operate and what requirements are placed on the people writing the architecture. The key is that it ticks off the points above and gives the engineers clear guidance on what to build and how it will all stick together.

Architecture is a vast and fascinating subject in itself, so we will not go much further into the details of this here, but we will now focus on what architecture means in an ML engineering context.

Exploring the unreasonable effectiveness of patterns

In this book, we have already mentioned a few times that we should not attempt to *reinvent* the wheel and we should reuse, repeat, and recycle what works according to the wider software and ML community. This is also true about your deployment architectures. When we discuss architectures that can be reused for a variety of different use cases with similar characteristics, we often refer to these as *patterns*. Using standard (or at least well-known) patterns can really help you speed up the time to value of your project and help you engineer your ML solution in a way that is robust and extensible.

Given this, we will spend the next few sections summarizing some of the most important architectural patterns that have become increasingly successful in the ML space over the past few years.

Swimming in data lakes

The single most important asset for anyone trying to use ML is, of course, the data that we can analyze and train our models on. The era of **big data** meant that the sheer size and variability in the format of this data became an increasing challenge. If you are a large organization (or even not-so-large), it is not viable to store all of the data you will want to use for ML applications in a structured relational database. Just the complexity of modeling the data for storage in such a format would be very high. So, what can you do?

Well, this problem was initially tackled with the introduction of **data warehouses**, which let you bring all of your relational data storage into one solution and create a single point of access. This helps alleviate, to some extent, the problem of data volumes, as each database can store relatively small amounts of data even if the total is large. These warehouses were designed with the integration of multiple data sources in mind. However, they are still relatively restrictive as they usually bundle together the infrastructure for compute and storage. This means they can't be scaled very well, and they can be expensive investments that create vendor lock-in. Most importantly for ML, data warehouses cannot store raw and semi-structured or unstructured data (for example, images). This automatically rules out a lot of good ML use cases if warehouses are used as your main data store. Now, with tools such as **Apache Spark**, which we've already used extensively throughout this book, if we have the clusters available, we can feasibly analyze and model any size or structure of data. The question then becomes, how should we store it?

Data lakes are technologies that allow you to store any type of data at any scale you feasibly need. There are a variety of providers of data lake solutions, including the main public cloud providers such as **Microsoft Azure**, **Google Cloud Platform (GCP)**, and AWS. Since we have met AWS before, let's focus on that.

The main storage solution in AWS is called the **Simple Storage Service**, or **S3**. Like all of the core data lake technologies, you can effectively load anything into it since it is based on the concept of *object storage*. This means that every instance of data you load up is treated as its own object with a unique identifier and associated metadata. It allows your S3 bucket to simultaneously contain photographs, JSON files, .txt files, Parquet files, and any other number of data formats.

If you work in an organization that does not have a data lake, this does not automatically exclude you from doing machine learning, but it can definitely make it an easier journey since you always know how you can store the data you need for your problem, no matter the format.

Microservices

Your ML project's code base will start small – just a few lines at first. But as your team expends more and more effort in building the solution required, this will quickly grow. If your solution has to have a few different capabilities and perform some quite distinct actions and you keep all of this in the same code base, your solution can become incredibly complex. In fact, software in which the components are all tightly coupled and non-separable like this is called **monolithic**, as it is akin to single big blocks that can exist independently of other applications. This sort of approach may fit the bill for your use case, but as the complexity of solutions continues to increase, a much more resilient and extensible design pattern is often required.

Microservice architectures are those in which the functional components of your solution are cleanly separated, potentially in completely different code bases or running on completely different infrastructure. For example, if we are building a user-facing web application that allows users to browse, select, and purchase products, we may have a variety of ML capabilities we wish to deploy in quick succession. We may want to recommend new products based on what they have just been looking at, we may want to retrieve forecasts of when their recently ordered items will arrive, and we may want to highlight some discounts we think they will benefit from (based on our analysis of their historic account behavior). This would be a very tall order, maybe even impossible, for a monolithic application. However, it is something that quite naturally falls into microservice architecture like that in *Figure 5.1*:

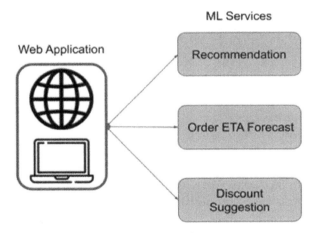

Figure 5.1 – An example of some ML microservices

The implementation of a microservice architecture can be accomplished using a few tools, some of which we will cover in the section on *Hosting your own microservice on AWS*. The main idea is that you always separate out the elements of your solution into their own services that are not tightly coupled together.

Microservice architectures are particularly good at allowing our development teams to achieve the following:

- Independently debug, patch, or deploy individual services rather than tearing down the whole system.

- Avoid a single point of failure.

- Increase maintainability.

- Allow separate services to be owned by distinct teams with clearer responsibilities.

- Accelerate the development of complex products.

Like every architecture pattern or design style, it is, of course, not a silver bullet, but we would do well to remember the microservice architecture when designing our next solution.

Next, we will discuss event-based designs.

Event-based designs

You do not always want to operate in scheduled batches. As we have seen, even just in the previous section, *Microservices*, not all use cases align with running a large batch prediction from a model on a set schedule, storing the results, and then retrieving them later. What happens if the data volumes you need are not there for a training run? What if no new data to run predictions in has arrived? What if other systems could make use of a prediction based on individual data points at the earliest time they become available rather than at a specific time every day?

In an event-based architecture, individual actions produce results that then trigger other individual actions in the system, and so on and so forth. This means that processes can happen as early as they can and no earlier. It also allows for a more dynamic or stochastic data flow, which can be beneficial if other systems are not running on scheduled batches either.

Event-based patterns could be mixed with others, for example, microservices or batch processing. The benefits still stand, and, in fact, event-based components allow for more sophisticated orchestration and management of your solution.

There are two types of event-based patterns:

- **Pub/sub**: In this case, event data is published to a message broker or event bus to be consumed by other applications. In one variant of the pub/sub pattern, the broker or buses used are organized by some appropriate classification and are designated as **topics**. An example of a tool that does this is **Apache Kafka**.

- **Event streaming**: Streaming use cases are ones where we want to process a continuous flow of data in something very close to real time. We can think of this as working with data as it *moves through* the system. This means it is not persisted *at rest* in a database but processed as it is created or received by the streaming solution. An example tool to use for event streaming applications would be **Apache Storm**.

Figure 5.2 shows an example event-based architecture applied to the case of **IoT** and mobile devices that have their data passed into classification and anomaly detection algorithms:

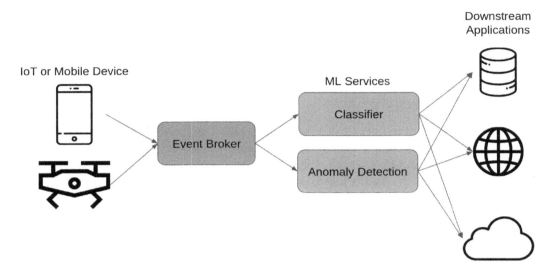

Figure 5.2 – A basic event-based architecture where a stream of data is accessed by different services via a broker

The next section will touch on designs where we do the opposite of processing one data point at a time and instead work with large chunks or batches at any one time.

Batching

Batches of work may not sound like the most sophisticated concept, but it is one of the most common pattern flavors out there in the world of machine learning.

If the data you require for prediction comes in at regular time intervals in batches, it can be efficient to schedule your prediction runs with a similar cadence. This type of pattern can also be useful if you do not have to create a low-latency solution.

This concept can also be made to run quite efficiently for a few reasons:

- Running in scheduled batches means that we know exactly when we will need compute resources, so we can plan accordingly. For example, we may be able to shut down our clusters for most of the day or repurpose them for other activities.

- Batches allow for the use of larger numbers of data points at runtime, so you can run things such as anomaly detection or clustering at the batch level if desired.

- The size of your batches of data can often be chosen to optimize some criterion. For example, using large batches and running parallelized logic and algorithms on it could be more efficient.

Software solutions where ML algorithms are run in batches often look very similar to classic **Extract, Transform, Load** (**ETL**) systems. These are systems where data is extracted from a source or sources, before being processed on route to a target system where it is then uploaded. In the case of an ML solution, the processing is not standard data transformation such as joins and filters, but is instead the application of feature engineering and ML algorithm pipelines. This is why, in this book, we will term these designs **Extract Transform Machine Learn** (**ETML**) patterns. ETML will be discussed more in *Chapter 8, Building an Extract Transform Machine Learning Use Case.*

We will now discuss a key piece of technology that is critical to making modern architectures applicable to a wide range of platforms – containers.

Containerizing

If you develop software that you want to deploy somewhere, which is the core aim of an ML engineer, then you have to be very aware of the environmental requirements of your code, and how different environments might affect the ability of your solution to run. This is particularly important for **Python**, which does not have a core capability for exporting programs as standalone executables (although there are options for doing this). This means that Python code needs a Python interpreter to run and needs to exist in a general Python environment where the relevant libraries and supporting packages have been installed.

A great way to avoid headaches from this point of view is to ask the question: *Why can't I just put everything I need into something that is relatively isolated from the host environment, which I can ship and then run as a standalone application or program?* The answer to this question is that you can and that you do this through **containerization**. This is a process whereby an application and its dependencies can be packaged together in a standalone unit that can effectively run on any computing platform.

The most popular container technology is **Docker**, which is open source and very easy to use. Let's learn about it by using it to containerize a simple **Flask** web application that could act as an interface to a forecasting model like that created in the *Example 2: Forecasting API* section in *Chapter 1, Introduction to ML Engineering.*

The next few sections will use a similar simple Flask application that has a forecast serving endpoint. As a proxy for a full ML model, we will first work with a skeleton application that simply returns a short list of random numbers when requested for a forecast. The detailed code for the application can be found in this book's GitHub repo at `https://github.com/PacktPublishing/Machine-Learning-Engineering-with-Python/tree/main/Chapter05/mleip-web-service-main`. The only points required for the following discussion are that the Flask app successfully returns the forecast output when queried against the `/forecast` endpoint.

An example is shown in *Figure 5.3*:

Figure 5.3 – The result of querying our skeleton ML microservice

Now, we move on to discuss how to containerize this application. First, you need to install Docker on your platform by using the documentation at `https://docs.docker.com/engine/install/`:

1. Once you have Docker installed, you need to tell it how to build the container image, which you do by creating a `Dockerfile` in your project. The `Dockerfile` specifies all of the build steps in text so that the process of building the image is automated and easily configurable. We will now walk through building a simple example `Dockerfile`, which will be built on in the next section, *Hosting your own microservice on AWS*. First, we need to specify the base image we are working from. It usually makes sense to use one of the official Docker images as a base, so here we will use the `python:3.8-slim` environment to keep things lean and mean. This base image will be used in all commands following the FROM keyword, which signifies we are entering a build stage. We can actually name this stage for later use, calling it `builder` using the FROM ... as syntax:

   ```
   FROM python:3.8-slim as builder
   ```

2. Then, we copy all the files we need from the current directory to a directory labeled `src` in the build stage and install all of our requirements using our `requirements.txt` file (if you want to run this step without specifying any requirements, you can just use an empty `requirements.txt` file):

   ```
   COPY . /src
   RUN pip install --user --no-cache-dir -r requirements.txt
   ```

3. The next stage involves similar steps but is aliased to the word app since we are now creating our application. Notice the reference to the `builder` stage from steps *1* and *2* here:

   ```
   FROM python:3.8-slim as app
   COPY --from=builder /root/.local /root/.local
   COPY --from=builder /src .
   ```

4. We can define or add to environment variables as we are used to in a bash environment:

   ```
   ENV PATH=/root/.local:$PATH
   ```

5. Since in this example we are going to be running a simple Flask web application (more on this later), we need to tell the system which port to expose:

```
EXPOSE 5000
```

6. We can execute commands during the Docker build using the CMD keyword. Here, we use this to run app.py, which is the main entry point to the Flask app, and will start the service we will call via REST API to get ML results later:

```
CMD ["python3", "app.py"]
```

7. Then we can build the image with the docker build command. Here, we create an image named basic-ml-webservice and tag it with the latest label:

```
docker build -t basic-ml-webservice:latest
```

8. To check the build was successful, run the following command in the Terminal:

```
docker images --format "table {{.ID}}\t{{.CreatedAt}}\t{{.Repository}}"
```

You should see an output like that in *Figure 5.4*:

```
IMAGE ID        CREATED AT                      REPOSITORY
cfc60d3d8055    2021-08-22 21:28:21 +0100 BST   basic-ml-webservice
cfc60d3d8055    2021-08-22 21:28:21 +0100 BST   508972911348.dkr.ecr.eu-west-1.amazonaws.com/basic-ml-microservice
cfc60d3d8055    2021-08-22 21:28:21 +0100 BST   basic-ml-microservice
c369d19a3e8f    2021-08-22 21:28:03 +0100 BST   <none>
4e8f4d160116    2021-08-07 19:40:11 +0100 BST   ml-microservice
06f5a53dccfb    2021-08-07 19:39:52 +0100 BST   <none>
9d753150d71e    2021-08-07 19:32:29 +0100 BST   <none>
f68dc7fd2a66    2021-08-07 19:32:16 +0100 BST   <none>
dd8edfcc5a84    2021-08-07 19:09:58 +0100 BST   <none>
0589078a401c    2021-08-07 19:09:45 +0100 BST   <none>
aa27d063bdae    2021-07-13 16:09:49 +0100 BST   inferencefunction
b5712d3d8d03    2021-07-13 16:05:55 +0100 BST   508972911348.dkr.ecr.eu-west-2.amazonaws.com/mleip-lambda-example-repo
b5712d3d8d03    2021-07-13 16:05:55 +0100 BST   inferencefunction
e6f9b123f9a0    2021-07-13 13:52:37 +0100 BST   public.ecr.aws/lambda/python
```

Figure 5.4 – Output from the Docker images command

9. Finally, you can run your Docker image with the following command in your Terminal:

```
docker run basic-ml-webservice:latest
```

Now that you have containerized some basic applications and can run your Docker image, we need to answer the question of how can we use this to build an ML solution hosted on an appropriate platform? The next section covers how we can do this on AWS.

Hosting your own microservice on AWS

A classic way to surface your ML models is via a lightweight web service hosted on a server. This can be a very flexible pattern of deployment. You can run a web service on any server with access to the internet (roughly) and, if designed well, it is often easy to add further functionality to your web service and expose it via new endpoints.

In Python, the two most used web frameworks have always been **Django** and Flask. In this section, we will focus on Flask as it is the simpler of the two and has been written about extensively for ML deployments on the web, so you will be able to find plenty of material to build on what you learn here.

On AWS, one of the simplest ways you can host your Flask web solution is as a containerized application on an appropriate platform. We will go through the basics of doing this here, but we will not spend time on the detailed aspects of maintaining good web security for your service. To fully discuss this may require an entire book in itself, and there are excellent, more focused resources elsewhere.

We will assume that you have your AWS account set up from *Chapter 2*, *The Machine Learning Development Process*. If you do not, then go back and refresh yourself on what you need to do.

We will need the AWS **Command Line Interface (CLI)**. This can be installed on a **Linux x86_64** system with the following commands:

```
$ curl "https://awscli.amazonaws.com/awscli-exe-linux-x86_64.
zip" -o "awscliv2.zip"
unzip awscliv2.zip
sudo ./aws/install
```

You can find the appropriate commands for installing and configuring the AWS CLI, as well as a lot of other useful information, on the AWS CLI documentation pages at https://docs.aws.amazon.com/cli/index.html.

Specifically, configure your Amazon CLI by following the steps in this tutorial: https://docs.aws.amazon.com/cli/latest/userguide/cli-configure-quickstart.html.

The documentation specifies how to install the CLI for a variety of different computer architectures. On a Linux-based system, this means running the preceding commands, which are shown in the documentation as in *Figure 5.5*:

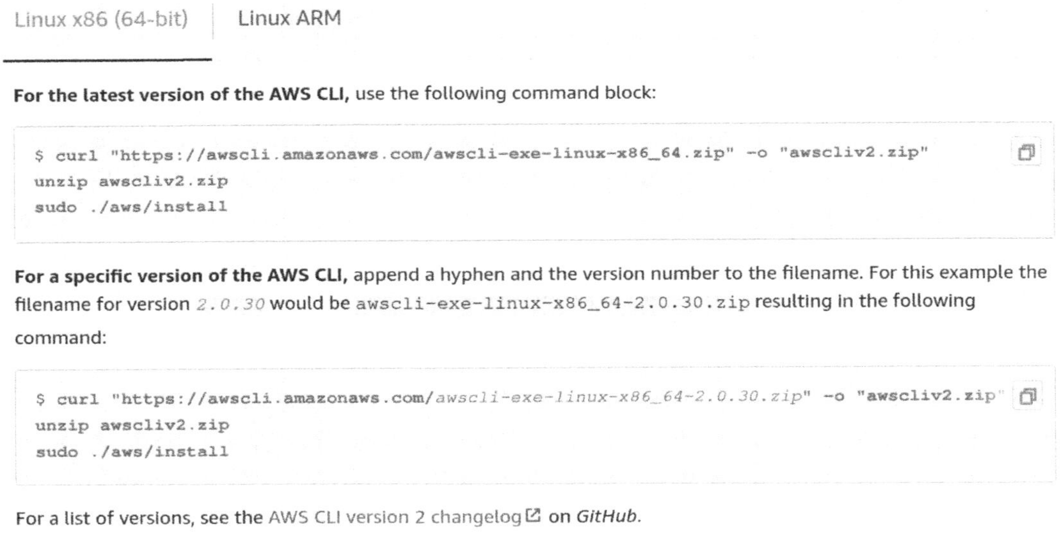

Linux x86 (64-bit) | Linux ARM

For the latest version of the AWS CLI, use the following command block:

```
$ curl "https://awscli.amazonaws.com/awscli-exe-linux-x86_64.zip" -o "awscliv2.zip"
unzip awscliv2.zip
sudo ./aws/install
```

For a specific version of the AWS CLI, append a hyphen and the version number to the filename. For this example the filename for version *2.0.30* would be `awscli-exe-linux-x86_64-2.0.30.zip` resulting in the following command:

```
$ curl "https://awscli.amazonaws.com/awscli-exe-linux-x86_64-2.0.30.zip" -o "awscliv2.zip"
unzip awscliv2.zip
sudo ./aws/install
```

For a list of versions, see the AWS CLI version 2 changelog ⤢ on *GitHub*.

Figure 5.5 – The AWS CLI documentation

In the following example, we will use the Amazon **Elastic Container Registry (ECR)** and **Elastic Container Service (ECS)** to host a skeleton containerized web application. In *Chapter 7*, *Building an Example ML Microservice*, we will fill in the details of the ML model to complete the ML engineering solution.

Deploying our service on ECS will require a few different components, which we will walk through in the next few sections:

- Our container hosted inside a repository on ECR
- A cluster and service created on ECS
- An application load balancer created via the **Elastic Compute Cloud (EC2)** service

First, let's tackle pushing the container to ECR.

Pushing to ECR

Let's look at the following steps:

1. We have the following Dockerfile defined within the project directory from the *Containerizing* section:

```
FROM python:3.8-slim as builder
COPY . /src
RUN pip install --user --no-cache-dir -r requirements.txt
FROM python:3.8-slim as app
COPY --from=builder /root/.local /root/.local
COPY --from=builder /src .

ENV PATH=/root/.local:$PATH
EXPOSE 5000


CMD ["python3", "app.py"]
```

2. We can then use the AWS **CLI** to create an ECR repository for hosting our container. We will call the repository `basic-ml-microservice` and will set the region as `eu-west-1`, but this should be changed to what region seems most appropriate:

```
aws ecr create-repository \
    --repository-name basic-ml-microservice \
    --image-scanning-configuration scanOnPush=true \
    --region eu-west-1
```

3. We can then log in to the container registry with the following command in the Terminal:

```
aws ecr get-login-password --region eu-west-1 | docker
login --username AWS --password-stdin <YOUR_AWS_ID>.dkr.
ecr.eu-west-1.amazonaws.com/basic-ml-microservice
```

4. Then, if we navigate to the directory containing the Dockerfile (app), we can run the following command to build the container:

```
docker build --tag basic-ml-microservice .
```

5. The next step tags the image:

```
docker tag flask-docker-demo-app:latest <YOUR_
AWS_ID>.dkr.ecr.eu-west-1.amazonaws.com/basic-ml-
microservice:latest
```

6. We then deploy the Docker image we have just built to the container registry with the following command:

```
docker push <YOUR_AWS_ID>.dkr.ecr.eu-west-1.amazonaws.
com/basic-ml-microservice:latest
```

In the next section, we set up our cluster on ECS.

Hosting on ECS

Now, let's start with the setup!

1. We then create an ECS cluster with the **EC2 Linux + Networking** configuration. To do this, first, navigate to **ECS** on the AWS Management Console and click **Create Cluster**:

Figure 5.6 – Creating a cluster in the Elastic Container Service

2.   Then, at the next step, select **EC2 Linux + Networking**:

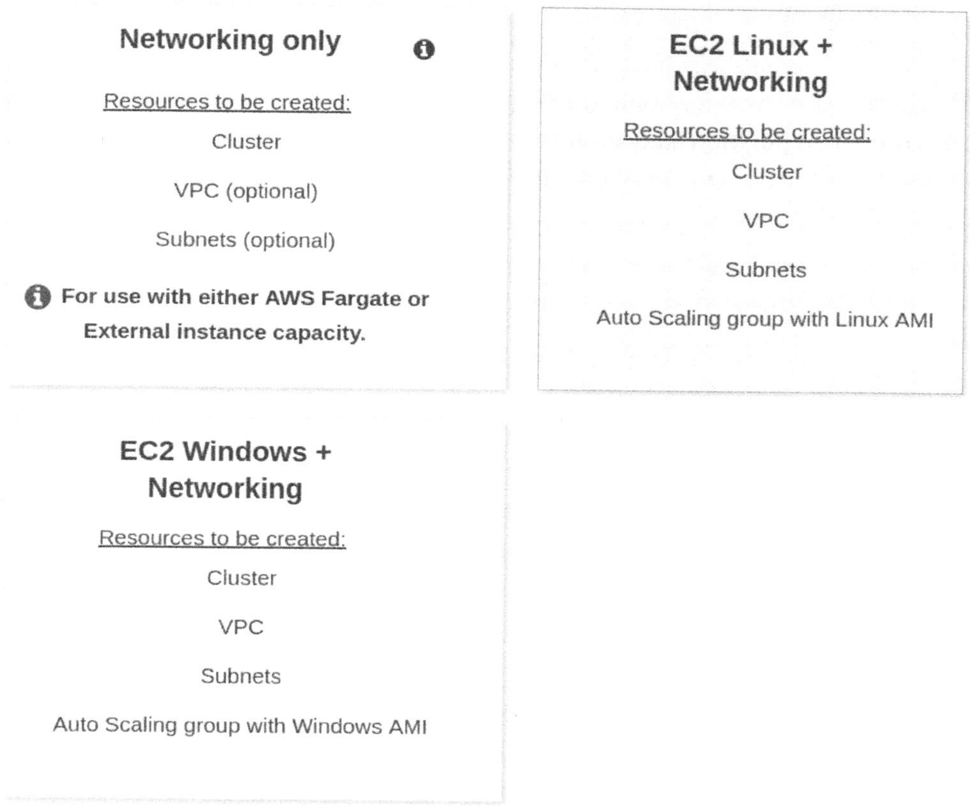

Networking only   ℹ

Resources to be created:

Cluster

VPC (optional)

Subnets (optional)

ℹ **For use with either AWS Fargate or External instance capacity.**

EC2 Linux + Networking

Resources to be created:

Cluster

VPC

Subnets

Auto Scaling group with Linux AMI

EC2 Windows + Networking

Resources to be created:

Cluster

VPC

Subnets

Auto Scaling group with Windows AMI

Figure 5.7 – Configuring our cluster in the AWS ECS

3.   We are then given options for configuring our cluster. Here, we call the cluster **mleip-web-app-demos** (or anything we like!) and specify that the EC2 instances used be **On-Demand** since this is a microservice where we likely do not want to allow for downtime while we wait for spot instances. We select a relatively small machine as the instance type, a **t2.micro**, which is good for lightweight, general-purpose computation, and so suits a small ML prediction service quite nicely. Since this is a demo, we only need one instance and can use the default configurations for the rest of the steps:

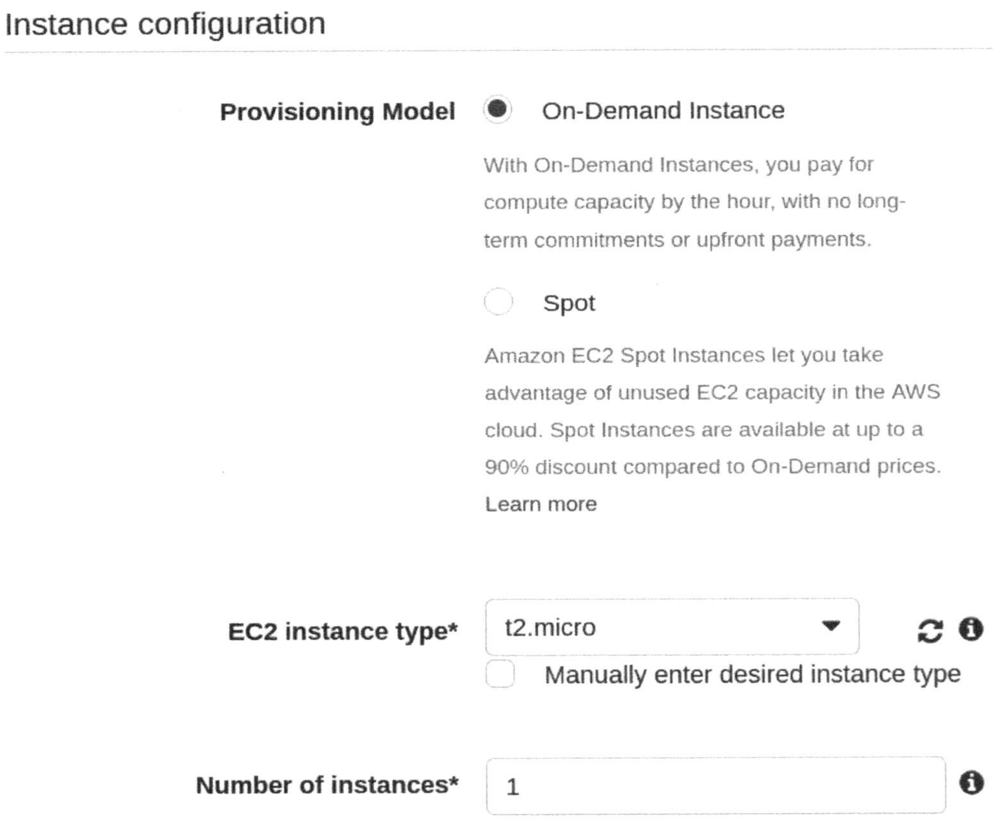

Instance configuration

Provisioning Model   ● On-Demand Instance

With On-Demand Instances, you pay for compute capacity by the hour, with no long-term commitments or upfront payments.

○ Spot

Amazon EC2 Spot Instances let you take advantage of unused EC2 capacity in the AWS cloud. Spot Instances are available at up to a 90% discount compared to On-Demand prices. Learn more

EC2 instance type*   t2.micro   ▼   ↻ ⓘ
○ Manually enter desired instance type

Number of instances*   1   ⓘ

Figure 5.8 – Selecting our instance type and provisioning the model and cluster name in the ECS

4. The next step is to configure the networking for our cluster. We can choose to create a new **Virtual Private Cloud** (**VPC**) and security groups for this VPC with appropriate settings or reuse previously defined ones. There is much more information on VPCs in AWS at `https://docs.amazonaws.cn/en_us/vpc/latest/userguide/what-is-amazon-vpc.html`:

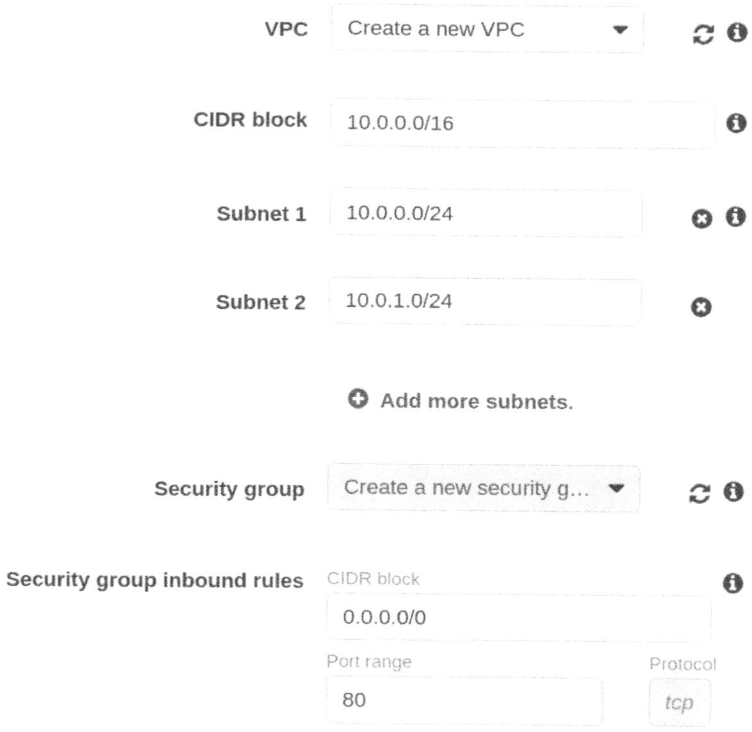

Figure 5.9 – Setting up the networking for our ECS-hosted microservic.

5. Once we have done this, if we click **Create Cluster** at the bottom of the page, we are directed to a status page that shows the progress of the cluster instantiation:

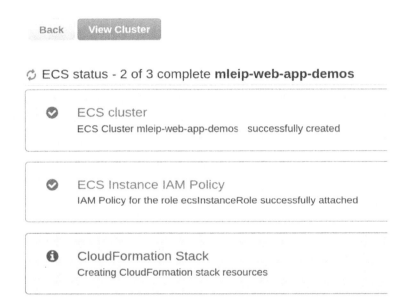

Figure 5.10 – Creating our ECS cluster

6. Once complete, if we navigate back to the ECS page, we can see a summary view of the cluster we just created, as in *Figure 5.10*:

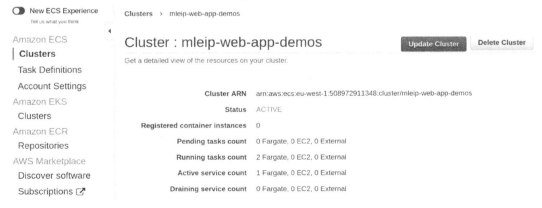

Figure 5.11 – We can now access our instantiated ECS cluster

7. We now need to create a task definition in the cluster. We do this by selecting **Task Definitions** on the left-hand side menu and then selecting **Create new Task Definition**, which you can see in *Figure 5.11*:

Figure 5.12 – Defining a task inside our ECS cluster

8. We then select the **Fargate** compatibility type for the cluster, which helps us to manage a lot of the backend infrastructure without thinking about it and only pay for the compute resources that we use:

Create new Task Definition

Step 1: Select launch type compatibility	Select launch type compatibility
Step 2: Configure task and container definitions	Select which launch type you want your task definition to be compatible with based on where you want to launch your task.

FARGATE

Price based on task size

Requires network mode awsvpc

AWS-managed infrastructure, no Amazon EC2 instances to manage

EC2

Price based on resource usage

Multiple network modes available

Self-managed infrastructure using Amazon EC2 instances

EXTERNAL

Price based on instance-hours and additional charges for other AWS services used

Self-managed on-premise infrastructure with ECS Anywhere

Figure 5.13 – Selecting Fargate as the task launch type for our ECS task

9. We then fill in some details for the task definition, as shown in *Figure 5.13*. For example, we will call the task definition **microservice-forecast-task** and we will use a task role created in the AWS Management Console called **ecsTaskExecutionRole**. For more details on **Identity Access Management (IAM)** roles, please see `https://aws.amazon.com/iam/`:

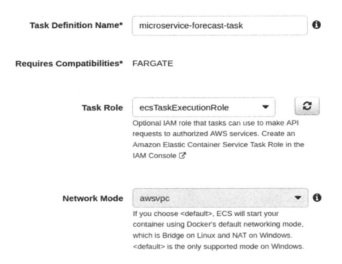

Figure 5.14 – Task definition in the ECS

10. The next step is to define the task size. Here we select the lowest values of 0.5 GB and 0.25 vCPU:

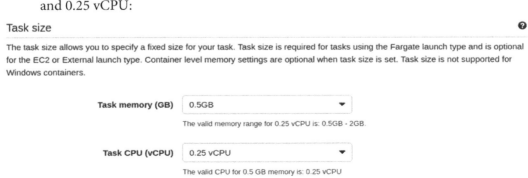

Figure 5.15 – Defining ECS task size

11. Now, we add a container to the setup by clicking the **Add container** option on the page and then filling in details for the container name and image URI. We can also add memory limits to the task and provide the container port we wish to expose to incoming internet traffic (here we will use port 5000). This is shown in *Figure 5.15*. These are the same container names and image URIs we used for pushing the container to ECR:

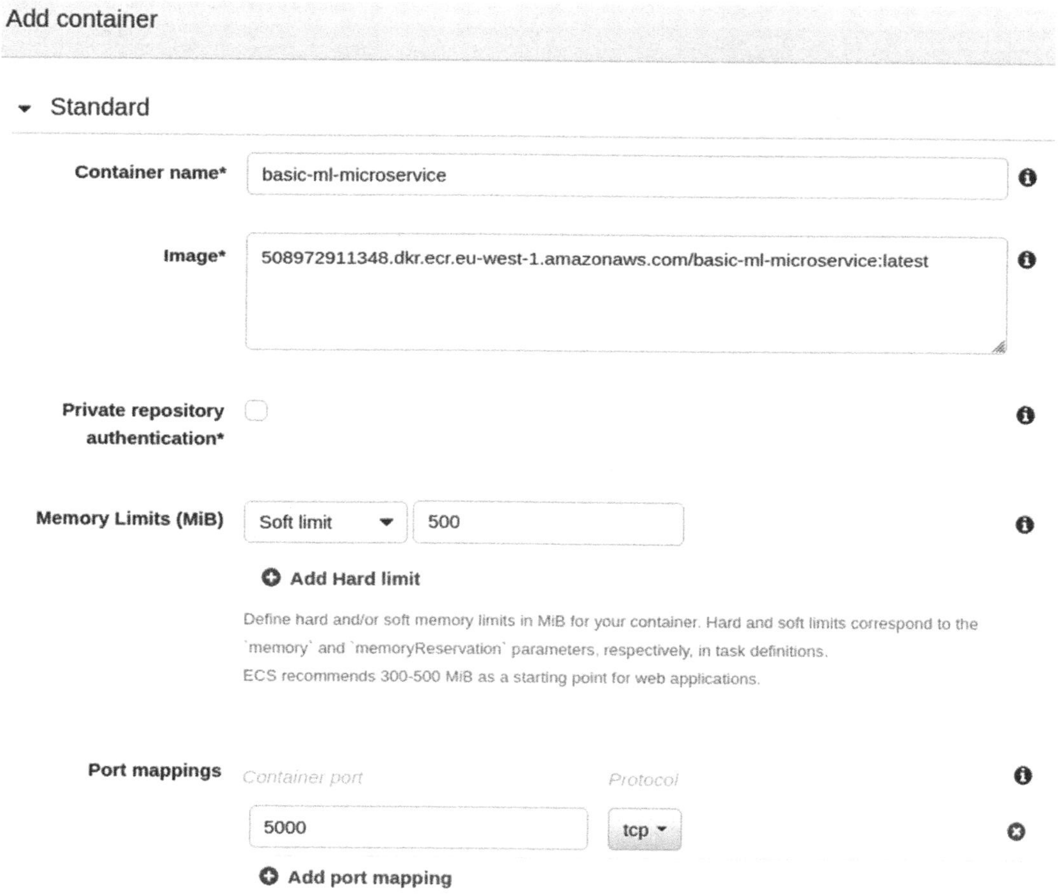

Add container

▼ Standard

| Container name* | basic-ml-microservice | ❶ |
| Image* | 508972911348.dkr.ecr.eu-west-1.amazonaws.com/basic-ml-microservice:latest | ❶ |

Private repository   ⬜   ❶
authentication*

Memory Limits (MiB) | Soft limit ▼ | 500 | ❶

   ⊕ **Add Hard limit**

Define hard and/or soft memory limits in MiB for your container. Hard and soft limits correspond to the
`memory` and `memoryReservation` parameters, respectively, in task definitions.
ECS recommends 300-500 MiB as a starting point for web applications.

Port mappings   Container port   Protocol   ❶

   | 5000 | tcp ▼ | ✖

   ⊕ **Add port mapping**

Figure 5.16 – Adding our container to the ECS cluster

12. After completing the above step, we can select **Create** at the bottom of the page to create the task. Successful creation means we should be able to see the new task definition in the ECS service when we select **Task Definitions** on the left-hand side. This should look like *Figure 5.16*:

Task Definitions

Task definitions specify the container information for your application, such as how many containers are part of your task, what resources they more

Create new Task Definition	Create new revision	Actions ▾	

Status: (ACTIVE) INACTIVE

▼ Filter in this page

Task Definition	Latest revision status
microservice-forecast-task	ACTIVE

Figure 5.17 – A successfully created ECS task

Now, the final step of setting up our ECS-hosted solution is the creation of a service. We will now walk through how to do this:

1. First, navigate back to the ECS page and then the **Clusters** section. Select the **mleip-web-app-demos** cluster and then the **Create Service** button. We are then presented with a page asking for various configuration values. In this example, we will select **Launch Type** to be **Fargate** and then give the name of the cluster and task definition to match the names of the items we have just created in the previous steps. You can see these values in *Figure 5.17*:

Configure service

A service lets you specify how many copies of your task definition to run and maintain in a cluster. You can optionally use an Elastic Load Balancing load balancer to distribute incoming traffic to containers in your service. Amazon ECS maintains that number of tasks and coordinates task scheduling with the load balancer. You can also optionally use Service Auto Scaling to adjust the number of tasks in your service.

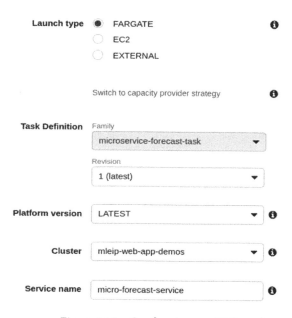

Figure 5.18 – Configuring our ECS service

2. On the same configuration page, we also have to define some values around how the service will be scaled, monitored, and deployed, as shown in *Figure 5.18*. For this simple demonstration, we can create a **REPLICA service type** that instantiates two tasks. This effectively means you will have two instances of your containerized application available at any one time to help build in some redundancy. We also define the minimum and maximum percent of our tasks, which should be healthy and running for this service during our **Rolling Update** type deployment:

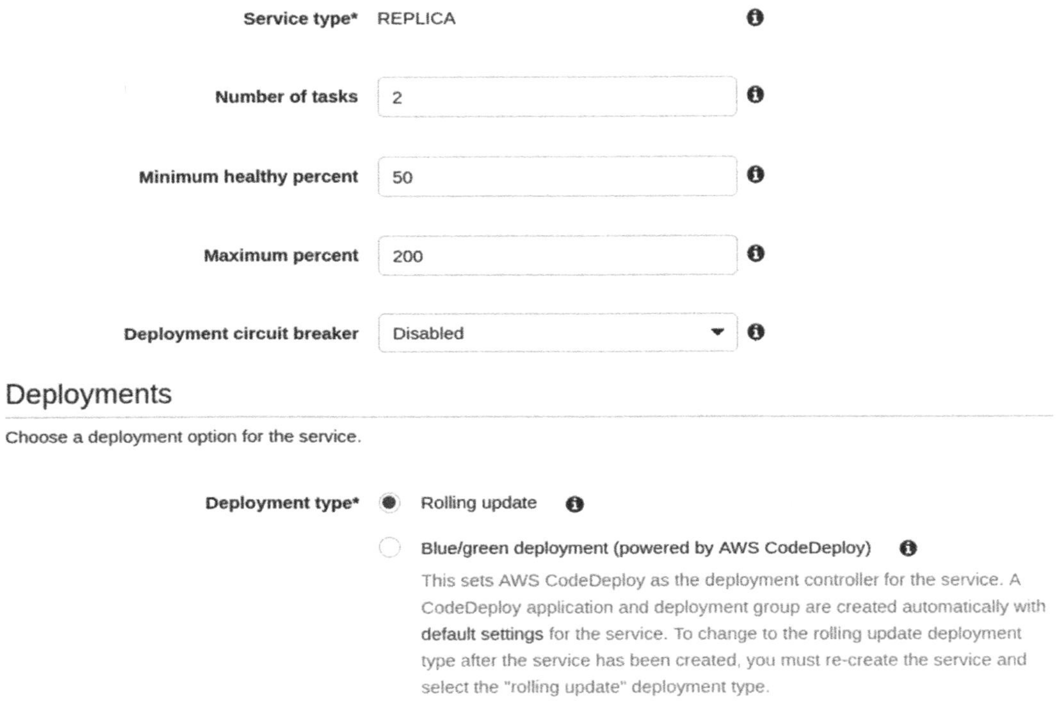

Service type*	REPLICA
Number of tasks	2
Minimum healthy percent	50
Maximum percent	200
Deployment circuit breaker	Disabled

Deployments

Choose a deployment option for the service.

Deployment type*   ● Rolling update

○ Blue/green deployment (powered by AWS CodeDeploy)

This sets AWS CodeDeploy as the deployment controller for the service. A CodeDeploy application and deployment group are created automatically with **default settings** for the service. To change to the rolling update deployment type after the service has been created, you must re-create the service and select the "rolling update" deployment type.

Figure 5.19 – Configuring service deployment and scaling behavior

3. There is then a section on load balancing that we must fill in. Here, select **Application Load Balancer** and then select an appropriate load balancer if you already have one defined. If you do not, then you can use the next section on **Creating a Load Balancer** to help. We then select the container solution we wish to load balance, which here is our **basic-ml-microservice** solution with port 5000 exposed. The same section also requires the definition of new listener ports and what is known as a **Target group** name. A target group is used by your load balancer to route requests to appropriate endpoint targets. We can create a new one here, but we need to make sure that our load balancer knows about it (see the next section), so you may need to update the load balancer. Finally, we define a path pattern for the listener, which here we have to ensure ends in /forecast as this is the default path that our Flask app uses. All of these value assignments are shown in *Figure 5.20*:

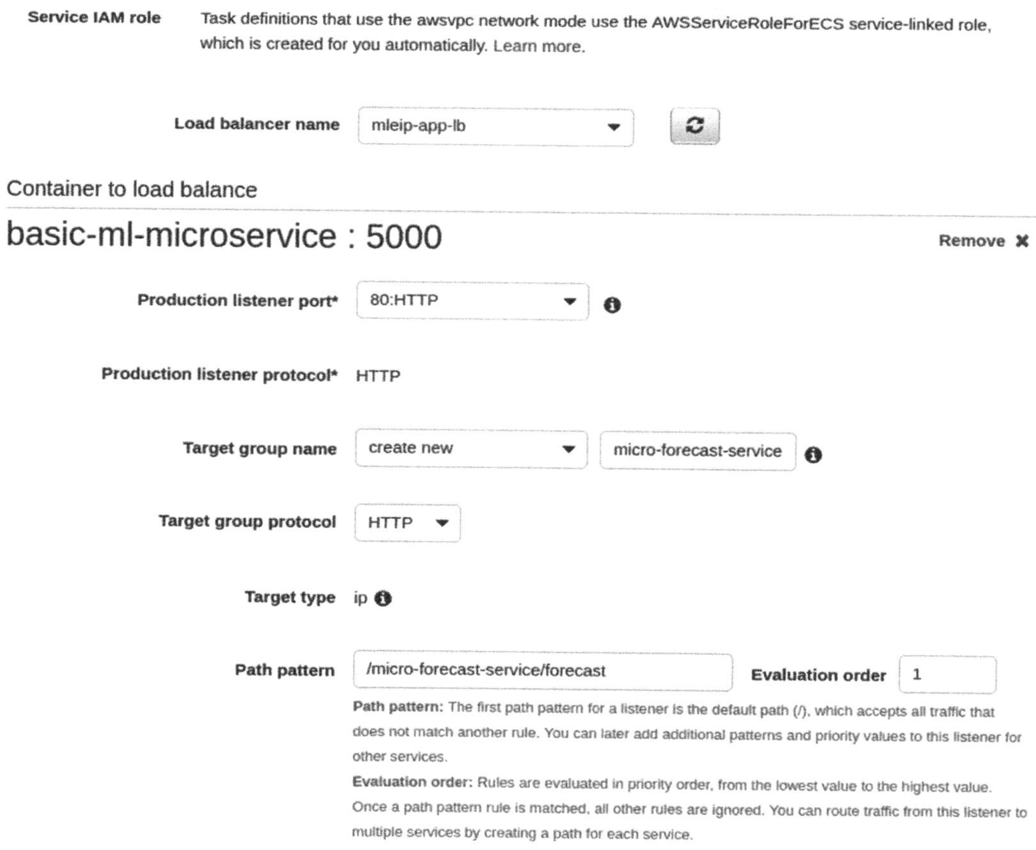

Service IAM role   Task definitions that use the awsvpc network mode use the AWSServiceRoleForECS service-linked role, which is created for you automatically. Learn more.

Load balancer name   mleip-app-lb

Container to load balance

basic-ml-microservice : 5000   Remove ✖

Production listener port*   80:HTTP   ❶

Production listener protocol*   HTTP

Target group name   create new   micro-forecast-service ❶

Target group protocol   HTTP

Target type   ip ❶

Path pattern   /micro-forecast-service/forecast   **Evaluation order**   1

Path pattern: The first path pattern for a listener is the default path (/), which accepts all traffic that does not match another rule. You can later add additional patterns and priority values to this listener for other services.
Evaluation order: Rules are evaluated in priority order, from the lowest value to the highest value. Once a path pattern rule is matched, all other rules are ignored. You can route traffic from this listener to multiple services by creating a path for each service.

Figure 5.20 – Setting up load balancing for our ECS service

4. You can now select **Create Service** and sit back happily as you have just deployed a neat little microservice. You can test this by calling your application via **Postman**. The URI you need to call has its first part determined by the DNS of your application load balancer (here beginning `http://mleip-app-lb`), which you can find in the EC2 service. The rest of the URI is defined by the required endpoint defined in your Flask application, here, `/forecast`. Calling the solution gives the result shown in *Figure 5.21*:

Figure 5.21 – Requesting an example forecast from our ECS-hosted microservice

Let's now move on to discuss how to create a load balancer!

Creating a load balancer

In the *Hosting on ECS* section, we used a load balancer called `mleip-app-lb`. This section will help you understand how to create this if you have not done this before in AWS.

Load balancers are pieces of software that efficiently route network traffic, such as incoming HTTP requests, between multiple servers to ensure service stability. They are an important piece of any architecture that dynamically serves requests.

Thankfully, AWS makes the creation of load balancers relatively easy, as we will now see. The next few steps will outline how to create an **application load balancer** that can be used in the creation of several different web applications:

1. First, we navigate to the **EC2 Management Console** in AWS, then we select **Load Balancers** in the left-hand side menu, and finally click **Create Load Balancer**. We should then be offered several options for different types of load balancer. Here, we will select **Application Load Balancer**, like in *Figure 5.22*:

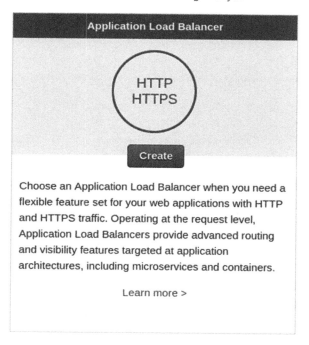

Figure 5.22 – Choosing to create an application load balancer in the AWS EC2 service

2. The next step is to configure the load balancer. Here, we will give it the name of **mleip-app-lb**, which matches the load balancer used in the *Hosting on ECS section*. We also add a listener using the HTTP protocol on port 80. It is important that the listener created here is on the same port selected when we provided load balancing information for the creation of our ECS service. Finally, we select VPC availability zones, which again should match with the VPC zones applicable to our ECS service. This is all shown in *Figure 5.23*:

Step 1: Configure Load Balancer

Basic Configuration

To configure your load balancer, provide a name, select a scheme, specify one or more listeners, and select a network. The default configuration is an Internet-facin

Name (i)	mleip-app-lb
Scheme (i)	⦿ internet-facing ◯ internal
IP address type (i)	ipv4

Listeners

A listener is a process that checks for connection requests, using the protocol and port that you configured.

Load Balancer Protocol	Load Balancer Port
HTTP ⌄	80

Add listener

Availability Zones

Specify the Availability Zones to enable for your load balancer. The load balancer routes traffic to the targets in these Availability Zones only. You can specify only on increase the availability of your load balancer.

VPC (i)	vpc-422d8f3b (172.31.0.0/16) (default)
Availability Zones	☑ eu-west-1a subnet-80223de6
	IPv4 address (i) Assigned by AWS

Figure 5.23 - The first step of configuration for our application load balancer

3. We next configure the security for the load balancer. If we have only created a listener on the HTTP protocol (as we did in *Step 2*), then we will get a warning about not having a secure listener on the next page, which you can alleviate by using the HTTPS protocol. This requires the management of SSL certificates, which we will not cover here. For more information, see https://docs.aws.amazon.com/elasticloadbalancing/latest/application/create-https-listener.html. For now, we can move on to the next step with the HTTP protocol in place, and either create a new security group or select an existing one, as shown in *Figure 5.24*:

Step 3: Configure Security Groups
A security group is a set of firewall rules that control the traffic to your load balancer. On this page, you can add rules to allow specific traffic to reach your load balancer. First, decide whether to create a new security group or select an existing one.

Assign a security group	◉ Create a **new** security group
	○ Select an **existing** security group
Security group name	mleip-app-lb-sg-wizard
Description	mleip-app-lb-sg-wizard-1 created on 2021-08-22T20:03:31.275+01:00

Type ⓘ	Protocol ⓘ	Port Range ⓘ	Source ⓘ	
Custom TCP I ∨	TCP	80	Custom ∨ 0.0.0.0/0, ::/0	✕

Add Rule

Figure 5.24 – Configuring the security groups for the load balancer

4. The next step requires us to configure the routing of requests via the load balancer. This is done by selecting or creating a **Target group** (already discussed in the *Hosting on ECS* section) with the appropriate routing protocol and health check paths (see *Figure 5.25*). We create a new target group here and then later edit this to ensure routing to the appropriate service as needed:

Step 4: Configure Routing

Your load balancer routes requests to the targets in this target group using the protocol and port that you specify here. It also performs health checks on this load balancer. You can edit or add listeners after the load balancer is created.

Target group

Target group ⓘ	New target group ⬦
Name ⓘ	mleip-app-lb-tg
Target type	◉ Instance
	○ IP
	○ Lambda function
Protocol ⓘ	HTTP ⬦
Port ⓘ	5000
Protocol version ⓘ	◉ HTTP1
	Send requests to targets using HTTP/1.1. Supported when the request protocol is HTTP/1.1 or HTTP/2.
	○ HTTP2
	Send requests to targets using HTTP/2. Supported when the request protocol is HTTP/2 or gRPC, but gRPC-specific features are not available.
	○ gRPC
	Send requests to targets using gRPC. Supported when the request protocol is gRPC.

Health checks

Protocol ⓘ	HTTP ⬦
Path ⓘ	/

Figure 5.25 – Defining the routing behavior of the load balancer

5. Navigating to the next step in the process asks for you to **Register Targets**, but this can be skipped for now and targets registered later by selecting **Add Listener** to your load balancer once it is created. We can then navigate to the final page, which shows a review of the load balancer you are about to create. This will look similar to *Figure 5.26*. Select **Create** to complete the process:

Step 6: Review
Please review the load balancer details before continuing

▼ Load balancer

Name	mleip-app-lb
Scheme	internet-facing
Listeners	Port:80 - Protocol:HTTP
IP address type	ipv4
VPC	vpc-422d8f3b
Subnets	subnet-80223de6, subnet-23806e68, subnet-f70159ad
Tags	

▼ Security groups

Security groups	mleip-app-lb-sg-wizard

▼ Routing

Target group	New target group
Target group name	mleip-app-lb-tg
Port	5000
Target type	instance
Protocol	HTTP
Protocol version	HTTP1
Health check protocol	HTTP
Path	/
Health check port	traffic port
Healthy threshold	5
Unhealthy threshold	2
Timeout	5
Interval	30
Success codes	200

Figure 5.26 – Reviewing our load balancer before creation

6. Confirmation of successful creation of the load balancer should then appear on the page, as shown in *Figure 5.27*:

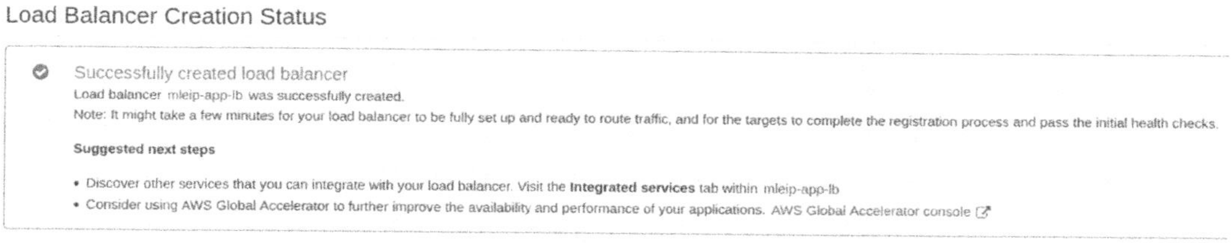

Load Balancer Creation Status

Figure 5.27 – The successful creation of our application load balancer

And that's it! We now have all of the pieces in place and hooked up to have a working microservice suitable for serving ML models.

The next section will now move on to discuss how we can use production-ready pipelining tools to deploy and orchestrate our ML jobs.

Pipelining 2.0

In *Chapter 4, Packaging Up*, we discussed the benefits of writing our ML code as pipelines. We discussed how to implement some basic ML pipelines using tools such as **sklearn** and **Spark MLlib**. The pipelines we were concerned with there were very nice ways of streamlining your code and making several processes available to use within a single object to simplify an application. However, everything we discussed then was very much focused within one Python file and not necessarily something we could extend very flexibly outside the confines of the package we were using. With the techniques we discussed, for example, it would be very difficult to create pipelines where each step was using a different package or even where they were entirely different programs. They did not allow us to build much sophistication into our data flows or application logic either, as if one of the steps failed, the pipeline failed, and that was that.

The tools we are about to discuss take these concepts to the next level. They allow you to manage the workflows of your ML solutions so that you can organize, coordinate, and orchestrate elements with the appropriate level of complexity to get the job done.

Airflow

Apache Airflow is the workflow management tool that was initially developed by **Airbnb** in the 2010s and has been open source since its inception. It gives data scientists, data engineers, and ML engineers the capability of programmatically creating complex pipelines through Python scripts. Airflow's task management is based on the definition and then execution of a **Directed Acyclic Graph (DAG)** with nodes as the tasks to be run. DAGs are also used in **TensorFlow** and **Spark**, so you may have heard of these before.

Airflow contains a variety of default operators to allow you to define DAGs that can call and use multiple components as tasks, without caring about the specific details of that task. It also provides functionality for scheduling your pipelines:

1. As an example, let's build an Apache Airflow pipeline that will get data, perform some feature engineering, train a model, and then persist it to **MLFlow**. We won't cover the detailed implementation of each command, but simply show you how these hang together in an Airflow DAG. First, we import the relevant Airflow packages and any utility packages we need:

```
from datetime import timedelta
from airflow import DAG
from airflow.operators.bash_operator import BashOperator
from airflow.utils.dates import days_ago
```

2. Next, Airflow allows you to define default arguments that can be referenced by all of the following tasks, with the option to overwrite at the same level:

```
default_args = {
    'owner': 'Andrew McMahon',
    'depends_on_past': False,
    'start_date': days_ago(31),
    'email': ['example@example.com'],
    'email_on_failure': False,
    'email_on_retry': False,
    'retries': 1,
    'retry_delay': timedelta(minutes=2)
}
```

3. We then have to instantiate our DAG and provide the relevant metadata, including our scheduling interval:

```
dag = DAG(
    'classification_pipeline',
    default_args=default_args,
    description='Basic pipeline for classifying the Wine
Dataset',
    schedule_interval=timedelta(days=1), # run daily?
check
    )
```

4. Then, all that is required is to define your tasks. Here, we define an initial task that runs a Python script that gets our dataset:

```
get_data = BashOperator(
    task_id='get_data',
    bash_command='python3 /usr/local/airflow/scripts/get_
data.py',
    dag=dag,
)
```

5. We then perform a task that takes this data and performs our model training steps. This task could, for example, encapsulate one of the pipeline types we covered in *Chapter 3, From Model to Model Factory*; for example, a Spark MLlib pipeline:

```
train_model= BashOperator(
    task_id='train_model',
    depends_on_past=False,
    bash_command='python3 /usr/local/airflow/scripts/
train_model.py',
    retries=3,
    dag=dag,
)
```

6. The final step of this process will take the resultant trained model and publish it to MLFlow. This means that other services or pipelines can use this model for prediction:

```
persist_model = BashOperator(
    task_id='persist_model',
    depends_on_past=False,
    bash_command='python /usr/local/airflow/scripts /
persist_model.py,
    retries=3,
    dag=dag,
)
```

7. Finally, we define the running order of the task nodes that we have defined in the DAG using the >> operator. The tasks above could have been defined in any order, but the following syntax stipulates how they must run:

```
get_data >> train_model >> persist_model
```

In the next sections, we will briefly cover how to set up an Airflow pipeline on AWS using **CI/CD** principles. This will bring together some of the setup and work we have been doing in previous chapters in the book.

Airflow on AWS

AWS provides a cloud-hosted service called **Managed Workflows for Apache Airflow (MWAA)** that allows you to deploy and host your Airflow pipelines easily and robustly. Here, we will briefly cover how to do this.

You then complete the following steps:

1. Select **Create environment** on the MWAA landing page. This is shown in *Figure 5.28*:

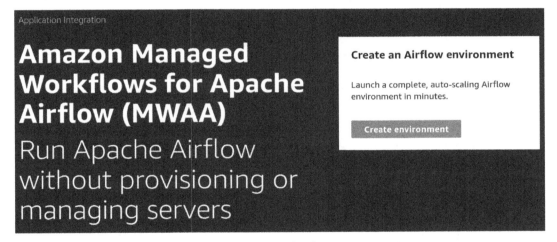

Figure 5.28 – The MWAA landing page on AWS

2. You will then be provided with a screen asking for the details of your new Airflow environment. *Figure 5.29* shows the high-level steps that the website takes you through:

▼ How Amazon MWAA works

Create an environment

An environment contains your Airflow cluster, including your scheduler, workers, and web server.

Upload your DAGs to Amazon S3

Package and upload your DAG (Directed Acyclic Graph) code to Amazon S3. Amazon MWAA loads the code into Airflow.

Run your DAGs in Airflow

Run your DAGs from the Airflow UI or CLI. Monitor your environment with Amazon CloudWatch.

Figure 5.29 – The high-level steps for setting up an MWAA environment and associated managed Airflow runs

Environment details, as shown in *Figure 5.30*, is where we specify our environment name. Here we have called it **mleip-airflow-dev-env**:

Environment details Info

Name

mleip-airflow-dev-env

Use only letters, numbers, dashes, or underscores. Max 80 characters.

Airflow version

2.0.2 (Latest) ▼

Figure 5.30 – Naming your MWAA environment

3. For MWAA to run, it needs to be able to access code defining the DAG and any associated requirements or plugins files. The system then asks for an AWS S3 bucket where these pieces of code and configuration reside. In this example, we create a bucket called **mleip-airflow-example** that will contain these pieces. *Figure 5.31* shows the creation of the bucket:

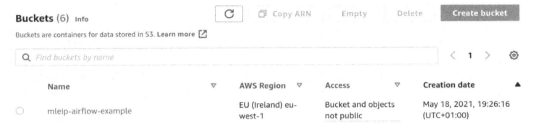

Figure 5.31 – The successful creation of our AWS S3 bucket for storing our Airflow code and supporting configuration elements

Figure 5.32 shows how we point MWAA to the correct bucket, folders, and plugins or requirements files if we have them too:

DAG code in Amazon S3 Info

Amazon MWAA uses your Amazon S3 bucket to load your DAGs and supporting files. Specify your S3 bucket, and the paths of your DAG folder, plugins.zip, and requirements.txt.

- DAG folder
- Plugins zip file
- Requirements file

S3 bucket

ⓘ Create or specify an S3 bucket to store your DAG code. The bucket name must have versioning enabled. You can create a new bucket in the Amazon S3 console ☑

S3 Bucket
The S3 bucket where your source code is stored. Enter an S3 URI or browse and select a bucket.

> Q s3://mleip-airflow-example   ✕ | View ☑ | | Browse S3 |

Format: s3://mybucketname

DAGs folder
The S3 bucket folder that contains your DAG code. Enter an S3 URI or browse and select a folder.

> Q s3://mleip-airflow-example/dags   ✕ | View ☑ | | Browse S3 |

Format: s3://mybucketname/mydagfolder

Plugins file - optional
The S3 bucket ZIP file that contains your DAG plugins. Enter an S3 URI or browse and select a file object and version.

> Q s3://mleip-airflow-example/plugins.zip ✕ Choose a version ▼ | View ☑ | | Browse S3 |

Format: s3://mybucketname/myplugins.zip

Requirements file - optional
The S3 bucket file that contains your DAG requirements.txt. Enter an S3 URI or browse and select a file object and version.

> Q //mleip-airflow-example/requirements.txt ✕ Choose a version ▼ | View ☑ | | Browse S3 |

Figure 5.32 – We reference the bucket we created in the previous step in the configuration of the MWAA instance

4. We then have to define the configuration of the network that the managed instance of Airflow will use. This can get a bit confusing if you are new to networking, so it might be good to read around the topics of subnets, IP addresses, and VPCs. Creating a new MWAA VPC is the easiest approach for getting started in terms of networking here, but your organization will have networking specialists who can help you use the appropriate settings for your situation. We will go with this simplest route and click **Create MWAA VPC**, which opens a new window where we can quickly spin up a new VPC and network setup based on a standard stack definition provided by AWS, as shown in *Figure 5.33*:

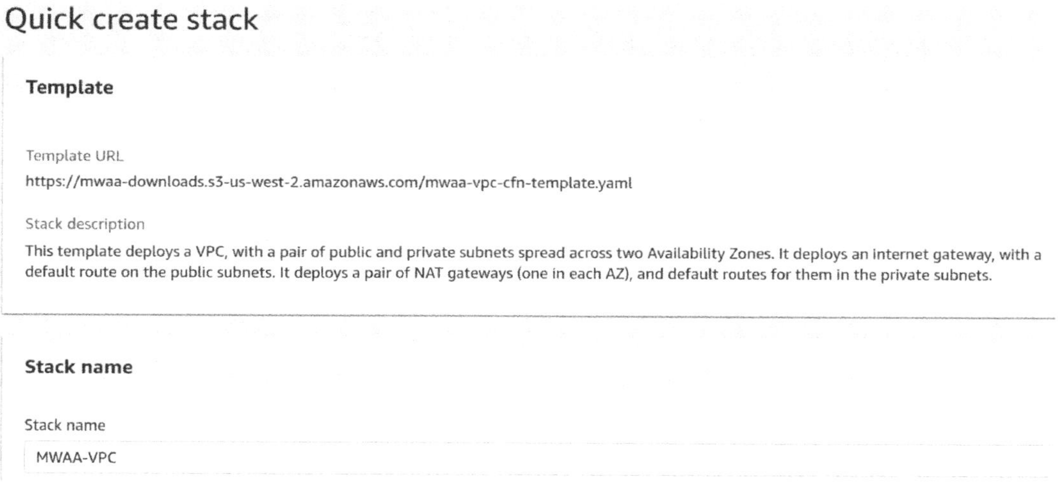

Quick create stack

Template

Template URL

https://mwaa-downloads.s3-us-west-2.amazonaws.com/mwaa-vpc-cfn-template.yaml

Stack description

This template deploys a VPC, with a pair of public and private subnets spread across two Availability Zones. It deploys an internet gateway, with a default route on the public subnets. It deploys a pair of NAT gateways (one in each AZ), and default routes for them in the private subnets.

Stack name

Stack name

MWAA-VPC

Figure 5.33 – An example stack template for creating your new VPC

5.   We are then taken to a page where we are asked for more details on networking:

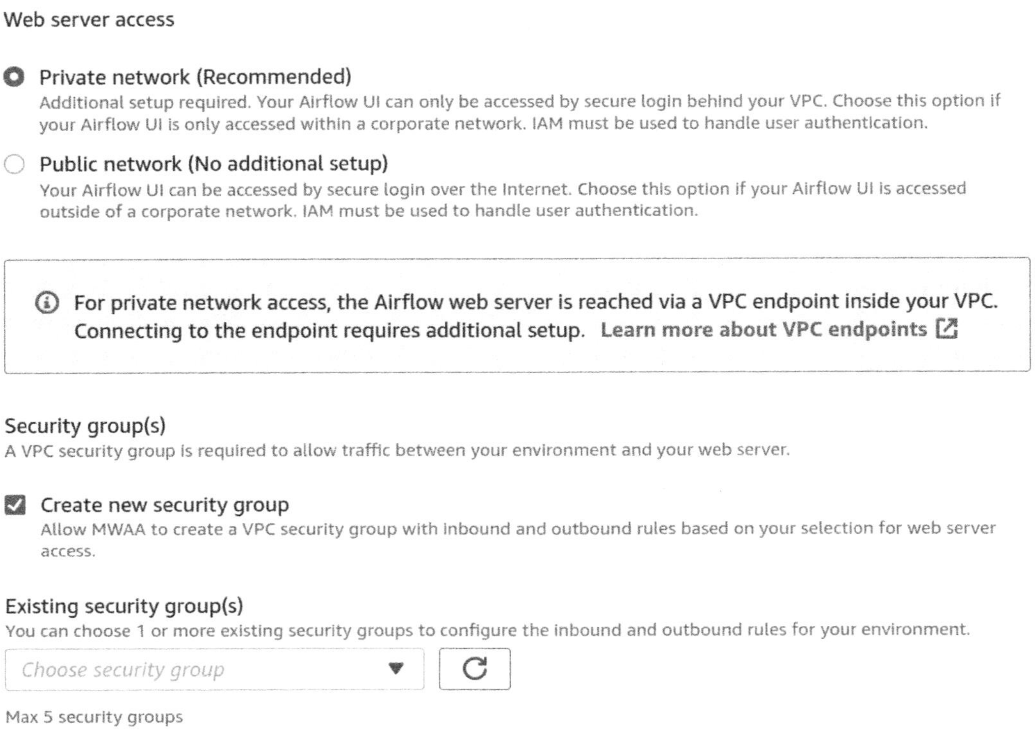

Web server access

⦿ **Private network (Recommended)**
Additional setup required. Your Airflow UI can only be accessed by secure login behind your VPC. Choose this option if your Airflow UI is only accessed within a corporate network. IAM must be used to handle user authentication.

◯ **Public network (No additional setup)**
Your Airflow UI can be accessed by secure login over the Internet. Choose this option if your Airflow UI is accessed outside of a corporate network. IAM must be used to handle user authentication.

> ⓘ For private network access, the Airflow web server is reached via a VPC endpoint inside your VPC. Connecting to the endpoint requires additional setup. **Learn more about VPC endpoints** ⬀

Security group(s)
A VPC security group is required to allow traffic between your environment and your web server.

☑ **Create new security group**
Allow MWAA to create a VPC security group with inbound and outbound rules based on your selection for web server access.

Existing security group(s)
You can choose 1 or more existing security groups to configure the inbound and outbound rules for your environment.

| Choose security group ▼ | C |

Max 5 security groups

Figure 5.34 – Finalizing the networking for our MWAA setup

6. Next, we have to define the **Environment class** that we want to spin up. Currently, there are three options. Here, we use the smallest, but you can choose the environment that best suits your needs (always ask the billpayer's permission!). *Figure 5.35* shows that we can select the **mw1.small** environment class with a min to max worker count of 1-10. MWAA does allow you to change the environment class after instantiating if you need to, so it can often be better to start small and scale up as needed from a cost point of view:

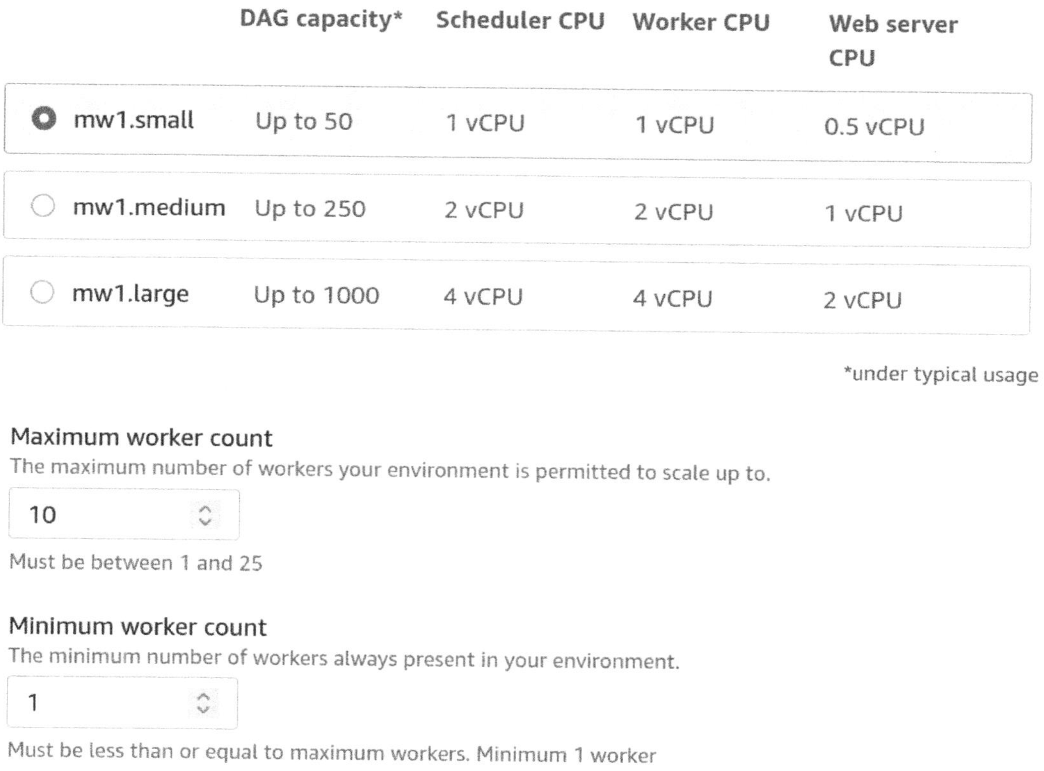

	DAG capacity*	Scheduler CPU	Worker CPU	Web server CPU
⦿ mw1.small	Up to 50	1 vCPU	1 vCPU	0.5 vCPU
○ mw1.medium	Up to 250	2 vCPU	2 vCPU	1 vCPU
○ mw1.large	Up to 1000	4 vCPU	4 vCPU	2 vCPU

*under typical usage

Maximum worker count

The maximum number of workers your environment is permitted to scale up to.

10	⌃⌄

Must be between 1 and 25

Minimum worker count

The minimum number of workers always present in your environment.

1	⌃⌄

Must be less than or equal to maximum workers. Minimum 1 worker

Figure 5.35 – Selecting an environment class and worker sizes

7. Now, if desired, we confirm some optional configuration parameters (or leave these blank, as done here) and confirm that we are happy for AWS to create and use a new execution role. *Figure 5.36* shows an example of this (and don't worry, the security group will have long been deleted by the time you are reading this page!):

Permissions Info

Execution role
The IAM role used by your environment to access your DAG code, write logs, and perform other actions.

```
Create a new role                              ▼        C
```

Role name

```
AmazonMWAA-mleip-airflow-dev-env-IyAb8s
```

Use alphanumeric and '+=,.@-_' characters. Maximum 64 characters.

ⓘ Amazon MWAA will create and assume the execution role in IAM named **AmazonMWAA-mleip-airflow-dev-env-IyAb8s** on your behalf. This role is configured with permission to retrieve code from your Amazon S3 bucket, use your KMS key, and send data to Amazon CloudWatch. You must add permissions to your execution role if your Airflow DAGs require access to any other AWS services. Info

Figure 5.36 – The creation of the execution role used by AWS for the MWAA environment

8. The next page will supply you with a final summary before allowing you to create your MWAA environment. Once you do this, you will be able to see in the MWAA service your newly created environment, like in *Figure 5.37*. This process can take some time, and for this example took around 30 minutes:

Airflow environments

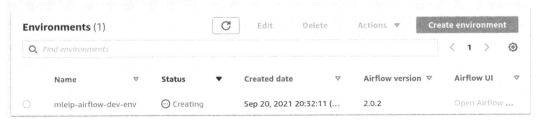

Figure 5.37 – Our newly minted MWAA environment

Now that you have this MWAA environment and you have supplied your DAG to the S3 bucket that it points to, you can open the Airflow UI and see the scheduled jobs defined by your DAG. You have now deployed a basic running service that we can build upon in later work.

> **Important note**
>
> Once you have created this MWAA environment, you cannot pause it, as it costs a small amount to run per hour (around 0.5 USD per hour for the environment configuration above). MWAA does not currently contain a feature for pausing and resuming an environment, so you will have to delete the environment and re-instantiate a new one with the same configuration when required. This can be automated using tools such as **Terraform** or AWS **CloudFormation**, which we will not cover here. So, a word of warning – *DO NOT ACCIDENTALLY LEAVE YOUR ENVIRONMENT RUNNING.* For example, definitely do not leave it running for a week, like I may or may not have done.

Revisiting CI/CD

We introduced the basics of CI/CD in *Chapter 2, The Machine Learning Development Process*, and discussed how this can be achieved by using **GitHub Actions**. We will now take this a step further and start to set up CI/CD pipelines that deploy code to the cloud.

First, we will start with an important example where we will push some code to an AWS S3 bucket. This can be done by creating a `yml` file in your GitHub repo under your `.github./workflows` directory called `aws-s3-deploy.yml`. This will be the nucleus around which we will form our CI/CD pipeline.

The `yml` file in our case will upload the Airflow DAG and contain the following pieces:

1. We name the process using the syntax for `name` and express that we want the deployment process to be triggered on a push to the main branch or a pull request to the main branch:

```
name: Upload DAGS to S3
on:
  push:
    branches: [ main ]
  pull_request:
    branches: [ main ]
```

2. We then define the jobs we want to occur during the deployment process. In this case, we want to upload our DAG files to an S3 bucket we have already created, and we want to use the appropriate AWS credentials we have configured in our GitHub secrets store:

```
jobs:
  deploy:
    name: Upload DAGS to Amazon S3
    runs-on: ubuntu-latest


    steps:
    - name: Checkout
      uses: actions/checkout@v2


    - name: Configure AWS credentials from account
      uses: aws-actions/configure-aws-credentials@v1
      with:
        aws-access-key-id: ${{ secrets.AWS_ACCESS_KEY_ID
}}
        aws-secret-access-key: ${{ secrets.AWS_SECRET_
ACCESS_KEY }}
        aws-region: us-east-1
```

Then, as part of the job, we run the step that copies the relevant files to our specified AWS S3 bucket. In this case, we are also specifying some details around how to make the copy using the AWS CLI. Specifically, here we want to copy over all the Python files to the `dags` folder of the repo:

```
    - name: Copy files to bucket with the AWS CLI
      run: |
        aws s3 cp ./dags s3://github-actions-ci-cd-tests
--recursive --include "*.py"
```

3. Once we perform a `git push` command with updated code, this will then execute the action and push the `dag` Python code to the specified S3 bucket. In the GitHub UI, you will be able to see something like *Figure 5.38* on a successful run:

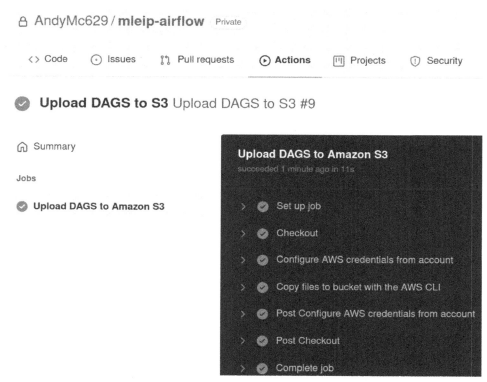

Figure 5.38 – A successful CI/CD process run via GitHub Actions and using the AWS CLI

This process then allows you to successfully push new updates to your Airflow service into AWS to be run by your MWAA instance. This is real CI/CD and allows for you to continually update the service you are providing without downtime.

Summary

In this chapter, we have discussed some of the most important concepts when it comes to deploying your ML solutions. In particular, we focused on the concepts of architecture and what tools we could potentially use when deploying solutions to the cloud. We covered some of the most important patterns used in modern ML engineering and how these can be implemented with tools such as containers and AWS Elastic Container Registry and Elastic Container Service, as well as how to create scheduled pipelines in AWS using Managed Workflows for Apache Airflow. We also explored how to hook up the MWAA example with GitHub Actions, so that changes to your code can directly trigger updates of running services, providing a template to use in future CI/CD processes.

In the next chapter, we will look at the question of how to scale up our solutions so that we can deal with large volumes of data and high throughput calculations.

6
Scaling Up

The previous chapter was all about starting the conversation around how we get our solutions out into the world through different deployment patterns, as well as some of the tools we can use to do this. This chapter will aim to build on that conversation by discussing the concepts and tools we can use to scale up our solutions to cope with large volumes of data or traffic.

Running some simple **Machine Learning** (**ML**) models on a few thousand data points on your laptop is a good exercise, especially when you're performing the discovery and proof-of-concept steps we outlined previously at the beginning of any ML development project. This approach, however, is not appropriate if we have to run millions upon millions of data points at a relatively high frequency, or if we have to train thousands of models of a similar scale at any one time. This requires a different approach, mindset, and toolkit.

In the following pages, we will cover some details of the most popular framework for distributing data computations in use today: Apache Spark. In particular, we will discuss some of the key points about how it works under the hood so that, in development, we can make some good decisions about how to use it, before moving on to discuss some of the approaches to ML that we can employ with Spark. This will help you build on some of the practical examples we already looked at earlier in this book, when we used Spark to solve our ML problems, with some more concrete theoretical understanding and further detailed practical examples provided. After this, you will learn how to scale out your infrastructure by using serverless functions. We will then briefly introduce some of the theory behind using **Kubernetes (K8s)** clusters. The first of these provides a mechanism to get simple models to scale out very quickly. The second allows you to keep the benefits of containerization but scale horizontally as well. Finally, we will wrap up, as usual, by providing a summary of what we've learned.

In this chapter, we will cover the following topics:

- Scaling with Spark
- Spinning up serverless infrastructure
- Containerizing at scale with Kubernetes

Technical requirements

To run the examples in this chapter you will require the following tools and packages be installed:

- Apache Spark (version 3.0.0 or higher)
- Git
- AWS CLI v2

Scaling with Spark

Apache Spark came from the work of some brilliant researchers at the *University of California, Berkeley* in 2012 and since then, it has revolutionized how we tackle problems with large datasets. Before Spark, the dominant paradigm for **big data** was **Hadoop MapReduce**, which is a lot less popular now.

Spark is a cluster computing framework, which means it works on the principle that several computers are linked together in a way that allows computational tasks to be shared. This allows us to coordinate these tasks effectively. Whenever we discuss running Spark jobs, we always talk about *the cluster* we are running on. This is the collection of computers that perform the tasks, the worker nodes, and the computer that hosts the organizational workload, known as the head node.

Spark is written in Scala, a language with a strong functional flavor and that compiles down to **Java Virtual Machines (JVMs)**. Since this is a book about ML engineering in Python, we don't discuss too much about the underlying Scala components of Spark, except where they help us use it in our work. Spark has several popular APIs that allow programmers to develop with it in a variety of languages, including Python. This gives rise to the PySpark syntax we have been using in several examples throughout this book.

So, how is this all put together?

Well, first of all, one of the things that makes Apache Spark so incredibly popular is the large array of connectors, components, and APIs it has available. For example, four main components interface with *Spark Core*:

- **Spark SQL, DataFrames, and Datasets**: This component allows you to create very scalable programs that deal with structured data. The ability to write SQL-compliant queries and create data tables that leverage the underlying Spark engine through one of the main **structured APIs** of Spark (Python, Java, Scala, or R) gives very easy access to the main bulk of Spark's functionality.

- **Spark Structured Streaming**: This component allows engineers to work with streaming data that's, for example, provided by a solution such as Apache Kafka. The design is incredibly simple and allows developers to simply work with streaming data as if it is a growing Spark structured table, with the same querying and manipulation functionality as for a standard one. This provides a low entry barrier for creating scalable streaming solutions.

- **GraphX**: This is a library that allows you to implement graph parallel processing and apply standard algorithms to graph-based data (for example, algorithms such as PageRank or Triangle Counting). The `GraphFrames` project from Databricks makes this functionality even easier to use by allowing us to work with DataFrame-based APIs in Spark and still analyse graph data.

- **Spark MLlib**: Last but not least, we have the component that's most appropriate for us as ML engineers: Spark's native library for ML. This library contains the implementation of many algorithms and feature engineering capabilities we have already seen in this book. Being able to use `DataFrame` APIs in the library this extremely easy to use, while still giving us a route to creating very powerful code. The potential speedups you can gain for your ML training by using Spark MLlib on a Spark cluster versus running another ML library on a single thread can be tremendous. There are other tricks we can apply to our favorite ML implementations and then use Spark to scale them out; we'll look at this later.

Spark's architecture is based on the driver/executor architecture. The driver is the program that acts as the main entry point for the Spark application and is where the `SparkContext` object is created. `SparkContext` sends tasks to the executors (which run on their own JVMs) and communicates with the cluster manager in a manner appropriate to the given manager and what mode the solution is running in. One of the driver's main tasks is to convert the code we write into a logical set of steps in a **Directed Acyclic Graph** (**DAG**) (the same concept that we used with Apache Airflow in *Chapter 5, Deployment Patterns and Tools*), and then convert that DAG into a set of tasks that need to be executed across the available compute resources.

In the pages that follow, we will assume we are running Spark with the **Hadoop YARN** resource manager, which is one of the most popular options and is also used by the *AWS Elastic Map Reduce* solution by default (more on this later). When running with **YARN** in *cluster mode*, the driver program runs in a container on the YARN cluster, which allows a client to submit jobs or requests through the driver and then exit (rather than requiring the client to remain connected to the cluster manager, which can happen when you're running in so-called *client mode*, which we will not discuss here).

The cluster manager is responsible for launching the executors across the resources that are available on the cluster.

Spark's architecture allows us, as ML engineers, to build solutions with the same API and syntax, regardless of whether we are working locally on our laptop or a cluster with thousands of nodes. The connection between the driver, the resource manager, and the executors is what allows this magic to happen.

Spark tips and tricks

In this subsection, we will cover some simple but effective tips for writing performant solutions with Spark. We will focus on key pieces of syntax aimed at data manipulation and preparation, which, as discussed elsewhere in this book, is always the first step in any ML-based solution pipeline. Let's get started:

1. First, we will cover the basics of writing good Spark SQL. The entry point for any Spark program is the `SparkSession` object, which we need to import an instance of in our application. It is often instantiated with the `spark` variable:

```
from pyspark.sql import SparkSession


spark = SparkSession \
    .builder \
    .appName("Spark SQL Example") \
    .config("spark.some.config.option", "some-value") \
    .getOrCreate()
```

2. You can then run Spark SQL commands against your available data using the `spark` object and the `sql` method:

```
spark.sql('''select * from data_table''')
```

There are a variety of ways to make the data you need available inside your Spark programs, depending on where they exist. The following example has been taken from some of the code we went through in *Chapter 3*, *From Model to Model Factory*, and shows how to pull data into a `dataframe` from a `csv` file:

```
data = spark.read.format("csv")\
.option("sep", ";")\
.option("inferSchema", "true")\
.option("header", "true").load(
"../../chapter1/stream-classifier/data/bank/bank.csv")
```

3. Now, we can create a temporary view of this data using the following syntax:

```
data.createOrReplaceTempView('data_view')
```

4. Then, we can query against this data using the methods mentioned previously to see the records or create new DataFrames:

```
new_data = spark.sql('''select …''')
```

When writing Spark SQL, some standard practices help your code to be efficient:

- Try not to join big tables on the left with small tables on the right (and vice versa) as this is inefficient.

- Avoid query syntax that will scan full datasets if they are very large; for example, `select max(date_time_value)`.

Some other good practices when working with Spark are as follows:

- **Avoid data skew**: Do what you can to understand how your data will be split across executors. If your data is partitioned on a date column, this may be a good choice if volumes of data are comparable for each day but bad if some days have most of your data and others very little. Repartitioning on a more appropriate column (or on a Spark-generated ID from the `repartition` command) will be required.

- **Avoid data shuffling**: This is when data is redistributed across different partitions. For example, we may have a dataset that is partitioned at the day level and then we ask Spark to sum over one column of the dataset for all of time. This will cause all of the daily partitions to be accessed and the result to be written to a new partition. For this to occur, disk writes and a network transfer have to occur, which can often lead to performance bottlenecks for your Spark job.

- **Avoid actions in large datasets**: For example, when you run the `collect()` command, you will bring all of your data back onto the driver node. This can be very bad if it is a large dataset but may be needed to convert the result of a calculation into something else. Note that the `toPandas()` command, which converts your Spark `DataFrame` into a pandas `DataFrame`, also collects all the data in the driver's memory.

Another excellent tool to have in your arsenal, as an ML engineer using Apache Spark, is the **User-Defined Function** (**UDF**). UDFs allow you to wrap up more complex and bespoke logic and apply it at scale in a variety of ways. An important aspect of this is that if you write a standard PySpark (or Scala) UDF, then you can apply this *inside* Spark SQL syntax, which allows you to efficiently reuse your code and even simplify the application of your ML models.

As a concrete example, let's build a UDF that looks at the banking data we worked with in *Chapter 3*, *From Model to Model Factory*, to create a new column called `'month_as_int'` that converts the current string representation of the month into an integer for processing later. We will not concern ourselves with train/test splits or what this might be used for; instead, we will just highlight how to apply some logic to a PySpark UDF. Let's get started:

1. First, we must read the data. Note that the relative path given here is consistent with the `spark_example_udfs.py` script, which can be found in this book's GitHub repository at `https://github.com/PacktPublishing/Machine-Learning-Engineering-with-Python/blob/main/Chapter06/spark_example_udfs.py`:

```python
from pyspark.sql import SparkSession
from pyspark import SparkContext
from pyspark.sql import functions as f


sc = SparkContext("local", "Ch6BasicExampleApp")
# Get spark session
spark = SparkSession.builder.getOrCreate()


# Get the data and place it in a spark dataframe
data = spark.read.format("csv").option("sep", ";").
option("inferSchema", "true").option("header", "true").
load(
    "../chapter1/stream-classifier/data/bank/bank.csv")
```

2. If we show the current data with the `data.show()` command, we will see something like this:

```
+---+------------+-------+---------+-------+-------+-------+----+--------+---+-----+--------+--------+-----+--------+--------+---+
|age|         job|marital|education|default|balance|housing|loan| contact|day|month|duration|campaign|pdays|previous|poutcome|  y|
+---+------------+-------+---------+-------+-------+-------+----+--------+---+-----+--------+--------+-----+--------+--------+---+
| 30|  unemployed|married|  primary|     no|   1787|     no|  no|cellular| 19|  oct|      79|       1|   -1|       0| unknown| no|
| 33|    services|married|secondary|     no|   4789|    yes| yes|cellular| 11|  may|     220|       1|  339|       4| failure| no|
| 35|  management| single| tertiary|     no|   1350|    yes|  no|cellular| 16|  apr|     185|       1|  330|       1| failure| no|
| 30|  management|married| tertiary|     no|   1476|    yes| yes| unknown|  3|  jun|     199|       4|   -1|       0| unknown| no|
| 59| blue-collar|married|secondary|     no|      0|    yes|  no| unknown|  5|  may|     226|       1|   -1|       0| unknown| no|
| 35|  management| single| tertiary|     no|    747|     no|  no|cellular| 23|  feb|     141|       2|  176|       3| failure| no|
| 36|self-employed|married| tertiary|     no|    307|    yes|  no|cellular| 14|  may|     341|       1|  330|       2|   other| no|
| 39|  technician|married|secondary|     no|    147|    yes|  no|cellular|  6|  may|     151|       2|   -1|       0| unknown| no|
| 41|entrepreneur|married| tertiary|     no|    221|    yes|  no| unknown| 14|  may|      57|       2|   -1|       0| unknown| no|
| 43|    services|married|  primary|     no|    -88|    yes| yes|cellular| 17|  apr|     313|       1|  147|       2| failure| no|
```

Figure 6.1 – A sample of the data from the initial DataFrame in the banking dataset

3. Now, we can double-check the schema of this DataFrame using the `data.printSchema()` command. This confirms that `month` is stored as a string currently, as shown here:

```
|-- age: integer (nullable = true)
|-- job: string (nullable = true)
|-- marital: string (nullable = true)
|-- education: string (nullable = true)
|-- default: string (nullable = true)
|-- balance: integer (nullable = true)
|-- housing: string (nullable = true)
|-- loan: string (nullable = true)
|-- contact: string (nullable = true)
|-- day: integer (nullable = true)
|-- month: string (nullable = true)
|-- duration: integer (nullable = true)
|-- campaign: integer (nullable = true)
|-- pdays: integer (nullable = true)
|-- previous: integer (nullable = true)
|-- poutcome: string (nullable = true)
|-- y: string (nullable = true)
```

Figure 6.2 – The schema of the read in bank dataset

4. Now, we can define our UDF, which will use the Python `datetime` library to convert the string representation of the month into an integer:

```
import datetime
def month_as_int(month):
    month_number = datetime.datetime.strptime(month,
"%b").month
    return month_number
```

5. If we want to apply our function inside Spark SQL, then we must register the function as a UDF. The arguments for the `register()` function are the registered name of the function, the name of the Python function we have just written, and the return type. The return type is `StringType()` by default, but we have made this explicit here:

```
from pyspark.sql.types import StringType
spark.udf.register("monthAsInt", month_as_int,
StringType())
```

6. Finally, now that we have registered the function, we can apply it to our data. First, we will create a temporary view of the bank dataset and then run a Spark SQL query against it that references our UDF. Running the following syntax with the `show()` command gives the result shown in *Figure 6.3*, which is our desired output:

```
data.createOrReplaceTempView('bank_data_view')

spark.sql('''
select *, monthAsInt(month) as month_as_int from bank_
data_view
''').show()
```

Running the preceding syntax with the `show()` command shows that we have successfully calculated the new column. The last few columns of the resulting `DataFrame` are shown here:

```
+-----+--------+--------+---+------------+
|pdays|previous|poutcome|  y|month_as_int|
+-----+--------+--------+---+------------+
|   -1|       0| unknown| no|          10|
|  339|       4| failure| no|           5|
|  330|       1| failure| no|           4|
|   -1|       0| unknown| no|           6|
|   -1|       0| unknown| no|           5|
|  176|       3| failure| no|           2|
|  330|       2|   other| no|           5|
|   -1|       0| unknown| no|           5|
|   -1|       0| unknown| no|           5|
|  147|       2| failure| no|           4|
|   -1|       0| unknown| no|           5|
|   -1|       0| unknown| no|           4|
|   -1|       0| unknown| no|           8|
|   -1|       0| unknown|yes|           4|
|  241|       1| failure| no|           1|
|   -1|       0| unknown| no|           8|
|   -1|       0| unknown| no|           8|
|  152|       2| failure| no|           4|
|   -1|       0| unknown| no|           5|
|  152|       1|   other| no|           7|
+-----+--------+--------+---+------------+
```

Figure 6.3 – The new column has been calculated successfully by applying our UDF

7. Alternatively, we can create our UDF with the following syntax and apply the result to a Spark `DataFrame`. This gives us the same result that's shown in the preceding screenshot:

```
from pyspark.sql.functions import udf
month_as_int_udf = udf(month_as_int, StringType())

df = spark.table("bank_data_view")
```

```
df.withColumn('month_as_int', month_as_int_udf("month")).
show()
```

8. Finally, PySpark also provides a nice decorator syntax for creating our UDF. The following code block also gives the same results as the preceding screenshot:

```
@udf("string")
def month_as_int_udf(month):
    month_number = datetime.datetime.strptime(month,
"%b").month
    return month_number
df.withColumn('month_as_int', month_as_int_udf("month")).
show()
```

This shows how we can apply some simple logic in a UDF, but for us to deploy a model at scale using this approach, we have to put the ML logic inside the function and apply it in the same manner. This can become a bit tricky if we want to work with some of the standard tools we are used to from the data science world, such as pandas and scikit-learn. Luckily, there is another option we can use that has a few benefits. We will discuss this now.

The UDFs currently being considered have a slight issue when we are working in Python in that translating data between the JVM and Python can take a while. One way to get around this is to use what is known as **pandas UDFs**, which use the Apache Arrow library under the hood to ensure that the data is read quickly for the execution of our UDFs. This gives us the flexibility of UDFs without any slowdown.

pandas UDFs are also extremely powerful because they work with the syntax of – you guessed it – pandas Series and DataFrame objects. This means that a lot of data scientists who are used to working with pandas to build models locally can easily adapt their code to scale up using Spark.

As an example, let's walk through how to apply a simple classifier to the wine dataset that we used earlier in this book. Note that the model was not optimized for this data; we are just showing an example of applying a pre-trained classifier.

1. First, let's create a simple **Support Vector Machine** (**SVM**)-based classifier on the wine dataset. We are not performing correct training/test splits, feature engineering, or other best practices here as we just want to show you how to apply any sklearn model:

```
import sklearn.svm
import sklearn.datasets
```

```
clf = sklearn.svm.SVC()
X, y = sklearn.datasets.load_wine(return_X_y=True) clf.
fit(X, y)
```

2. We can then bring the feature data into a Spark DataFrame to show you how to apply the pandas UDF in later stages:

```
df = spark.createDataFrame(X.tolist())
```

3. pandas UDFs are very easy to define. We just write our logic in a function and then add the @pandas_udf decorator, where we also have to provide the output type for the function. In the simplest case, we can just wrap the (normally serial or only locally parallelized) process of performing a prediction with the trained model:

```
import pandas as pd
from pyspark.sql.types import IntegerType
from pyspark.sql.functions import pandas_udf


@pandas_udf(returnType=IntegerType())
def predict_pd_udf(*cols):
    X = pd.concat(cols, axis=1)
    return pd.Series(clf.predict(X))
```

4. Finally, we can apply this to the Spark DataFrame containing the data by passing in the appropriate inputs we needed for our function. In this case, we will be passing in the column names of the features, of which there are 13:

```
col_names = ['_{}'.format(x) for x in range(1, 14)]
df_pred = df.select('*', predict_pd_udf(*col_names).
alias('class'))
```

5. Now, if you look at the results of this, you will see the following for the first few rows of the df_pred DataFrame:

```
+-----+----+----+----+-----+----+----+----+----+----+----+----+------+-----+
|  _1|  _2|  _3|  _4|  _5|  _6|  _7|  _8|  _9| _10| _11| _12|   _13|class|
+-----+----+----+----+-----+----+----+----+----+----+----+----+------+-----+
|14.23|1.71|2.43|15.6|127.0| 2.8|3.06|0.28|2.29|5.64|1.04|3.92|1065.0|    0|
| 13.2|1.78|2.14|11.2|100.0|2.65|2.76|0.26|1.28|4.38|1.05| 3.4|1050.0|    0|
|13.16|2.36|2.67|18.6|101.0| 2.8|3.24| 0.3|2.81|5.68|1.03|3.17|1185.0|    0|
|14.37|1.95| 2.5|16.8|113.0|3.85|3.49|0.24|2.18| 7.8|0.86|3.45|1480.0|    0|
|13.24|2.59|2.87|21.0|118.0| 2.8|2.69|0.39|1.82|4.32|1.04|2.93| 735.0|    2|
```

Figure 6.4 – The result of applying a simple pandas UDF

And that completes our whirlwind tour of UDFs and pandas UDFs in Spark, which allow us to take serial Python logic, such as, data transformations or our ML models, and apply them in a manifestly parallel way.

In the next section, we will focus on how to set ourselves up to perform Spark-based computations in the cloud.

Spark on the cloud

As should be clear from the preceding discussion, writing and deploying PySpark-based ML solutions can be done on your laptop, but for you to see the benefits when working at scale, you must have an appropriately sized computing cluster to hand. Provisioning this sort of infrastructure can be a long and painful process but as discussed already in this book, a plethora of options for infrastructure are available from the main public cloud providers.

For Spark, AWS has a particularly nice solution called **Elastic Map Reduce** (**EMR**), which is a managed big data platform that allows you to easily configure clusters of a few different flavors across the big data ecosystem. In this book, we will focus on Spark-based solutions, so we will focus on creating and using clusters that have Spark tooling to hand.

In the next section, we will go through a concrete example of spinning up a Spark cluster on EMR and then deploying a simple Spark MLlib-based application onto it.

So, with that, let's explore Spark on the cloud with **AWS EMR**!

AWS EMR example

To understand how EMR works, we will continue in the practical vein that the rest of this book will follow and dive into an example. We will begin by learning how to create a brand-new cluster before discussing how to write and deploy our first PySpark ML solution to it. Let's get started:

1. First, navigate to the **EMR** page on AWS and find the **Create Cluster** button:

Figure 6.5 – Creating our EMR cluster

2. Next, specify the S3 bucket where we will store our logs and other metadata:

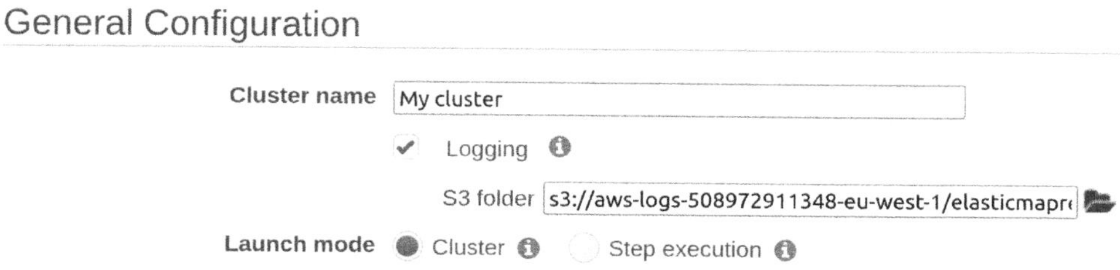

General Configuration

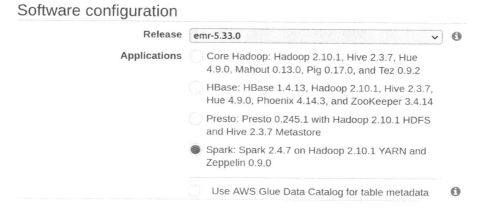

Figure 6.6 – Assigning S3 storage to our EMR cluster

3. Then, define the application type. We will select the **Spark** option:

Software configuration

Figure 6.7 – Configuring the type of EMR cluster we want

4. Next, we must select the hardware for our cluster. Here, we can just select a small **m1.medium** machine specification and create the smallest cluster possible (1 master and 1 core node) since this is for demonstration purposes. You can also choose to scale your clusters based on workload if required but beware of the cost implications of this!

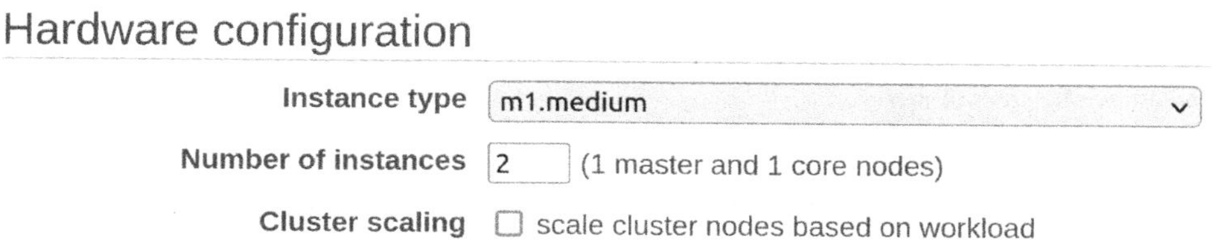

Hardware configuration

Figure 6.8 – Defining the specifications of our cluster hardware

5. Finally, we can configure the security if we wish to. In this case, we will just let AWS define some default values and not define an EC2 key pair. When you use this in production, it is advised that you make sure you understand how to make your services secure for your network and tenancy (or seek the advice of someone in your organization who knows how):

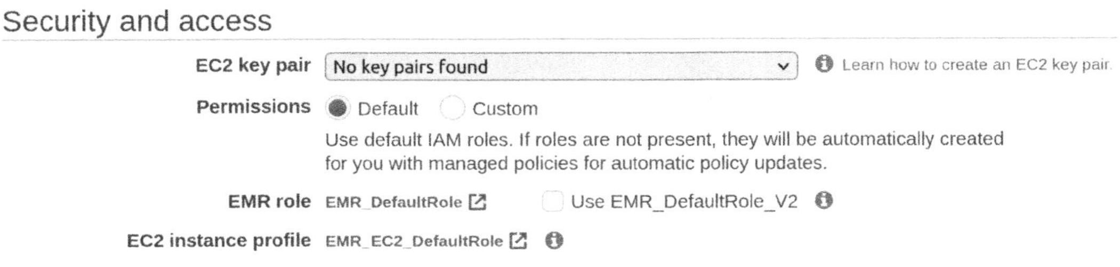

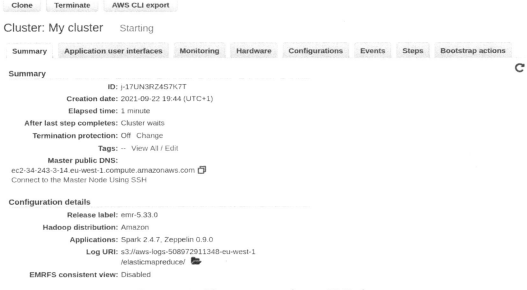

Figure 6.9 – Configuring the security for our cluster

6. And that's it! Our EMR cluster is now created. We will be redirected to the following page:

Figure 6.10 – The review page for our EMR cluster

After spinning up our EMR cluster, we want to be able to submit work to it. Here, we will adapt the example Spark MLlib pipeline we produced in *Chapter 3, From Model to Model Factory*, to analyze the banking dataset and submit this as a step to our newly created cluster. We will do this as a standalone single PySpark script that acts as the one step in our application, but it is easy to build on this to make far more complex applications.

7. First, we will take the code from *Chapter 3, From Model to Model Factory*, and perform some nice refactoring based on our discussions around good practices. First, we can more effectively modularize the code so that it contains a function that provides all our modeling steps (not all of the steps have been reproduced here for brevity). We have also included a final step that writes the results of the modeling to a parquet file:

```python
def model_bank_data(spark, input_path, output_path):
    data = spark.read.format("csv")\
        .option("sep", ";")\
        .option("inferSchema", "true")\
        .option("header", "true")\
        .load(input_path)


    data = data.withColumn('label', f.when((f.col("y") ==
"yes"), 1).otherwise(0))


    # ...


    data.write.format('parquet')\
        .mode('overwrite')\
        .save(output_path)
```

8. Building on this, we will wrap all of the main boilerplate code into a main function that can be called at the if __name__ == "__main__": entry point to the program:

```python
def main():
    parser = argparse.ArgumentParser()
    parser.add_argument(
        '--input_path', help='S3 bucket path for the
input data. Assume to be csv for this case.'
    )
    parser.add_argument(
        '--output_path', help='S3 bucket path for the
output data. Assume to be parquet for this case'
```

```
    )
    args = parser.parse_args()



    # Create spark context
    sc = SparkContext("local", "pipelines")
    # Get spark session
    spark = SparkSession\
        .builder\
        .appName('MLEIP Bank Data Classifier EMR
Example')\
        .getOrCreate()



    model_bank_data(
        spark,
        input_path=args.input_path,#"s3://mleip-emr-ml-
simple/bank.csv",
        output_path=args.output_path#"s3://mleip-emr-ml-
simple/results.parquet"
    )
```

9. We put the preceding functions into a script called `emr_sparkmllib.py` that we will submit to our EMR cluster later:

```
import argparse



from pyspark.sql import SparkSession
from pyspark import SparkContext



from pyspark.sql import functions as f
from pyspark.mllib.evaluation import
BinaryClassificationMetrics, MulticlassMetrics
from pyspark.ml.feature import StandardScaler,
OneHotEncoder, StringIndexer, Imputer, VectorAssembler
```

```
from pyspark.ml import Pipeline, PipelineModel
from pyspark.ml.classification import LogisticRegression


def model_bank_data(spark, input_path, output_path):
    ...


def main():
    ...


if __name__ == "__main__":
    main()
```

10. Now, to submit this script to the EMR cluster we have just created, we need to find out the cluster ID, which we can get from the AWS UI or by running the following command:

```
aws emr list-clusters --cluster-states WAITING
```

11. Then, we need to send the emr_sparkmllib.py script to S3 to be read in by the cluster. We can create an S3 bucket called mleip-emr-ml-simple to store this and our other artifacts using either the CLI or the AWS console (see *Chapter 5, Deployment Patterns and Tools*). Once copied over, we are ready for the final steps.

12. Now, we must submit the script using the following command, with <CLUSTER_ID> replaced with the ID of the cluster we just created. After a few minutes, the step should have completed and written the outputs to the results.parquet file in the same S3 bucket:

```
aws emr add-steps \
--cluster-id <CLUSTER_ID> \
--steps Type=Spark, Name="Spark Application
Step",ActionOnFailure=CONTINUE,Args=[s3://mleip-emr-ml-
simple/emr_sparkmllib.py,--input_path,s3://mleip-emr-ml-
simple/bank.csv --output_path,s3://mleip-emr-ml-simple/
results.parquet]
```

And that is it – that is how we can start developing PySpark ML pipelines on the cloud using **AWS EMR**!

In the next section, we will explore another method of scaling up our solutions by using so-called serverless tools.

Spinning up serverless infrastructure

Whenever we do any ML or software engineering, we have to run the requisite tasks and computations on computers, often with appropriate networking, security, and other protocols and software already in place, which we have often referred to already as constituting our *infrastructure*. A big part of our infrastructure is the servers we use to run the actual computations. This might seem a bit strange, so let's start by talking about *serverless* infrastructure (how can there be such a thing?). This section will explain this concept and show you how to use it to scale out your ML solutions.

Serverless is a bit misleading as a term as it does not mean that no physical servers are running your programs. It does mean, however, that the programs you are running should not be thought of as being statically hosted on one machine, but as ephemeral instances on another layer on top of the underlying hardware.

The benefits of serverless tools for your ML solution include (but are not limited to) the following:

- **No servers!** Don't underestimate the savings in time and energy you can get by offloading infrastructure management to your cloud provider.

- **Simplified scaling**: It's usually very easy to define the scaling behavior of your serverless components by using clearly defined maximum instances, for example.

- **Low barrier to entry**: These components are usually extremely easy to set up and run, allowing you and your team members to focus on writing high-quality code, logic, and models.

- **Natural integration points**: Serverless tools are often nice to use for handovers between other tools and components. Their ease of setup means you can be up and running with simple jobs that pass data or trigger other services in no time.

- **Simplified serving**: Some serverless tools are excellent for providing a serving layer for your ML models. The scaling and low barrier to entry mentioned previously mean you can quickly create a very scalable service that provides predictions upon request or upon being triggered by some other event.

One of the best and most widely used examples of serverless functionality is **AWS Lambda**, which allows us to write programs in a variety of languages with a simple web browser interface or through our usual development tools, and then have them run completely independently of any infrastructure that's been set up. Lambda is an amazing low entry barrier solution to getting some code up and running and scaling it up. However, it is very much aimed at creating simple APIs that can be hit over an HTTP request. Deploying your ML model with Lambda is particularly useful if you are aiming for an event- or request-driven system.

To see this in action, let's build a basic system that takes incoming image data as an HTTP request with a JSON body and returns a similar message containing the classification of the data using a pre-built scikit-learn model. This walkthrough is based on the AWS example at `https://aws.amazon.com/blogs/compute/deploying-machine-learning-models-with-serverless-templates/`.

For this, we can save a lot of time by leveraging templates already built and maintained as part of the AWS **Serverless Application Model (SAM)** framework (`https://aws.amazon.com/about-aws/whats-new/2021/06/aws-sam-launches-machine-learning-inference-templates-for-aws-lambda/`).

To install the AWS SAM CLI on your relevant platform, follow the instructions at `https://docs.aws.amazon.com/serverless-application-model/latest/developerguide/serverless-sam-cli-install.html`.

Now, let's perform the following steps to set up a template Lambda deployment for hosting and serving a ML model on serverless infrastructure:

1. First, we must run the `sam init` command and select the AWS `Quick Start Templates` option:

    ```
    Which template source would you like to use?
            1 - AWS Quick Start Templates
            2 - Custom Template Location
    Choice: []
    ```

    Figure 6.11 – Selecting a template from the AWS SAM framework

2. We will be offered a choice of `package type` Select `image` so that we can create a Docker container hosted on **Elastic Container Registry (ECR)**:

    ```
    What package type would you like to use?
            1 - Zip (artifact is a zip uploaded to S3)
            2 - Image (artifact is an image uploaded to an ECR image repository)
    Package type: []
    ```

    Figure 6.12 – Selecting a package type for the SAM template

3. Next, we have to select the base image we want to use. In line with all the other examples in this book, let's choose `python3.8-base`:

```
Which base image would you like to use?
        1 - amazon/nodejs14.x-base
        2 - amazon/nodejs12.x-base
        3 - amazon/nodejs10.x-base
        4 - amazon/python3.8-base
        5 - amazon/python3.7-base
        6 - amazon/python3.6-base
        7 - amazon/python2.7-base
        8 - amazon/ruby2.7-base
        9 - amazon/ruby2.5-base
       10 - amazon/go1.x-base
       11 - amazon/java11-base
       12 - amazon/java8.al2-base
       13 - amazon/java8-base
       14 - amazon/dotnet5.0-base
       15 - amazon/dotnetcore3.1-base
       16 - amazon/dotnetcore2.1-base
Base image: 4
```

Figure 6.13 – Selecting a base image for the SAM template

4. Now, we must give the project a name. We shall call ours `mleip-lambda-example`:

Project name [sam-app]: mleip-lambda-example

Figure 6.14 – Assigning our project name

5. You will see that the repository is cloned from the remote repository where all of the SAM templates are hosted, before being prompted for the template you wish to use. We will select the scikit-learn API option here:

```
AWS quick start application templates:
        1 - Hello World Lambda Image Example
        2 - PyTorch Machine Learning Inference API
        3 - Scikit-learn Machine Learning Inference API
        4 - Tensorflow Machine Learning Inference API
        5 - XGBoost Machine Learning Inference API
Template selection: 3
```

Figure 6.15 – Cloning the scikit-learn SAM application template

6. If the previous step was successful, a folder should have been generated in your current directory with the chosen name that contains the code template:

```
---------------------
Generating application:
---------------------
Name: mleip-lambda-example
Base Image: amazon/python3.8-base
Dependency Manager: pip
Output Directory: .

Next steps can be found in the README file at ./mleip-lambda-example/README.md
```

Figure 6.16 – Successfully creating our SAM application template folder

Note that the preceding steps have created a template for a scikit-learn-based system that classifies handwritten digits.

If you want to deploy this example, follow the next few steps.

7. First, we must build the container locally by running `.aws-sam/build` in the `mleip-lambda-example` directory. Upon a successful build, you should receive a success message similar to the following in your Terminal:

```
Build Succeeded


Built Artifacts    : .aws-sam/build
Built Template     : .aws-sam/build/template.yaml


Commands you can use next
=========================
[*] Invoke Function: sam local invoke
[*] Deploy: sam deploy –guided
```

Now, we can test the service locally to ensure that everything is working well with the mock data that's supplied with the repository. This uses a JSON file that encodes a basic image and runs the inference step for the service. If this has worked, you will see an output that looks something like the following for your Lambda call:

```
$sam local invoke InferenceFunction --event events/event.
json



Invoking Container created from
inferencefunction:python3.8-v1
Image was not found.
Building image................
Skip pulling image and use local one:
```

```
inferencefunction:rapid-1.26.0.


START RequestId: bef853a2-c0cc-478c-8b11-d3805632d72f
Version: $LATEST
END RequestId: bef853a2-c0cc-478c-8b11-d3805632d72f
REPORT RequestId: bef853a2-c0cc-478c-8b11-d3805632d72f
Init Duration: 0.09 ms    Duration: 1838.22 ms    Billed
Duration: 1900 ms    Memory Size: 5000 MB    Max Memory
Used: 5000 MB
{"statusCode": 200, "body": "{\"predicted_label\": 3}"}
(mleng)
```

8. Since we have gone the Docker image route, deploying our Lambda function will require the use of ECR. To authenticate the Docker client with the ECR registry, run the following command with your region and account ID in the appropriately marked places:

    ```
    aws --region <region> ecr get-login-password | docker
    login --username AWS --password-stdin <accountID>.dkr.
    ecr.<region>.amazonaws.com
    ```

    You will then get a message saying the following:

    ```
    Login Succeeded
    ```

9. Now, we must create an ECR repository for our solution. Let's call ours `mleip-lambda-example-repo` so that it's in line with our naming for the code base:

    ```
    aws ecr create-repository --repository-name mleip-lambda-
    example-repo --image-tag-mutability MUTABLE --image-
    scanning-configuration scanOnPush=true
    ```

10. If this step is successful, you should see something like the following code block returned in your Terminal (once again, with `<region>` and `<accountID>` replaced by their respective values for your AWS account):

    ```
    {
        "repository": {
            "repositoryArn":
    "arn:aws:ecr:<region>:<accountID>:repository/mleip-
    lambda-example-repo",
            "registryId": "<accountID>",
    ```

```
        "repositoryName": "mleip-lambda-example-repo",
        "repositoryUri": "<accountID>.dkr.ecr.<region>.
amazonaws.com/mleip-lambda-example-repo",
        "createdAt": "2021-07-14T19:06:25+01:00",
        "imageTagMutability": "MUTABLE",
        "imageScanningConfiguration": {
            "scanOnPush": true
        },
        "encryptionConfiguration": {
            "encryptionType": "AES256"
        }
    }
}
```

> **Important note**
> We will need `repositoryUri` for later steps, so keep this handy.

11. Now, we can trigger the guided deployment functionality that is packaged with SAM by running the following command:

```
sam deploy --guided
```

12. For the prompts that follow, we can just select the defaults by pressing *Enter* each time until we are asked for `Image Repository for InferenceFunction`, which we set aside in the previous step and can now copy in. For the remaining steps, we can hit *Enter* (or `yes`) until we are asked if we want to `Deploy this changeset?`. For example, the first few questions and responses will look something like this (with `<repositoryURI>` replaced with your ECR repository URI from *Step 5*):

```
Configuring SAM deploy
======================


        Looking for config file [samconfig.toml] :  Not found


        Setting default arguments for 'sam deploy'
        ==========================================
```

```
Stack Name [sam-app]:

AWS Region [eu-west-2]:

Image Repository for InferenceFunction:
<repositoryURI>
      inferencefunction:python3.8-v1 to be pushed
to <repositoryURI>:inferencefunction-b5712d3d8d03-
python3.8-v1



    #Shows you resources changes to be deployed and
require a 'Y' to initiate deploy
    Confirm changes before deploy [y/N]: y
    #SAM needs permission to be able to create roles to
connect to the resources in your template
    Allow SAM CLI IAM role creation [Y/n]: Y
    InferenceFunction may not have authorization defined,
Is this okay? [y/N]: y
    Save arguments to configuration file [Y/n]: Y
    SAM configuration file [samconfig.toml]:
    SAM configuration environment [default]:
```

13. Finally, upon completing these steps, you will get the following message, confirming that the deployment has been successful and that our Lambda function is up and running!

```
CloudFormation outputs from deployed stack
-------------------------------------------------------------------------------------------
Outputs
-------------------------------------------------------------------------------------------
Key             InferenceApi
Description     API Gateway endpoint URL for Prod stage for Inference function
Value           https://biwapzz3y5.execute-api.eu-west-2.amazonaws.com/Prod/classify_digit/

Key             InferenceFunctionIamRole
Description     Implicit IAM Role created for Inference function
Value           arn:aws:lambda:eu-west-2:508972911348:function:sam-app-InferenceFunction-WKDKOefcLIWn

Key             InferenceFunction
Description     Inference Lambda Function ARN
Value           arn:aws:lambda:eu-west-2:508972911348:function:sam-app-InferenceFunction-WKDKOefcLIWn
-------------------------------------------------------------------------------------------

Successfully created/updated stack - sam-app in eu-west-2
```

Figure 6.17 – Successfully deploying our AWS Lambda function

14. As a quick test to confirm this is working, we can use a tool such as Postman to hit our shiny new Lambda API. Simply copy the `InferenceApi` URL from the output screen from *Step 8* as the destination for the request, select **POST** for the request type, and then choose **binary** as the body type. Then, you can choose any image to send up to the API (in this case, small images are more likely to work; larger images can cause errors for this standard template):

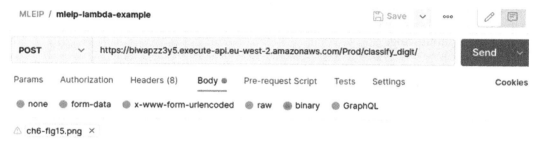

Figure 6.18 – Calling our Lambda function's endpoint with Postman

15. You can also test this more programmatically with a CURL command like the following – just replace the URL and image locations with the appropriate values and you are good to go:

```
curl --location --request POST 'https://biwapzz3y5.
execute-api.eu-west-2.amazonaws.com/Prod/classify_digit/'
\
--header 'Content-Type: image/png' \
--data-binary '@/home/andrew/dev/github/Machine-Learning-
Engineering-with-Python/chapter6/lambda/mleip-lambda-
example/events/ch6-fig15.png'
```

In this step and *Step 9*, the body of the response from the Lambda function is as follows:

```
{
    "predicted_label": 5
}
```

And that's it – we have just built and deployed a simple ML inference service using AWS Lambda!

In the next section, we will touch upon the final way of scaling our solutions that we will discuss in this chapter, which is using K8s and Kubeflow to horizontally scale containerized applications.

Containerizing at scale with Kubernetes

We have already covered how to use containers for building and deploying our ML solutions. The next step is understanding how to orchestrate and manage several containers to deploy and run applications at scale. This is where the open source tool **K8s** comes in.

K8s is an extremely powerful tool that provides a variety of different functionalities that help us create and manage very scalable containerized applications, including (but not limited to) the following:

- **Load Balancing**: K8s will manage routing incoming traffic to your containers for you so that the load is split evenly.

- **Horizontal Scaling**: K8s provides simple interfaces so that you can control the number of container instances you have at any one time, allowing you to scale massively if needed.

- **Self Healing**: There is built-in management for replacing or rescheduling components that are not passing health checks.

- **Automated Rollbacks**: K8s stores the history of your system so that you can revert to a previous working version if something goes wrong.

All of these features help ensure that your deployed solutions are robust and able to perform as required under all circumstances.

K8s is designed to ensure the preceding features are embedded from the ground up by using a microservice architecture, with a control plane interacting with nodes (servers), each of which host pods (one or more containers) that run the components of your application.

The key thing that K8s gives you is the ability to scale your application based on load by creating replicas of the base solution. This is extremely useful if you are building services with API endpoints that could feasibly face surges in demand at different times. To learn about some of the ways you can do this, see `https://kubernetes.io/docs/concepts/workloads/controllers/deployment/#scaling-a-deployment`:

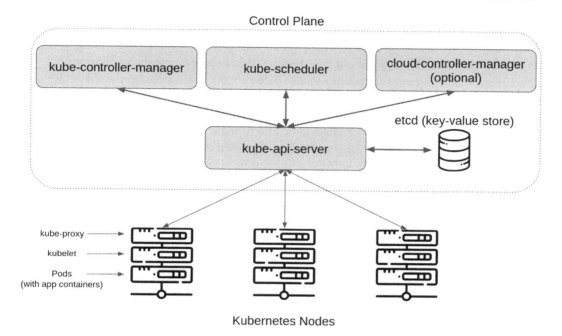

Figure 6.19 – The K8s architecture

But what about ML? In this case, we can look to a newer piece of the K8s ecosystem: **Kubeflow**.

Kubeflow styles itself as the *ML toolkit for K8s* (https://www.kubeflow.org/), so as ML engineers, it makes sense for us to be aware of this rapidly developing solution. This is a very exciting tool and an active area of development. The concept of horizontal scaling for K8s generally still applies here, but Kubeflow provides some standardized tools for converting the pipelines you build into standard K8s resources, which can then be managed and resourced in the ways described previously. This can help reduce *boilerplate* and lets us, as ML engineers, focus on building our modeling logic rather than setting up the infrastructure, even though K8s is already a nice abstraction.

This section only touched on K8s and Kubeflow very briefly, to make sure you are aware of these tools for your exploration. For more details on K8s and Kubeflow, consult the documentation and follow the tutorials at https://kubernetes.io/ and https://www.kubeflow.org/docs/. I would also recommend another Packt title called *Kubernetes in Production Best Practices* by *Aly Saleh* and *Murat Karslioglu*: https://www.packtpub.com/product/kubernetes-in-production-best-practices/9781800202450.

Summary

In this chapter, we looked at how to take the ML solutions we have been building in the past few chapters and thought about how to scale them up to larger data volumes or higher numbers of requests for predictions. To do this, we mainly focused on **Apache Spark** as this is the most popular general-purpose engine for distributed computing. During our discussion of Apache Spark, we revisited some coding patterns and syntax we used previously in this book. By doing so, we developed a more thorough understanding of how and why to do certain things when developing in PySpark. We discussed the concept of **UDFs** in detail and how these can be used to create massively scalable ML workflows.

After this, we explored how to work with Spark on the cloud, specifically through the **Elastic Map Reduce (EMR)** service provided by AWS. Then, we looked at some of the other ways we can scale our solutions; that is, through serverless architectures and horizontal scaling with containers. In the former case, we walked through how to build a service for serving a ML model using **AWS Lambda**. This used standard templates provided by the AWS Serverless Application Management framework. Finally, we provided a high-level view of how to use K8s and Kubeflow to scale out ML pipelines horizontally, as well as some of the other benefits of using these tools.

In the next chapter, we will pull together many aspects of our new ML engineering knowledge to build a forecasting microservice, building upon the basic model example shown in *Chapter 1, Introduction to ML Engineering*.

Section 3: End-to-End Examples

This section has the objective of working through some concrete examples in a way that pulls together all of the previous discussions in the book. These examples can be used as templates by readers of the book for future applications in their own work. The examples will have a particular focus on what decisions need to be made to select the best engineering approach, given what has been learned in the rest of the book. Once you have completed this section, you will have seen two examples of how to apply your new knowledge to archetypal machine learning engineering projects.

This section comprises the following chapters:

- *Chapter 7, Building an Example ML Microservice*
- *Chapter 8, Building an Extract Transform Machine Learning Use Case*

7

Building an Example ML Microservice

This chapter will be all about bringing together some of what we have learned in the book so far with a realistic example. This will be based on one of the scenarios introduced in *Chapter 1, Introduction to ML Engineering*, where we are required to build a forecasting service for store item sales. We will discuss the scenario in a bit of detail and outline the key decisions that have to be made to make a solution a reality, before showing how we can employ the processes, tools, and techniques we have learned through this book to solve key parts of the problem from an ML engineering perspective. At the end of this chapter, you should come away with a clear view of how to build your own ML microservices for solving a variety of business problems.

In this chapter, we will cover the following topics:

- Understanding the forecasting problem
- Designing our forecasting service
- Selecting the tools
- Executing the build

Each topic will provide an opportunity for us to walk through the different decisions we have to make as engineers working on a complex ML delivery. This will provide us with a handy reference when we go out and do this in the real world!

With that, let's get started and build a forecasting microservice!

Technical requirements

To follow along with the examples in this chapter, you will need to have the following installed:

- AWS CLI v2
- Flask
- Postman

Understanding the forecasting problem

In *Chapter 1, Introduction to ML Engineering*, we considered the example of a ML team that has been tasked with providing forecasts of items at the level of individual stores in a retail business. The fictional business users had the following requirements:

- The forecasts should be rendered and accessible via a web-based dashboard.
- The user should be able to request updated forecasts if necessary.
- The forecasts should be carried out at the level of individual stores.
- Users will be interested in their own regions/stores in any one session and not be concerned with global trends.
- The number of requests for updated forecasts in any one session will be small.

Given these requirements, we can work with the business to create the following user stories, which we can put into a tool such as JIRA, as explained in *Chapter 2, The Machine Learning Development Process*. Some examples of user stories covering these requirements would be the following:

- **User Story 1**: As a local logistics planner, I want to log in to a dashboard in the morning and be able to see forecasts of item demand at store level for the next few days.

- **User Story 2**: As a local logistics planner, I want to be able to request an update of my forecast if I see it is out of date. I want the new forecast to be retrieved in a reasonable time.

- **User Story 3**: As a local logistics planner, I want to be able to filter for forecasts based on specific stores.

These user stories are very important for the development of the solution as a whole. As we are focused on the ML engineering aspects of the problem, we can now dive into what these mean for building the solution.

For example, the desire to *be able to see forecasts of item demand at store level* can be translated quite nicely into a few technical requirements for the ML part of the solution. This tells us that the target variable will be the quantity of items required on a particular day. It tells us that our ML model or models need to be able to work at store level, so either we have one model per store, or the concept of store can be taken in as some sort of feature.

Similarly, the requirement that the user wants to *be able to request an update of my forecast if I see it is out of date ... I want the new forecast to be retrieved in a reasonable time* places a strict latency requirement on training. We cannot build something that takes days to retrain, so this may suggest that one model built across all of the data may not be the best solution.

Finally, the request that the user wants to be able to filter for forecasts based on specific stores again supports the notion that whatever we build has to take in store as some sort of input, but not necessarily as a feature. This should get us thinking about how our application logic may want to take in these request values (store) and use them to pull in the appropriate ML model before performing inference.

Walking through this process, we can see how just a few lines of requirements have allowed us to start fleshing out how we will tackle the problem in practice. Some of these thoughts and others could be consolidated upon a little brainstorming among our team for the project in a table like that of *Figure 7.1*:

User story	Details	Technical requirements
1	As a local logistics planner, I want to log in to a dashboard in the morning and be able to see forecasts of item demand at store level for the next few days.	• Target variable = item demand • Forecast horizon = 1–7 days • Interface with dashboard required
2	As a local logistics planner, I want to be able to request an update of my forecast if I see it is out of date. I want the new forecast to be retrieved in a reasonable time.	• Lightweight retraining • Model per store?
3	As a local logistics planner, I want to be able to filter for forecasts based on specific stores.	• Model per store

Figure 7.1 – Translating user stories to technical requirements

Now we will build on our understanding of the problem by starting to pull together a design for the ML piece of the solution.

Designing our forecasting service

The requirements in the *Understanding the forecasting problem* section are the definitions of the targets we need to hit, but they are not the method for getting there. Drawing on our understanding of design and architecture from *Chapter 5, Deployment Patterns and Tools*, we can start building out our design.

First, we should confirm what kind of design we should be working to. Since we need dynamic requests, it makes sense that we follow the microservice architecture discussed in *Chapter 5, Deployment Patterns and Tools*. This will allow us to build a service that has the sole focus of retrieving the right model from our model store and performing the requested inference. The prediction service should therefore have interfaces available between the dashboard and the model store.

Furthermore, since a user may want to work with a few different store combinations in any one session and maybe switch back and forward between the forecasts of these, we should provide a mechanism for doing so that is performant.

It is also clear from the scenario that we can quite easily have a very high volume of requests for predictions but a lower request for model updates. This means that separating out training and prediction will make sense and that we can follow the train-persist process outlined in *Chapter 3, From Model to Model Factory*. This will mean that prediction will not be dependent on a full training run every time and that retrieval of models for prediction is relatively fast.

What we have also gathered from the requirements is that our training system doesn't necessarily need to be triggered by drift monitoring in this case, but by dynamic requests made by the user. This adds a bit of complexity as it means that our solution should not retrain for every request coming in but be able to determine whether a retrain is worth it for a given request or whether the model is already up to date. For example, if four users log on and are looking at the same region/store/item combination and all request a retrain, it is pretty clear that we do not need to retrain our model four times! Instead, what should happen is that the training system registers a request, performs a retrain, and then safely ignores the other requests.

We can bring these design points together into a high-level design diagram, for example, in *Figure 7.2*:

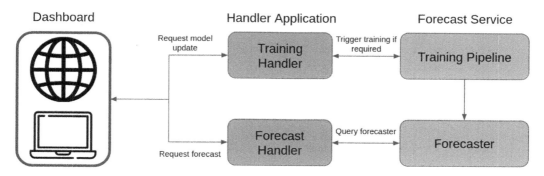

Figure 7.2 – High-level design for the forecasting microservice

The next section will focus on taking these high-level design considerations to a lower level of detail as we perform some tool selection ahead of development.

Selecting the tools

Now that we have a high-level design in mind and we have written down some clear technical requirements, we can begin to select the toolset we will use to implement our solution.

One of the most important considerations on this front will be what framework we use for modeling our data and building our forecasting functionality. Given that the problem is a time series modeling problem with a need for fast retraining and prediction, we can consider the pros and cons of a few options that may fit the bill before proceeding.

The results of this exercise are shown in *Figure 7.3*:

Tool/ framework	Pros	Cons
Sklearn	• Already understood by almost all data scientists • Very easy-to-use syntax • Lots of great community support • Good feature engineering and pipelining support	• No native time series modeling capabilities • Will require some more feature engineering to apply to models to time series data • More work and understanding required by engineer/scientist
Prophet	• Purely focused on forecasting • Has inbuilt hyperparameter optimization capabilities • Provides a lot of easy-to-use functionality out of the box • Often gives accurate results on a wide variety of problems • Provides confidence intervals out of the box	• Not as commonly used as sklearn (but still relatively popular) • Underlying methods are quite sophisticated – may lead to *black box* usage • Not inherently scalable
Spark MLlib	• Natively scalable to large volumes • Good feature engineering and pipelining support	• No native time series modeling capabilities • Algorithm options are relatively limited

Figure 7.3 – The considered pros and cons of some different ML toolkits
for solving this forecasting problem

Based on the information in *Figure 7.3*, it looks like the `Prophet` library would be a good choice and offer a nice balance between predictive power, desired time series capabilities, and experience among the developers and scientists on the team.

The data scientists could then use this information to build a proof-of-concept, with code much like that shown in *Chapter 1, Introduction to ML Engineering*, in the *Example 2: Forecasting API* section, which applies Prophet to a standard retail dataset.

Given this proof-of-concept, the next challenge is moving onto the later stages of the ML model development life cycle, which is covered in the next section.

Executing the build

As discussed in *Chapter 2, The Machine Learning Development Process*, there are several stages we have to go through on the ML project life cycle after performing discovery and building an initial proof-of-concept. These steps are focused on the development of the solution and then the deployment of that solution.

First, we will focus on how we would break down these stages into manageable tasks that could be executed by our engineering team. Each component in *Figure 7.2* roughly corresponds to one of these tasks, as follows:

- **Prediction Handler / Training Handler**: Each of these will consist of application logic that takes a request from the dashboard (via an API request over HTTP) and then triggers the appropriate process. These can be brought together as different endpoints in a simple web service that acts as the interface between the dashboard and the other components of the system.

- **Training Pipeline and Forecaster**: As discussed in the previous section and in the *Designing your training system section* in *Chapter 3, From Model to Model Factory*, this should be a standalone process that can be triggered, run the training of the model, and then output the model to the model store for reference by other parts of the system. For this, we can actually employ a service from AWS called **Forecast**, which provides a series of forecasters that can be trained and exposed programmatically via APIs. This is a nice example of *don't reinvent the wheel*, a philosophy we briefly discussed in *Chapter 4, Packaging Up*.

- **Model Store**: We need somewhere to store our model and reference it later. Conveniently, this is handled by the **Forecast** service.

In the next few sections, we will walk through some of the main considerations when building or interfacing with these components.

Training pipeline and forecaster

As discussed in the *Understanding the forecasting problem* section, the retraining process for this solution should be triggered via a user request and not based on any sort of drift monitoring. This means that the training setup here is in fact simpler than the case covered in detail in *Chapter 3, From Model to Model Factory*.

For this example, we will use a very handy service provided by AWS called **Forecast**, which is a managed service that allows for us to create, train, and predict from different time series forecasting models via API calls. This abstracts away a lot of the heavy lifting we would otherwise have to do and allows us to quickly create a forecasting service our training and prediction handler can interact with.

First, we have to set up our forecasting service using our AWS CLI and credentials. In order to do this, we can run the steps outlined in the tutorial at `https://docs.aws.amazon.com/forecast/latest/dg/gs-cli.html` but make the following variable swap-outs when running the command-line commands:

```
--dataset-name "store_demand"
--dataset-group-name "store_demand_group"
--dataset-import-job-name "store_demand_import_job"
```

The steps for setting up your first Forecast service are given in the shell scripts in the folder in the GitHub repository at `https://github.com/PacktPublishing/Machine-Learning-Engineering-with-Python/tree/main/Chapter07/forecast-service`. You can also use Python API equivalents of these commands, shown for example in the notebook at `https://github.com/PacktPublishing/Machine-Learning-Engineering-with-Python/blob/main/Chapter07/exploration/aws-forecast-training.ipynb`. After running these setup steps, we are ready to proceed to training a forecasting predictor.

We will now walk through creating and training our forecaster using the AWS Python SDK, as this will allow us to interact with the **Forecast** service via our handler web application:

1. First, we connect the CLI session to the forecasting service:

```python
import boto3
session = boto3.Session(region_name='eu-west-1')
forecast = session.client(service_name='forecast')
forecastquery = session.client(service_
name='forecastquery')
```

2. We can then create our predictor and start its training run:

```python
create_predictor_response = \
    forecast.create_predictor(PredictorName=predictor_
name,
                                AlgorithmArn=algorithm_arn,
                                ForecastHorizon=7,
                                PerformAutoML=False,
                                PerformHPO=False,
                                InputDataConfig=
{"DatasetGroupArn": dataset_group_arn},
                                FeaturizationConfig=
```

```
{"ForecastFrequency": DATASET_FREQUENCY}
                                       )
```

3. After submitting the preceding `create_predictor()` command, we can execute the `aws forecast` command with the predictor `arn` in order to determine the status of the training. This command will return a relatively large response but at the end will have a flag saying `"Status": "CREATE_IN_PROGRESS"`. We must wait until this has changed to `"Status": "ACTIVE"` in order to continue with prediction steps:

```
aws forecast --region eu-west-1 describe-
predictor --predictor-arn arn:aws:forecast:eu-west-
1:508972911348:predictor/store_demand_prophet
```

4. After the predictor has been trained, you can create a forecast:

```
forecast_name = f"store_demand_forecast"
create_forecast_response = \
    forecast.create_forecast(ForecastName=forecast_name,
                             PredictorArn=predictor_arn)

forecast_arn = create_forecast_response['ForecastArn']
```

5. Now we can query the forecast status in similar way as for the predictor:

```
forecast.describe_forecast(ForecastArn=forecast_arn)
{'ForecastArn': 'arn:aws:forecast:eu-west-
1:508972911348:forecast/store_demand_forecast',
 'ForecastName': 'store_demand_forecast',
 'ForecastTypes': ['0.1', '0.5', '0.9'],
 'PredictorArn': 'arn:aws:forecast:eu-west-
1:508972911348:predictor/store_demand_prophet',
 'DatasetGroupArn': 'arn:aws:forecast:eu-west-
1:508972911348:dataset-group/store_demand_group',
 'Status': 'ACTIVE',
 ...}}
```

6.   Finally, we can request a forecast result via the API. Here, `item_id` refers to the store number. The results of running this Python syntax are shown in the following code block:

```python
forecast_response = forecastquery.query_forecast(
    ForecastArn=forecast_arn,
    Filters={"item_id": "1"})
```

```
{'Forecast': {'Predictions': {'p10': [{'Timestamp':
'2015-08-01T00:00:00',
    'Value': 3238.8896484375},...],
  'p50': [{'Timestamp': '2015-08-01T00:00:00', 'Value':
4690.10107421875},...],
  'p90': [{'Timestamp': '2015-08-01T00:00:00', 'Value':
6157.83935546875},...]}},...}
```

We can use this sort of functionality in the solution to query and retrain the forecasting models. The key focus for building the solution is really in bringing together these tools and providing an interface to them through the training and prediction handler web service, which we now move on to discuss.

Training and forecast handlers

As alluded to in the previous section, the prediction and training handler for this system can be contained within a simple web application. We can do this using a simple Flask web app hosted on **Elastic Container Registry** (**ECR**) like in the *Hosting your own microservice on AWS* section in *Chapter 5, Deployment Patterns and Tools.*

The rest of this section will focus on what key pieces of code need to be implemented in order to progress with the solution, in a way that leverages the ML engineering practices we have discussed throughout this book.

In our web application, we will need to have endpoints that can be queried for either training or prediction purposes, so we will have endpoints named (imaginatively) `training` and `forecast`. The following sections will discuss these endpoints..

Training endpoint

The application logic behind the training endpoint should contain a check that the model that a retrain is being requested for has not already recently been updated before proceeding to request a new training job and model update. The exact details of this logic can very much depend on the customer's need, but we can cover a basic scenario here.

The rough flow of the logic could be something like the following:

- What is the date for this training request?

- Find the time the most recent predictor was trained.

- If the difference between date of training request (now) and the time of most recent predictor training is within tolerance (2 days for example) then return a message saying *training of new predictor not initiated, time elapsed within tolerance.*

- If the time elapsed between the date of the training request and the time of most recent predictor training is outside of tolerance, initiate training.

This logic can be handled via classes that wrap pieces of the AWS CLI functionality that we use for interacting with the Forecast service:

1. For example, we can create a simple class that wraps the connection to the Forecast service for later use by another functionality:

```
class ForecastSession(object):

    def __init__(self):
        self.session = boto3.Session(region_name=REGION)
        self.forecast = session.client(service_
name='forecast')
        self.forecastquery = session.client(service_
name='forecastquery')
```

2. We can then define classes that depend on an instance of the `ForecastSession` object for access to the AWS Forecast service and perform the steps we need. First, we can define a `Trainer` class that handles training of new predictors in the service. We do not show the full class here for brevity but show the use of an instance of the `ForecastSession` object, here called `forecast_session`, and the method names for the class:

```
class Trainer(object):
    def __init__(self, forecast_session):
```

```
        self.forecast_session = forecast_session
...
    def get_df_pred_metadata(self):
...
    def get_latest_predictor(self):
...
    def latest_predictor_in_tolerance(self, tolerance_
days=2):
...
    def train_new_predictor(self):
...
    def create_latest_forecast(self):
...
```

Example logic for all of this functionality is given in the repository, but the key point is that here we have already leveraged many of the object-oriented programming techniques we explored in *Chapter 4*, *Packaging Up*.

We will now continue with a brief discussion on what has to be included in the forecast endpoint.

Forecast endpoint

The application logic behind the forecast endpoint should first of all ensure that the model required for forecasting is available within the context of the handler service; if it is not, then it should retrieve it from our model store. After doing this, it should use the model to produce a forecast that can be rendered and stored within the user's dashboard.

We will now walk through the steps for creating the forecast endpoint in our containerized web application:

1. Contained in a submodule called resources within the main application directory, we have a file called forecast.py. This includes a simple ForecastHandler, which manages the outputs of the Forecaster object:

```
class ForecastHandler(Resource):
    def __init__(self, **kwargs):
        self.forecaster = kwargs['forecaster']


    def get(self):
        return {}
```

```
    def post(self):
        args = post_parser.parse_args()
        print(args)
        result = {"store_number": args["store_
number"], "result": self.forecaster.get_forecast(store_
id=args["store_number"])}
        return jsonify(result)
```

2. The forecast.py file also includes the Forecaster class, which interacts with the Forecast service similarly to the Trainer class discussed in the *Training endpoint* section:

```
class Forecaster(object):

    def __init__(self, forecast_session):
    ...
    def get_df_forecast_metadata(self):
    ...
    def get_latest_forecast(self):
        ...
    def get_forecast(self, store_id):
        ...
```

The ForecastHandler and Forecaster objects are then all that we need to connect to and retrieve forecasts from the service.

The final section will discuss how we bring all of this together into the handler service.

Bringing it together

The handler service has to be brought together now by deploying the training and forecasting pieces as endpoints within the web application. We will show how to do this for the forecast endpoint; the training endpoint is essentially a copy of this:

1. We import all of the libraries we will need to create a Flask web app in a file called app.py:

```
from flask import Flask
from flask_restful import Api, Resource
from resources.forecast import ForecastHandler,
```

```
Forecaster
import logging
```

2. In app.py, we instantiate the Flask app using the flask_restful functionality:

```
app = Flask(__name__)
api = Api(app)
```

3. We add a forecast endpoint to the app. This endpoint uses a class that we call ForecastHandler, which itself leverages functionality in a class called Forecaster:

```
forecaster = Forecaster()
api.add_resource(ForecastHandler, '/forecast', resource_
class_kwargs={'forecaster': forecaster})
```

4. We then define the main entry point of the app, where logging will be configured and where the application can be run:

```
if __name__ == '__main__':
    logging.basicConfig(filename='app.log',
level=logging.INFO, format='%(asctime)s | %(name)s |
%(levelname)s | %(message)s')
    logging.info('Main app sequence begun')
    app.run(debug=True, host='0.0.0.0', port=5000) #
change debug=False in production
    logging.info('App finished')
```

5. We can then test this basic forecast handling service by triggering the application with python app.py and then querying the endpoint with **Postman**:

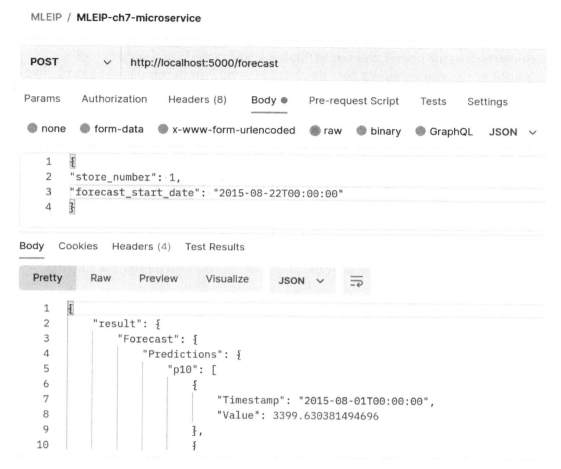

Figure 7.4 – The result of querying the forecast endpoint in our forecasting microservice

And that's it. Our handler service is quite simple. Since we are working to a microservice architecture, we do not need to build anything very complicated and can focus on each of the separate components required. This is one of the reasons to use this architecture, as we discussed in *Chapter 5, Deployment Patterns and Tools*.

We now conclude with a summary of what we have covered in this chapter.

Summary

In this chapter, we have walked through an example of how to take the tools and techniques from the first six chapters of this book and apply them together to solve a realistic business problem. We have discussed in detail how the need for a dynamically triggered forecasting algorithm can lead very quickly to a design that requires several small services to interact seamlessly. In particular, we created a design with components responsible for handling events, training models, storing models, and performing predictions. We then walked through how we would choose our toolset to build to this design in a real-world scenario, by considering things such as appropriateness for the task at hand as well as likely developer familiarity. Finally, we carefully defined the key pieces of code that would be required to build the solution in a way that could solve the problem repeatedly and robustly.

In the next, and final, chapter, we will build out an example of a batch ML process. We will term the pattern that this adheres to as Extract, Transform, Machine Learn, and explore what key points should be covered in any project aiming to build this type of solution.

8

Building an Extract Transform Machine Learning Use Case

Similar to *Chapter 7, Building an Example ML Microservice*, the aim of this chapter will be to try to crystallize a lot of the tools and techniques we have learned about throughout this book and apply them to a realistic scenario. This will be based on another use case introduced in *Chapter 1, Introduction to ML Engineering*, where we imagined the need to cluster taxi-ride data on a scheduled basis. We will explore this scenario so that we can outline the key decisions we would make if building a solution in reality, as well as discussing how to implement it by leveraging what has been covered in other chapters.

This use case will allow us to explore what is perhaps the most used pattern in **Machine Learning (ML)** solutions across the world—that of the batch inference process. Due to the nature of retrieving, transforming, and then performing ML on data, I have termed this **Extract Transform Machine Learning (ETML)**.

We will follow the same high-level format as for the use case in *Chapter 7, Building an Example ML Microservice*, and discuss the following topics in this chapter:

- Understanding the batch processing problem
- Designing an ETML solution
- Selecting the tools
- Executing the build

All of these topics will help us understand the particular decisions and steps we need to take in order to build a successful ETML solution.

In the next section, we will revisit the high-level problem introduced in *Chapter 1, Introduction to ML Engineering*, and explore how to map the business requirements to technical solution requirements, given everything we have learned in the book so far.

Technical requirements

To apply the examples from this chapter, you will need the following tools installed or available:

- JIRA Atlassian account
- Github account
- scikit-learn
- logging Python Library

Understanding the batch processing problem

In *Chapter 1, Introduction to ML Engineering*, we saw the scenario of a taxi firm that wanted to analyze anomalous rides at the end of every day. The customer had the following requirements:

- Rides should be clustered based on ride distance and time and anomalies/outliers identified.
- Speed (distance/time) was not to be used, as analysts would like to understand long-distance rides or those of long duration.
- The analysis should be carried out on a daily schedule.
- The data for inference should be consumed from the company's data lake.
- The results should be made available for consumption by other company systems.

As we did in *Chapter 2, The Machine Learning Development Process*, and *Chapter 7, Building an Example ML Microservice*, we can now build out some user stories from these requirements, as follows:

- **User story 1**: As an operations analyst, I want to be given clear labels of rides that have anomalously long ride times or distances.

- **User story 2**: As an internal application developer, I want to have a clear access point for data with anomalous labels. This data should be stored in the cloud.

- **User story 3**: As an operations analyst, I would like to see labels for the previous day's rides every morning.

User story 1 should be taken care of by our general clustering approach, especially since we are using the **Density-Based Spatial Clustering of Applications with Noise (DBSCAN)** algorithm, which provides a label of *-1* for outliers.

User story 2 means that we have to push the results to a location on the cloud that can then be picked up either by a data engineering pipeline or by a web application pipeline. To make this as flexible as possible, we will push results to an assigned **Amazon Web Services (AWS) Simple Storage Service (S3)** bucket. We will initially export the data in **JavaScript Object Notation (JSON)** format as this is a format that is often used in application development and that can be read in by most data engineering tools.

The final user story, user story 3, gives us guidance on the scheduling we require for the system. In this case, the requirements mean we should run in a daily batch job.

Let's tabulate these thoughts in terms of some ML solution technical requirements, as follows:

User Story	Details	Technical Requirements
1	As an operations analyst, I want to be given clear labels of rides that have anomalously long ride times or distances.	• Algorithm type = anomaly detection/ clustering/outlier detection • Features = ride time and distance
2	As an internal application developer, I want to have a clear access point for data with anomalous labels. This data should be stored in the cloud.	• System output destination = S3 on AWS
3	As an operations analyst, I would like to see labels for the previous day's rides every morning.	• Batch frequency = daily

Figure 8.1 – Translating user stories to technical requirements

In the next section, we will map these technical requirements to a high-level design.

Designing an ETML solution

The requirements clearly point us to a solution that takes in some data and augments it with ML inference, before outputting the data to a target location. Any design we come up with must encapsulate these steps.

The key elements our design has to cover can be articulated by expanding out what we wrote down in *Figure 8.1*; this is shown in the following diagram:

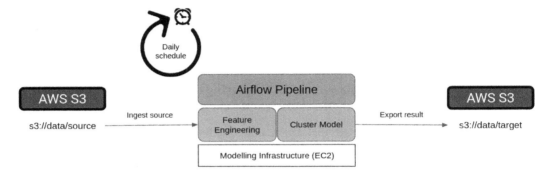

Figure 8.2 – High-level design for the ETML clustering system

In the next section, we will look at some potential tools we can use to solve this problem, given everything we have learned in previous chapters.

Selecting the tools

For this example, and pretty much for whenever we have an ETML problem, our main considerations boil down to a few simple things, which we will cover in the following sections.

Interfaces

When we execute the extract and load parts of ETML, we need to consider how to interface with the systems that store our data. It is important that whichever database or data technology we are extracting from, we use the appropriate tools to extract at whatever scale and pace we need. In this example, our interfacing can be taken care of by the AWS `boto3` library and the S3 **Application Programming Interface (API)** it surfaces.

The following table shows the pros and cons of using this option:

Solution Aspect	Potential Tools	Pros	Cons
Interfaces	AWS **Command-Line Interface (CLI)** and boto3	• Simple to use • Connects to a wide variety of other AWS tools and services	• Not cloud-agnostic • Not applicable outside of AWS (on-premises systems, for example)

Figure 8.3 – Pros and cons of using the AWS CLI and boto3 for interfacing with our data sources

In the next section, we will consider the decisions we must make around the scalability of our modeling approach. This is very important when working with batches of data, which could be extremely large in some cases.

Scaling of models

In *Chapter 6, Scaling Up*, we discussed some of the mechanisms for scaling up our analytics and ML workloads. We should ask ourselves whether any of these, or even other methods, apply to the use case at hand and use them accordingly. This works the other way too: if we are looking at relatively small amounts of data, there is no need to provision a large amount of infrastructure, and there may be no need to spend time creating very optimized processing. Each case should be examined on its own merits and within its own context.

We tabulate some of the options and their pros and cons here:

Potential Tools	Pros	Cons
Spark MLlib	Can scale to very large datasets	• Requires cluster management • Overkill for smaller datasets/processing requirements • Limited algorithm set
Spark with pandas **User-Defined Function (UDF)**	• Can scale to very large datasets • Can use any Python-based algorithm	Might not make sense for some problems where parallelization is not easily applicable
Scikit-learn	• Well known by many data scientists • Can run on many different types of infrastructure	Not very scalable

Figure 8.4 – Options for the modeling part of the ETML solution, with their pros and cons and with a particular focus on scalability

Now we have explored the tooling decisions we have to make around scalable ML models; we move on to another important topic for ETML solutions—how we manage the scheduling of batch processing.

Scheduling of ETML pipelines

The kind of batch process that ETML corresponds to is often something that ties in quite nicely with daily batches, but given the other two points outlined previously, we may need to be careful about when we schedule our jobs—for example, a step in our pipeline may need to connect to a production database that does not have a read replica (a copy of the database specifically just for reading). If this were the case, then we may cause major performance issues for users of any solutions utilizing that database if we start hammering it with queries at 9 a.m. on a Monday morning. Similarly, if we run overnight and want to load into a system that is undergoing other batch upload processes, we may create resource contention, slowing down the process. There is no *one-size-fits-all* answer here; it is just important to consider your options. We look at the pros and cons of using Apache Airflow, which we introduced in *Chapter 5, Deployment Patterns and Tools*, for the scheduling and job management of this problem in the following table:

Potential Tools	Pros	Cons
Apache Airflow	• Good scheduling management • Ability to build relatively complex pipelines • Good documentation • Cloud-hosted services available, such as AWS **Managed Workflows for Apache Airflow (MWAA)**	• Learning curve for usage • Takes time to test pipelines and scheduling • Cloud services (MWAA) can be expensive

Figure 8.5 – Pros and cons of using Apache Airflow for managing our scheduling

Given some of the points in *Figure 8.5*, it seems that actually, for a relatively small dataset, a combination of scikit-learn modeling with Apache Airflow could cover all of our requirements.

The next section will discuss how we can proceed with the execution of the solution, given this information.

Executing the build

Execution of the build, in this case, will be very much about how we take the **Proof-Of-Concept** code shown in *Chapter 1, Introduction to ML Engineering*, and then split this out into components that can be called by another scheduling tool such as Apache Airflow. This will provide a showcase of how we can apply the skills we learned in *Chapter 4, Packaging Up*.

In the next few sections, we will walk through how to inject some engineering best practices into the code base, and we will discuss some coding examples to help bring this to reality. We will not focus on the scheduling and pipelining aspect for Apache Airflow (please refer to *Chapter 5, Deployment Patterns and Tools,* for this) but will focus instead on how some simple adaptations to an existing code base can dramatically improve its production readiness.

Not reinventing the wheel in practice

As discussed in *Chapter 3, From Model to Model Factory*, whether we run our ML pipeline in a train-run or train-persist mode, we still require a feature engineering step! Since the datasets used are relatively small and we have decided to use `sklearn` here, we can just use that package's feature engineering capabilities.

This has the added benefit of remaining very close to the original POC developed by our (imaginary) data scientists!

In terms of modeling, again, our use of `sklearn` in production will mean that the base functionality provided by our data scientists in the POC phase will be an excellent start to our development work.

What we can do, however, is add some of the engineering techniques we discussed in *Chapter 4, Packaging Up*, in order to help harden this code. And to be honest, there is no better way to do that than to leverage a lot of the hard work we already did in that chapter! Specifically, we developed a package that detected outliers, which is very much what we want to do here. The only thing that we have to do is add the new functionality developed by our data scientists using ML engineering best practices.

This is a good example of the principle that we should not reinvent the wheel when we do our work, as emphasized at the end of *Chapter 4, Packaging Up*.

The next section walks through how we can add to the `outliers` package developed in *Chapter 4, Packaging Up,* by leveraging the Gitflow workflow explained in *Chapter 2, The Machine Learning Development Process.*

Using the Gitflow workflow

First, in order for us to work on the library, we navigate to the GitHub repository for it at `https://github.com/AndyMc629/mleip-outliers`. At the time of writing, this repository only contains the code developed during *Chapter 4, Packaging Up,* in the main branch.

Next, we can integrate our Jira instance, created in *Chapter 1, Introduction to ML Engineering,* into this GitHub repository. We do this by taking the following steps:

1. We install the GitHub integration plugin in Atlassian Marketplace, given here: `https://marketplace.atlassian.com/apps/1224265/github-integration-for-jira?hosting=cloud&tab=overview`. When prompted, provide the repository name. This is shown in the following screenshot:

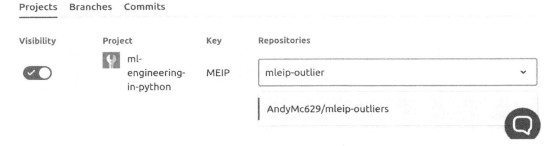

Figure 8.6 – Configuring JIRA with our package repository

2. Now the GitHub integration plugin is installed, we can create branches or trigger **Pull Requests (PRs)** via JIRA. First, we navigate to the relevant user story and click the **GitHub toolkit** button in the lower-right corner of the screen, as illustrated in the following screenshot:

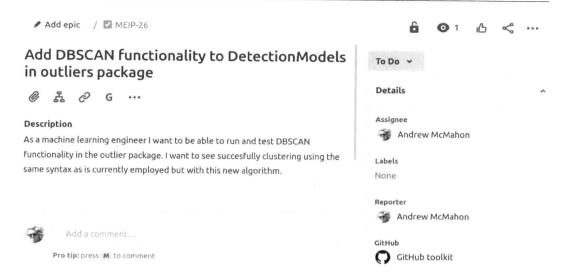

Figure 8.7 – Selecting the GitHub toolkit option to create a new feature branch based on the Jira ticket

3. After clicking this, a new part of the window opens with some options. We select Create and the branch name is auto-populated with a suggestion. This can be edited. Finally, we push the **Create branch** button on the bottom right. A view of these steps is shown in the following screenshot:

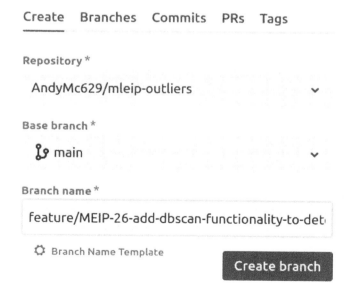

Figure 8.8 – Creation of a feature branch via Jira

4.   The previous steps should have successfully created your feature branch. If you navigate to your GitHub repository and select the **branches** icon at the top of the repository, you should be able to see that your branch has indeed been created. An example is shown in the following screenshot:

Figure 8.9 – Confirmation that the feature branch has been created in GitHub

We've just discussed how to work with version control in a robust way for this use case. In the next section, we will walk through how we can take some of our previous learnings about engineering best practices and implement them here. We will also show how to continue using the Gitflow workflow for implementing these changes in the code base.

Injecting some engineering practices

For the use case presented here, we can proceed under the assumption that the business mainly wants the `outliers` package to be augmented with new functionality. We will also discuss how we can inject some engineering practices into the package as well. We will walk through how we, as ML engineers, can progress towards these goals. We'll proceed as follows:

1. First, the POC produced by the data scientists in the **Play** phase of the project utilized the DBSCAN clustering algorithm from scikit-learn. In order to add DBSCAN functionality to the `outliers` package, we must add some extra logic to deal with the case when this model type is passed into the `model_config.json` file. This logic again utilizes the `**kwargs` syntax explained in *Chapter 3, From Model to Model Factory*, to allow for the passing of variable numbers of parameters to the DBSCAN model instance, as illustrated in the following code snippet:

```python
def create_model(self, model_name=None, params=None):
    logging.debug(f"Creating model with params:
model_name:{model_name} and params:{params}")
    if model_name is None and params is None:
        return None
    if model_name == 'IsolationForest' and params is
not None:
        return IsolationForest(**params)
    if model_name == 'DBSCAN' and params is not None:
        return DBSCAN(**params)
```

2. The original version of the `outliers` package did not have a lot of logging in place. In the preceding code example and in other sections of the `outliers` package, we have added more logging functionality in order to help diagnose any issues that may occur in production. We have also added exception handling, another of the best practices identified in *Chapter 4, Packaging Up*. The code is illustrated in the following snippet:

```python
def detect(self, data):
    try:
        logging.debug("Fitting pipeline")
        return self.pipeline.fit_predict(data)
    except Exception as e:
        logging.debug(f"fit_predict() failed with
object {self.pipeline}")
```

```
        logging.debug(e)
        print(e)
```

3. Since the outliers package is mainly acting as a wrapper for **Unsupervised Learning (UL)** methods suited to outlier detection, it is naturally something that can be used in a **train-run** rather than a **train-persist** mode of operation (alluding back to earlier discussions in the *Designing an ETML solution* section). This means that the main() method, given in the package as an example of how to use this in an application, can simply focus on instantiating the appropriate models, applying them, and then outputting the results, as illustrated in the following code snippet:

```
        logging.info("Reading in models")
        models = DetectionModels(MODEL_CONFIG_PATH).get_
    models()

        logging.info("Iterating over models")
        for model in models:
            logging.info("Create detector")
            detector = detectors.pipelines.
    OutlierDetector(model=model)
            logging.info("Detector created")
            result = detector.detect(data)
            logging.info("Result calculated")
```

All of this taken together means that we now have code that is more production-ready in the outliers package that can be used with a variety of tools, including by being a script callable by an Apache Airflow pipeline in a scheduled ETML job.

We will now define the steps needed to merge the code changes into the master branch of the package, as follows:

1. Once the engineering team is happy with the changes to the package, a PR can be raised for merging in the changes to the master. This can be done via the Jira board for the original task, as shown in the following screenshot:

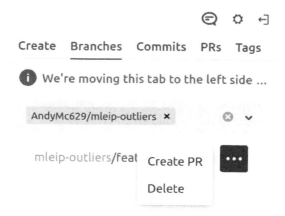

Figure 8.10 – Creating a PR via the Jira GitHub integration plugin

2. We are then redirected to the Git web **User Interface** (**UI**), and we can fill in the relevant details for our PR, including details of the changes being proposed. This is illustrated in the screenshot shown next. After this, we click **Create pull request**:

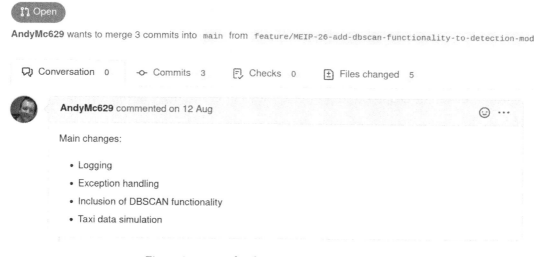

Feature/meip 26 add dbscan functionality to detection models in outliers package #1

`⟨⟩ Open`

AndyMc629 wants to merge 3 commits into `main` from `feature/MEIP-26-add-dbscan-functionality-to-detection-mod`

💬 Conversation 0   -o- Commits 3   ▣ Checks 0   ⊞ Files changed 5

AndyMc629 commented on 12 Aug

Main changes:

- Logging
- Exception handling
- Inclusion of DBSCAN functionality
- Taxi data simulation

Figure 8.11 – PR for the code changes in GitHub

3. After submission of the PR, if we navigate to the **pull requests** section in the web UI, we can see the active request and click on it to view details of the change. This includes options for viewing which commits were submitted within the PR, which checks have been performed through GitHub Actions (see *Chapter 4, Packaging Up*), and changes at an individual file and line level. Once happy with the changes, the reviewer of the request can push the **Merge pull request** button at the bottom of the screen, as illustrated in the following screenshot:

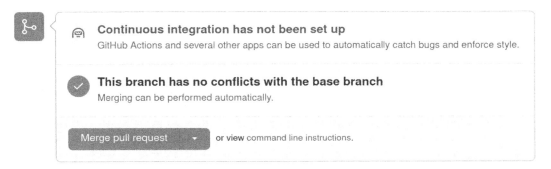

Figure 8.12 – Merging in our changes to the outliers package with a PR

And that's how we can make the `outliers` package more robust and ready to use in a production pipeline. All that is left to do is apply the relevant steps from the logic in an Airflow **Directed Acyclic Graph** (**DAG**), as shown in *Chapter 5, Deployment Patterns and Tools*. We will not repeat those steps here, but just emphasize that the augmentations made to the code base mean that the core logic for our ETML pipeline is ready to go.

We will now end the chapter, and the book, with a brief summary of what we have covered in this chapter.

Summary

This chapter has covered how to apply a lot of the techniques learned in this book, in particular from *Chapter 2*, *The Machine Learning Development Process*, *Chapter 3*, *From Model to Model Factory*, and *Chapter 4*, *Packaging Up*, to a real ML problem involving updating an existing ML package. This scenario was an example that could be solved using the ETML pattern, which was explained in detail. A design for a potential solution, as well as a discussion of some of the tooling choices any ML engineering team would have to go through, was covered. Finally, a deep dive into some of the key pieces of work that would be required to make this solution production-ready was performed. This focused on code changes that augmented the ML capabilities of the existing package and that hardened the solution. It also covered how to use Jira and Git to implement these changes using version control, as discussed in *Chapter 2* of this book, *The Machine Learning Development Process*.

With that, you have not only completed this chapter but also the book, so congratulations! Throughout this book, we have covered a wide variety of topics in ML engineering, from how to build your teams and what development processes could look like, all the way through to packaging, scaling, scheduling, deploying, testing, logging, and a whole bunch of stuff in between. There are so many topics we covered only briefly that could have entire books dedicated to them and so many other topics we did not have the space to cover. Despite this, it is my hope that you come away from reading this book feeling more equipped to go out and build software solutions that use ML to deliver real value every day. And, of course, I hope that it will help you do this using one of the most popular programming languages—and my favorite one—Python.

`Packt.com`

Subscribe to our online digital library for full access to over 7,000 books and videos, as well as industry leading tools to help you plan your personal development and advance your career. For more information, please visit our website.

Why subscribe?

- Spend less time learning and more time coding with practical eBooks and Videos from over 4,000 industry professionals

- Improve your learning with Skill Plans built especially for you

- Get a free eBook or video every month

- Fully searchable for easy access to vital information

- Copy and paste, print, and bookmark content

Did you know that Packt offers eBook versions of every book published, with PDF and ePub files available? You can upgrade to the eBook version at `packt.com` and as a print book customer, you are entitled to a discount on the eBook copy. Get in touch with us at `customercare@packtpub.com` for more details.

At `www.packt.com`, you can also read a collection of free technical articles, sign up for a range of free newsletters, and receive exclusive discounts and offers on Packt books and eBooks.

Other Books You May Enjoy

If you enjoyed this book, you may be interested in these other books by Packt:

Engineering MLOps

Emmanuel Raj

ISBN: 9781800562882

- Formulate data governance strategies and pipelines for ML training and deployment
- Get to grips with implementing ML pipelines, CI/CD pipelines, and ML monitoring pipelines
- Design a robust and scalable microservice and API for test and production environments
- Curate your custom CD processes for related use cases and organizations
- Monitor ML models, including monitoring data drift, model drift, and application performance
- Build and maintain automated ML systems

Machine Learning Engineering with MLflow.

Natu Lauchande

ISBN: 9781800560796

- Develop your machine learning project locally with MLflow's different features
- Set up a centralized MLflow tracking server to manage multiple MLflow experiments
- Create a model life cycle with MLflow by creating custom models
- Use feature streams to log model results with MLflow
- Develop the complete training pipeline infrastructure using MLflow features
- Set up an inference-based API pipeline and batch pipeline in MLflow

Packt is searching for authors like you

If you're interested in becoming an author for Packt, please visit authors.packtpub.com and apply today. We have worked with thousands of developers and tech professionals, just like you, to help them share their insight with the global tech community. You can make a general application, apply for a specific hot topic that we are recruiting an author for, or submit your own idea.

Share Your Thoughts

Now you've finished *Machine Learning Engineering with Python*, we'd love to hear your thoughts! Scan the QR code below to go straight to the Amazon review page for this book and share your feedback or leave a review on the site that you purchased it from.

https://packt.link/r/1-801-07925-0

Your review is important to us and the tech community and will help us make sure we're delivering excellent quality content.

Index

Made in the USA
Las Vegas, NV
17 May 2022

49024193R00155